Emptiness

Emptiness

Feeling Christian in America

John Corrigan

The University of Chicago Press
Chicago and London

John Corrigan is the Lucius Moody Bristol Distinguished Professor of Religion and professor of history at Florida State University.

The University of Chicago Press, Chicago 60637
The University of Chicago Press, Ltd., London

Printed in the United States of America

24 23 22 21 20 19 18 17 16 15   1 2 3 4 5

ISBN-13: 978-0-226-23746-6 (cloth)
ISBN-13: 978-0-226-23763-3 (e-book)
DOI: 10.7208/chicago/9780226237633.001.0001

Corrigan, John, 1952- author.
Emptiness : feeling Christian in America / John Corrigan.
pages cm
Includes bibliographical references and index.
ISBN 978-0-226-23746-6 (cloth : alkaline paper) —
ISBN 978-0-226-23763-3 (e-book) — 1. Christian life—United States. 2. Christianity—United States—Customs and practices. 3. Christian sects—United States—History. 4. Emotions—Religious aspects—Christianity. I. Title.
BR515.C67 2015
277.3—dc23
2014034469

♾ This paper meets the requirements of ANSI/NISO Z39.48-1992 (Permanence of Paper).

For John Kloos

Friend, collaborator, critic

Contents

Acknowledgments

It is a pleasure to thank the staff of the Strozier Library at Florida State University for their diligence in helping me track down and borrow obscure books and documents. A university endowment named for Lucius Moody Bristol, a Floridian whose professional interests in social systems and social justice resonate with my own, enabled me to travel to conduct research. Friends and critics who read the manuscript saved me from mistakes and pointed me in fruitful directions. I have been exceedingly lucky to share an office hallway with Amanda Porterfield, the most generous of colleagues and an inspirational scholar. Her detailed comments on an early draft led to many improvements, and her encouragements were much welcomed. John Kloos, with whom I have discussed religion in America for decades, delivered his typically painstaking reading and rereading and asked difficult questions. I acknowledge a long-term debt to him in the dedication of this book. I am grateful to Lauren Gray for her usual excellent job of indexing and proofreading. I am grateful to the anonymous readers for the University of Chicago Press for their deep critical engagement and their detailed reports. My friend and editor Alan Thomas has been a great sounding board for ideas, a reliable guide to my implementing them, and an excellent person to hang out with. Lois Crum expertly copyedited the book. Sheila as always listened and poured wine and, knowing firsthand what is best when one is writing, talked me into pausing, now and again.

Introduction

Emptiness and American Christianities

> The Greeks, who were perhaps the first humans to gaze unflinchingly into the heart of darkness and who understood, or at least some of them did, the meaninglessness and emptiness of the universe, pulled back from irrationality, as tempting as it was, by building an elaborate edifice of rationality and restraint. "Know thyself" and "nothing in excess" became the ideal ruling principles of their lives. As worthy as these maxims are, they only reveal their opposites: that human life is often about excesses, and that very seldom do we know ourselves.
> —Teofilo F. Ruiz

> The true fast . . . is the making of an emptiness about the soul that the higher fullness may fill it.
> —Phillips Brooks

Centuries before the colonization of North America, European Christians wrote about their feelings of emptiness and developed religious practice as a means of cultivating and cognizing those feelings. They correlated the feeling of emptiness with denial of self, and drawing upon an assortment of biblical texts and early Christian writings, they theologized it as a precondition for being filled with God's grace. The most striking of those theologies were tinged with mysticism and cast the feeling of emptiness as longing for God. Mystics, members of religious orders, and laypersons, in bold pursuit of the feeling of emptiness and equally keen to represent their emotional experiences, engaged in bodily disciplines conceptualized as pathways to emptying the self. Fasting was a means of emptying the body of food. During passionate prayer, droplets of fluid left the body through the eyes. Some drained their blood in violent solitary devotions or in periodic communal bloodletting rituals. Sweat left the body during work—*laborare est orare*. Silence made the throat empty of words. Those who did not bleed or fast or hold their tongues admired those who did. All hoped that God would fill them with joy.

While cherishing the feeling of emptiness as a preliminary to joyful connection with God, Christians were wary of emptiness that did not arise from self-denial. There was the emptiness of the world, which they understood in actuality to be a world so filled with self and selfishness that it disallowed the streaming of God's grace into the soul. Some Christians believed that time likewise was empty because it could not be filled by God, so corrupt in its harboring of sin and excess that only in apocalypse might one escape it. The body was empty in the same way, so drenched in lust as to be incapable of receiving what God offered. Some sought to escape such fullness-as-emptiness by retreating to deserts, forests, or mountaintops, to spaces thought to be empty of whatever clogged the portals of the soul and prevented union with God. For most who commented on their feelings, heedfulness about being wrongly filled remained partnered with the aspiration to emptiness, the longing for God. The emptier persons felt, the more distant they felt from God, and at the same time they could feel nearer to God. Exquisite longing bordered the joyful experience of gracious refreshment. Christians did not imagine emptiness apart from fullness. The complex conceptualization of each—either could be good or bad depending on the context—made such feelings both difficult and rich. The practice of Christianity that was grounded in the feeling of emptiness, however, was not ambiguous. Christians determinedly chased the feeling of emptiness, valorized it as longing for God, and performed devotions to prompt and deepen it.

European colonists arrived in North America bearing the bones of a

Christian culture of emptiness. In earliest New Spain, Christian converts venerated the Woman of the Apocalypse and anticipated escape from empty time into eternity. That piety remained fundamental to the Mexican Christianity that later so profoundly informed American Catholicism, shaping a sense of the poverty of the soul, the longing for God, and the difference between time and eternity. Catholics and Anglicans, in the Chesapeake and in some of the more northerly seaport towns, remained rooted in religious practice that included fasting and silence and took its bearings from the examples of virtuosos who, as portrayed in hagiographies, had pared the self to the bone. Puritans, among others, endeavored to redeem the time, fast and pray, and deny themselves in various ways, including through performances of conversion in which the human shell of awareness was imagined evacuated of its selfish contents and suffused with holiness. They and their descendants pictured the land as empty, a desert space that mirrored their empty souls and beckoned to them in the same way that they prayed God would fill their hollow hearts with grace. Constructed as empty, the space of North America relentlessly reminded Americans of their emptiness and their longing. Americans' efforts to fill it with emblems of themselves became an impossible mission to prove it fillable; and impossible also was the mission to prove that the longing in their souls was curable. Christians in colonial America felt the emptiness of space and time in their souls, were wary of empty words that could deceive them into errors of belief, and in a psychological and social drama of mirroring and substitutionary sacrifice, they emptied black bodies of blood, sweat, tears, food, and words. Instances of revival enthusiasm were clustered around orators who pressed upon their audiences images of the empty soul, the empty land, and the danger of following those who had not become empty enough. Those words also set the tone for thinking about religious others as conspirators set on subverting true Christianity and wickedly remaking the liberal mercantile and economically mobile late colonial society that Christianity had midwifed. The revivalism of the early nineteenth century added to those messages the promotion of new physical exercises—from anxious benches to protracted meetings—aimed at breaking the self and emptying the soul. Such innovation also included a growing confidence in the continental destiny of the regenerated, even as it broached denial of self.

As disestablishment gradually was implemented in the states of the new American Republic, religious groups learned to compete in order to survive. Protestant groups differentiated themselves from one another by innovating in theology, preaching, and worship. Roman Catholic congregations vied with one another only minimally, but as all denominations adjusted to the fact of competition, relations between Catholics and Protestants grew progressively more contentious, as did relations with emergent Mormonism. Disestablishment was the tipping point that prompted Christian groups to strategize their differentiation from other groups as a matter of aggressive boundary defense. That process was directed by the theological framing of Christian life that placed emptiness at its center. The emptiness of the group was an extension of the emptiness of the individual Christian. In the competitive arena of postestablishment antebellum America, Christian groups refined a practice of collective self-understanding that rested on marking out competitors as inferior or outrightly corrupt. As religious options proliferated—Mormons, Spiritualists, Shakers, Campbellites, Millerites, Adventists, Unitarians, and many others—Christians of all sorts set their markers of differentiation. Debate with competitors became a more transparent process of fostering in-group belonging through negative definition of out-groups. In a complex drama involving screened memory, self-doubt, fear of being deceived, the will to power, and the feeling of emptiness, groups constructed their identities by avowing what they were *not*. Outside of the leadership, members of a Christian group might not know much about what doctrines comprised the theological standpoint of the group, but they were willing to believe that the doctrines of opponents were wrong and were satisfied to experience the social rewards of standing together against common enemies.

American Christians by the early nineteenth century had assembled a store of cultural artifacts that expressed their feeling of emptiness and reminded them of it. Among those was what all referred to as The Great American Desert, an invented wasteland between the Mississippi River and the Rocky Mountains. A space of emptiness that challenged the imagination in its vastness, it carried forward Puritan thinking about the land and extended to Euro-Americans outside of New England the opportunity to glimpse in North American space their own emptiness. Emptiness, fullness, manifest destiny, the redeemer nation, the triumph of Christianity, all were encoded in the reports of the Great Desert, and all remained associated with the West after the Desert per se began to disappear from imagination toward the end of the century. American Christians continued to fast and pray, and to sweat, emulating the Jesus who as a carpenter emptied himself of sweat in honest labor and later shed his blood. During the Civil War, Americans emptied themselves of blood in the struggle over slavery. That sacrifice had strong religious undertones, a fact not lost on those who fought nor on those who wrote about the role of blood in sacralizing, they said, the nation. The latter, and perhaps many of the former, discerned in that bloodshed atonement and an act of pious self-sacrifice all at once, which emptied the self of its pride, served as punishment for sin, and cemented a national covenant with God.

The Civil War was not the only nineteenth-century conflict that invoked extreme theological language about emptiness. In antebellum America Christians became more wary of words, more anxious about the capability of words to deceive, and more inclined to point fingers at those whom they suspected of preaching empty doctrines. Christians' doubts about their religious opponents were intertwined with doubts about themselves, so that calls to battle on one front often involved action on the other. In such an environment, frictions blossomed. Christian denominations recited litanies of promises to defeat religious opponents and made good on their promises by fighting pitched battles with those they identified as enemies. In such encounters opposing groups reflected each other's concerns about emptiness both within and outside of the group. That dynamic, the recognition of one's own emptiness in another, was tragically visible when race was involved. Antebellum America was a formative period for the development of the ritual sacrifice of Africans, who, while being emptied of blood chained to a tree, drew both admiration and disgust from the lynch mob and reflected, for the white Christian, both the aspiration to be empty of self and the horror of that emptiness.

For some Christians, commitment to an apocalyptic reordering of the cosmos was preferable to living in history that was dead to God. History was empty, eternity was full, and Protestants across the spectrum of denominations—some more enthusiastically and with more forethought than others—anticipated the imminent return of Christ in an apocalyptic reordering of the world. Roman Catholics were less involved in the organization of millennial movements—communities such as the Saint Nazianz community in Wisconsin were exceptions—but they remained emotionally drawn to the end-time scenarios that were deeply etched in Catholic piety, a sensitivity they expressed more explicitly in their attention to Marianist apocalypses in the twentieth century. Like the empty space of the Great American Desert, the empty space of time was both a horror to be escaped and an emblem of Christian longing. Waiting for the end of time and the fullness of eternity, Christians went to Mass, prayed the rosary, listened to preaching, read the Bible, and retired to their prayer closets or sanctuaries to confront themselves about sin, feel the depth of their emptiness, and long for grace. All of this occurred during times of intermittent nineteenth-century collaborations among Christian denominations, during significant voluntary society activity undertaken to spread Christianity and to determine a moral course for the nation. It has taken place since then equally under the canopy of Christian promotion of the feeling of emptiness and the fostering of doubt about the doctrines and motives of religious others. As such it suggests how Christianity in America has worked at seeming cross-purposes in its practical organization of orthodoxy: Christian groups throughout American history have embraced austere premillennial visions and at the same time prosecuted ambitious programs of social reform and political involvement.

Feeling often was more important than doctrine, everyday vernacular practice more common than formal worship, and vocabularies of longing, emptiness, and striving more striking in their usage than the language of triumph, certainty, and closure. Authors leading an American literary renaissance and the writers who were influenced by them figured emptiness as creativity and experiment, but also as cultural morbidity, the absence of wonder, and the specter of death. In so doing, they helped to shape a metaphysical religion and liberal Protestantism that cultivated the feeling of emptiness in solitude and silence while it gazed confidently and often imperiously into the American future. At the same time that they dreamed of empire, those liberals fretted about the frailty of culture, perilously juggled self-reliance and self-surrender, and wailed about the hunger in the soul of the seeker. Other voices in the borderlands of American Christianity implied that to empty the body of self was not enough; they prescribed fresh spiritual technologies to leave the body itself behind—a full-on corporeal emptying—in order to enter a timeless and spaceless realm. Some such technologies managed communication with the disembodied dead; others were demonstrations of the illusion of the self, the body, and the physical world; and in one rapidly growing new denomination, marital partners could step out of time and be sealed in eternity.

Concern that space and time were overfilled with sin and that evil deceivers had polluted right doctrine with empty words led some to take refuge in the Bible, read as infallible and for many literally true in every word. Such fundamentalism played out on a charged social field a drama arising from numerous individual experiences of emptiness projected as collective self-understanding. Positive in-group identity accordingly was poorly elaborated because of the emphasis on negative definition at both the individual and the group levels. In consequence group solidarity was accomplished not as much through implementation of a systematic program of the progressive teasing out of applied "meanings" from a kernel of religious truth as by a blindly administered program of demonizing other groups. For more than a century, the fundamentalist orientation to social place has been determined by the identification of enemies who are imagined as conspiring against the Bible. Biblical literalism and the glossolalia of Pentecostal Christianity are central components of a worldview that incorporates fear of empty words and empty doctrines with continuously refreshed apocalyptic visions promising the passage from empty history to the fullness of eternity. It marshals a globally directed evangelical fervor that intends to fill the empty cultures of unconverted populations with lived Christian revelations and deploys a witchcraft cosmology geared to identify impostors. The successes of fundamentalist Christianities in gaining followers at the same time has been the syncing of such outlooks with social and ethical standpoints that translate the feeling of emptiness into personal self-denial read as holiness and with the persuasiveness of a promise that the empty soul will be filled.

Issues of doctrine and devotion that framed debate among Christians in America in the nineteenth century gave way in the twentieth to the identification of international enemies and the construction of science, big government, media, entertainment, gender and sexual equality, civil rights, and humanism as dangers to belief. Fundamentalist Protestantism and the antimodernist Catholicism of the turn of the century remained in force, in the agendas of groups ranging from the followers of Father Coughlin to the second coming of the Ku Klux Klan. Such Christianities, however, looking over the horizon to distant regions of the world that already had been missionized for decades or even centuries, recognized atheism, rather than Buddhism, Islam, Hinduism, papism, or paganism, as their most dangerous opponent. Atheism and its godless ideological stepchildren represented the empty soul at its worst. It was, for many mission-minded observers, also the paradigmatically empty soul almost at its best, yearning to be filled with the Christian message of redemption. Communism, socialism, and totalitarianism were cries for help. The American Christian mission to the world, which always has been dressed a bit more in Protestant clothes than in Catholic robes because of the enduring role of Rome in organizing world missions, accordingly coalesced by the mid-twentieth century as a mixed bag of motives and goals. At home, American Christians enthusiastically set out to tip the empty souls of Communists and the other godless toward God, and as that project gained traction partly for political reasons, Christians remembered anew other religious faiths as starved on empty doctrines and thus similarly poised to receive the gospel. A massive domestic and international missionary effort such as that of the Baptists at midcentury accordingly coordinated a message of emptiness at several levels: the empty souls of the godless; the empty beliefs of non-Christians; the empty space of the world that was not Christian, read as an invitation to fill it with Christian Americanness; the cooperation of American Christians in bringing forth the end of history and the fullness of eternity; the sacrifices of blood, sweat, and physical hunger performed by missionaries; and the demonization of those who appeared to stand in the way of the evangelical project.

In the twentieth century, *horror vacui* became the predominant American architectural style, a testament to the American Christian fascination with emptiness and to the inextinguishable need to fill it. Some groups built fearfully vacuous arena-sized houses of worship where the Sunday head count testified to the truth that empty was the precursor to filled. Emptiness was the central theme in American literature, in fiction and poetry, and after midcentury that literature began to disclose the extent to which Buddhist ideas of emptiness had been processed to coincide with deep-seated American Christian notions of the regeneration of the individual soul. The civil rights movement and second-wave feminism challenged the right of white patriarchs to determine who was empty, who could be filled, and how that should happen, all within the context of a refusal by African Americans and women to serve as living emblems of the empty vessel, as classic examples of pure emotional hungering and simple joy, as souls free of the full baggage of self-affirming critical thought or real agency. The reemergent Christian seeker culture blended a drug-laced call to empty the self of the corrupt materialist culture that frustrated spiritual aspiration with political awareness that conceptualized opponents as monsters. That movement later infused the nascent Christian Right. Christians negotiated paradoxical bargains with emptiness and fullness as self-emptying work became joyous flow, sex between a man and a woman became a threesome with an invisible God who filled both human souls with joy just as they were emptying into him and each other, and communication with God in prayer became a matter of sustaining silence. Christianity, an *orthodox* religion in the sense that it stresses "right words," remained, in America, deeply anxious about words. To an increasing extent, Americans avoided engaging doctrine, including the doctrines of churches to which they belonged.

Catholic nuns and priests, globe-trotting evangelical preachers, and leaders of local congregations developed ways of sustaining religious community that retained some older emphases while revising the tactics of public encounter. The ecumenical impulses of the 1950s recurred at century's end as a diminished interest in taking other Christian groups as opponents. Arguments against other Christian groups per se were less tenable in an environment where demonization of Islam was rejected by most Christians after 9/11 as counterproductive to political coexistence with rival faiths and to efforts to persuade to Christianity globally dispersed populations of non-Christians. At the same time, the central place of the feeling of emptiness and the practices and ideas associated with it continued to inform thinking about what made a person and a community Christian. The new enemies took the form of issues positions thought to represent sensibilities contrary to Christianity. Leaders of Christian groups increasingly phrased their warnings about sin in terms of their opposition to abortion, homosexuality, sex outside of marriage, divorce, the nontraditional family, and gender equality. The setting for such opposition differed from the evangelical campaign against evolution in the 1925 Scopes trial. In that debacle, the issue was made an emblem of conservative Christianity as a whole. By the end of the twentieth century, conservative Christian groups were disinclined to stake as much of their standing as churches on their resistance to abortion or gay marriage. Tactical battles replaced strategic campaigns. Christian denominations targeted issues and cast those who differed from them on those issues as threats to Christianity. In so doing they retained and even reinforced the practice of defining the group through alarm about external threats, and so secured a system of fostering solidarity that legitimated and built upon the interior emptiness of both individual and group. At the same time, they advanced the process—begun in the advent of competition between denominations immediately following disestablishment—of mobility of persons from one group to another. As Christian groups softened their critical rhetoric toward other Christian groups, they not only made the boundaries between such groups easier to cross but contributed to the enlarging of the weakly marked space between denominations, where seekers or the discontented could construct alternative Christian religious practice. At the beginning of the twenty-first century, that alternative practice might include fasting as part of Christian dieting, Protestant workshops on silence conducted at Roman Catholic Trappist monasteries, spilling blood for Jesus in nondenominational Christian martial arts competitions, Christian meditation that drew upon Buddhist traditions of emptiness, preparing for the apocalypse (as a Christian survivalist), striving to make work an extended prayer, or environmental activism dedicated to preserving seemingly empty space. Conservative Christian groups gained membership at the end of the twentieth century, but at the same time more Christianity was situated in the interstices between denominations.

In twenty-first-century America, there are more Christian denominations than ever before, more kinds of devotion that have developed outside of institutional boundaries, more styles of authority and communication, and less concern about doctrines among rank-and-file members. That does not mean, however, that Christian groups no longer exert a strong influence on public life or that they have in any way ceased to stake out their ground as social groups. As in the past, they do not refrain from defining themselves by pushing off from groups they oppose, although opposition more often is identified in terms of positions on social issues. In some cases, the demographics of that conflict signal that strong differences remain between Christian denominations, but those differences infrequently are brought to the foreground of debate. All American Christian groups, not just conservative ones, are engaged in the same project of endeavoring to construct and sustain a sense of affiliation among members of the community by differentiating from other social groups. Identifying those others in some cases as churches but more often as issues constituencies, they commonly name them as evil conspirators or wolves in sheep's clothing. Such characterizations of opponents are deeply rooted in the circumstances of the development of Christianity in America. But they are not solely the product of the American environment. Christianity in other parts of the world at various times and places evidences some similar features. The rapid proliferation of religious others after disestablishment, in the form of competitor Christian groups, has made the American context especially conducive to a style of solidarity that relies upon the *via negativa*. That process is grounded in the American Christian cultivation and representation of the feeling of emptiness. When the feeling of emptiness met the First Amendment, an aspect of Christian community formation with ancient roots was brought to the fore.

The culture of emptiness among American Christians is complex, varied, and constantly changing. It impresses as a process made up of many interconnected moving parts. Each group fosters the cultivation of the feeling of emptiness or of fullness in distinct ways. Even within a single group, the process can vary from one historical period to another. Feelings of emptiness arise and are sustained within an assortment of contexts. The social groups that define those contexts for their members rely upon complicated machinery to manage those feelings.

In America, the regulation of the feeling of emptiness, the management of that feeling, is accomplished through performance of a multifaceted social drama involving ongoing positioning and repositioning of the Christian in-group vis-á-vis groups perceived as competitors or opponents. Intense feelings of emptiness make difficult a positive sense of group identity (as well as personal identity). By defining itself *via negativa*—that is, by articulating what it is *not*—a group is able to mark its boundaries and in so doing offer to members a rationale for belonging. Aggressive attempts to identify opponents against whom it can push off occur in cases where a group's cultivation of emptiness is deep and broad. In cases where there is less active cultivation of the feeling of emptiness, and greater awareness of fullness, group identity typically arises from stronger collective affirmation of group principles alongside a less ambitious program of differentiation from competing out-groups. In such cases, a group conceptually (and sometimes physically) positions itself closer to out-groups and is less preoccupied with identifying opponents. The process of othering, then, is diminished in such cases. Feeling, group identity, and social boundary accordingly are interwoven as components in a process of othering that manages the emotional experiences of members of various Christian groups.

The regulating of the feeling of emptiness as a part of the broader dynamics of social differentiation can be observed in groups representing a wide range of Christian ideas and behaviors in America. The chapters that follow focus on five contexts of feeling in American Christianity. In the course of discussing emotion, body, space, time, and believers, they detail the many ways in which the feeling of emptiness is cultivated, promoted, and moderated and how those processes are related to the practices of boundary-drawing, criticism of competing social groups, and the construction of others.

In this book I discuss how Christian groups in America, committed to the cultivation of a feeling of emptiness, have defined themselves vis-à-vis other groups and how disestablishment abetted that process by creating the conditions for the proliferation of religious groups who could serve as foils. In thinking about group (and personal) identity, it also is useful, as we begin to estimate the importance of emptiness, to note that many writers, over many years, have approached the question "What is Christianity?" by describing what it is not. Even before the Republic, such a strategy is detectable. During the nineteenth century it became more common and pronounced. Sometimes, it swept everything from its path. In 1860, the *Mercersburg Review* attempted to define Christianity by invoking "the real principle of difference." Broaching the issue of "the essential nature of Christianity," the *Review* proposed:

> To the question: What is Christianity? we reply: It is not a method by which God maintains and vindicates His moral government over intelligent creatures. It is not a series of truths announced to the world from time to time by the Holy Spirit through inspired men. It is not a plan of infinite wisdom to fulfill eternal and immutable decrees. It is not simply an atonement for the sins of men accomplished by our Lord on the cross. Much less is it primarily a state of mind or a state of feeling experienced by believers. Nor is it a system of belief; nor a mode of worshipping God, nor a life of holiness.

None of those seeming attributes "express or represent its principle and essential nature." In the same way that the *Review* pushed off from a litany of statements of doctrine in blindly navigating toward presumed essential principles, many Christian groups pushed off from other groups in attempting to understand themselves as social entities. That process has been under-studied by historians of religion in America.[1]

Viewing the history of Christianity in America as the promotion of the feeling of emptiness turns our attention away from historical narratives that recount the progressive enlargement, refinement, alteration, erasure, and reinvention of a certain "positive" core set of principles and beliefs thought to comprise the essence of Christianity. It alternatively evokes fluidity, indefiniteness, contradictoriness, paradox, the anxious construction of appearances, the unreliability of language, and preoccupations with failure and loss. Some observers of the American religious scene have previously pointed us in that direction. The nineteenth-century American Roman Catholic convert Orestes Brownson, trying to puzzle out a way to narrate Christian history, complained: "But such are the variations and apparent inconsistencies of the historical representation it has received, that, while history enables us with ease to say what Christianity is not,—as for instance, that it is not Protestantism,—yet it does not without difficulty, enable us to say precisely what it is." James William Mendenhall, editor of the *Methodist Review* in the latter part of the nineteenth century, summarized his own perspective in similar terms: "The world must first be taught what Christianity is *not* before it will truly apprehend what Christianity is." In 1891 a Jewish observer of American Christianity, Rabbi Joseph Krauskopf, a member of the first class at Hebrew Union College in Cincinnati, saw the increased competition among Christian groups in America in the nineteenth century and reported: "What is Christianity? After long search and study and inquiry, I find it easier to tell what Christianity is not than what it is." Krauskopf explained that Protestants, Catholics, Calvinists, Swedenborgians, Episcopalians, Quakers, Methodists, Baptists, and Unitarians "indignantly and emphatically declare that" each of the others is not truly Christian. For Krauskopf, that realization was both instructive and disconcerting. The ruminations of leading Congregationalist theologian Lyman Abbott, moreover, would not have helped Krauskopf sort out the field. In a terse magazine article, "What Is a Christian?" (1908), he defined Christianity principally by what one did not need to believe, including the Westminster Confession of Faith, the Thirty-Nine Articles of the Episcopal Church, the Twenty-Five Articles of the Methodists, the Nine Articles of the Evangelical Alliance, the decrees of the Council of Trent, and the Nicene Creed. And even the most published writer in America, Charles Sheldon, author of *In His Steps*, a book advising persons to ask "What Would Jesus Do?" and then do it, confessed: "May I be pardoned if, in answer to a multitude of misunderstandings, I say this right here? I have never taught in any way the absurdity that others have claimed for me, that we could tell absolutely and dogmatically what Jesus would do in certain conditions!" Not knowing what Jesus would do, but endeavoring to do what Jesus would do accordingly was a challenge, and one that might be better approached (as Sheldon's fictional characters discovered) by not doing what Jesus would not do: not drinking, not engaging in unethical business practices, not retreating from the community, not being sexually loose, and other proscriptions. Beyond that, it was at least as difficult to know, for example, what it meant to be a Congregationalist when the "essence" of belonging to that group—to borrow a term from religious writers—was largely to cultivate a consciousness that one was not a Baptist, Catholic, Unitarian, Swedenborgian, or a member of another group that was believed to be different from Congregationalists.[2]

In the early twenty-first century, the pursuit of understanding what a Christian is, what the "essence of Christianity" is, remains a central concern for American Christians. Defining Christianity by saying what it is not remains an important part of that process, exemplified by ongoing explorations of Christian identity such as *What Christianity Is Not* (2013). Looking beneath that effort, we discover the emphasis placed upon the feeling of emptiness in American Christianity and the cascading consequences of that for the social identities of individuals and groups.[3]

Something and Nothing battle here.
One we never get to see at all,
The other we watch closely
Changing costumes and masks
In hope it'll add up to something.
—Charles Simic

1

Feeling

The Emotion of Emptiness

Emotion is more important than it used to be. In the past several decades, the humanities have rediscovered it and made it a prime concern. In areas such as religious studies, classics, philosophy, literary studies, and history, recent scholarship evidences a reorientation to emotion as a primary datum susceptible to scholarly analysis. There are new theories of emotion, its expression, its relation to cognition, the body, culture, and power. This renaissance in the study of emotion is characterized by bold interdisciplinary research and ambitious interpretation. It is changing the way we think about Mediterranean antiquity, the French Revolution, Pacific Islander communities, Egyptian Bedouins, memory, ethics, space, politics, and America.[1]

In the area of religion, this development has been noticeable even though the field has never been without some scholarship addressing feeling.[2] Overviews of recent work describe a turn within the field from theologically framed analyses of emotion to approaches that draw upon the social and behavioral sciences, biological sciences, and social and cultural history. Scholars have studied religious conceptualizations of emotion and its ritual performances, emotion in religious ethics and material culture, the gendering and racializing of emotion, language and embodiedness, the historical development of emotional religious cultures, and individual emotions such as anger, fear, and love.[3] In short, we know much more about emotion in religion than we did thirty years ago. As a result we are better positioned to appreciate the similarities and differences among religious groups in different parts of the world. We also are able to better understand religion in relation to other aspects of life, from politics to art, work, family, and institutions.

The surge of interest in emotion among religion scholars has opened opportunities for reconsiderations of American religious history. A focus on emotion enables interpretation that can track lives as they unfold in a wide range of contexts where similar emotional experiences are found. Rather than focusing primarily on doctrine or polity, study of American religion can pay attention to feelings that are important in religion and follow those feelings into other aspects of culture, observing the ways in which life experiences in various areas are interwoven around emotion. An investigation of emotion in religion in America accordingly notices human subjectivities that have been biologically framed and culturally shaped, identifies a key emotion or cluster of emotions and a set of cultural sites for their performance, and illustrates how emotional religion plays a role in the shaping of a national culture.

But what emotion? Of all of the emotions that have been associated with religion—wonder, awe, jealousy, love, shame, and many others—which one is best for a study of Christianity in America? The simple answer, and the obvious one, is that we should focus on an emotion that is prominent in religion but that also recurs in other contexts. The better answer is that we are less likely to see anything new in American Christianity by following the trail of an emotion that previously has been privileged in religious scholarship. Love is such an emotion. So is fear. So is hatred. It is possible that historians versed in emotions studies might one day reevaluate such emotions and by so doing fashion original historical narratives around them. For the present, however, we can endeavor to follow the trail of an emotion less familiar to readers of histories of American Christianity but crucially important to understanding American Christianity's history. That emotion is emptiness.

The experience of emptiness often is mentioned in psychoanalytic literature and is discussed in psychology journals, but less often has it been the focus of empirical investigation. Some researchers treat it as raw emotion, while others have described it as a highly cognized emotion, one that is related to existential concerns and involves philosophical and reflective thought. It has been linked to suicidal ideation, borderline personality disorder, and schizoid ego structure, and has been differentiated from depression. It is related to boredom in some psychological studies and in the writings of philosophers such as Jean Paul Sartre ("soul-destroying boredom") and Søren Kierkegaard. Virtually all psychological research agrees that it is a common human experience, and researchers employ the term "feeling of emptiness" to refer to it. The anthropologist Richard A. Shweder has argued for a cross-cultural understanding of feelings of emptiness as "soul loss," pointing out that the emotion of emptiness is common to cultures around the world and that it is associated with a similar cluster of ideas and related feelings in its various settings: death, vulnerability, blood stagnated in the veins, cold, darkness, a missing soul, and so forth, and that it is somatized similarly (i.e., sleep loss, weight loss, dizziness). The American psychologist James H. Leuba (1867–1946), among other American writers, became curious about emptiness in connection with religion in the early twentieth century, but little scientific research has followed from that.[4]

Those familiar with Buddhism will not be surprised by the focus here on emptiness (in some cases expressed as "nothingness") as an emotion central to religious lives. The experience of emptiness is fundamental to Buddhism and has been much discussed in Anglophone literature over the past half century, particularly in relation to Christianity. Recent scholarship has defined the Western engagement of Buddhism, as that religion gradually became known to Europeans following the sixteenth-century reports of Francis Xavier, as the invention of the "Oriental philosophy," a system characterized above all by "the cult of emptiness" or "the cult of nothingness." More pointedly, beginning in the 1960s and continuing for several decades, the influence of deconstructive theology, alongside growing American interest in Asian religious traditions generally, was felt in numerous studies arguing for similarity in Buddhist and Christian spirituality. The point of comparison in such work typically was that the experience of emptiness—the *sunyata* of Buddhism—was thought to occur not only in Christian mysticism but in the everyday religious practice of Western Christians. The writings of Japanese scholars Nishida Kitaro and his disciple Keiji Nishitani, among others, proved particularly alluring to Westerners who sought to advance postmodern inquiry about consciousness, logic, time, identity, and ethics through a focus on the feeling of emptiness.[5]

One endeavor eventuating from the Western interest in Buddhism was the attempt to demonstrate the theological compatibility of Buddhism with Christianity. Buddhist emptiness was compared, for example, to the Christian idea of *kenosis*. Drawing upon the writings of Christian mystics, some argued that *kenosis* as a kind of purposeful emptying of the self in expectation of being filled by God was a Christian expression of the cultivated emptiness that was central to Buddhist thought. A related scholarly project was the attempt to demonstrate that Christian apophatic theology, or negative theology (*via negativa*)—a spiritual path emphasizing awareness of what God is not, rather than what God is—was congruent with Buddhist emptiness. Among the most ambitious of scholarly efforts to bring the Buddhist experience of emptiness to the center of the study of religion—not just in comparison with Christianity but as a framework for understanding a range of traditions—was the work of Frederick J. Streng, an accomplished mid-twentieth-century translator of Mādhyamika texts and interpreter of Nagarjuna's (c. 150–250 CE) doctrine of emptiness. In *Emptiness: A Study in Religious Meaning*, Streng proposed, drawing on Nagarjuna, that emptiness was a "means of ultimate transformation," a process, and he asserted therein and in other writings that the term "religion" consequently had no fixed referent. The study of religion accordingly should set aside trust in language to identify a religious "essence" and pursue instead inquiry into the various networked social and cultural contexts from which "religious" meanings emerged. His approach, said one commentator, was to proffer "emptiness as a paradigm for understanding world religions."[6]

But Buddhism is not Christianity. Whatever the goals of research that seeks to harmonize those religions, and others with them, those are not our purpose here. We are interested in emptiness first of all as a feeling, and not primarily as a theological construct that might intersect with other such constructs. Feelings do not take place in a cultural vacuum and to some extent are cognized. The worlds of ideas in which people live are not distinct from people's experiences of emotion. There is some value, at some point, to compare Buddhist and Christian characterizations of the feeling of emptiness. But in inquiring into feeling and religion in American Christianity, we must avoid overlaying that Christianity with an Asian Buddhist conception of emptiness. It is the emotion itself that matters. It is what the psychologist and historian of religions Louise Sundararajan has emphasized in her writing about the "savoured" Chinese Buddhist emotion of *kong*, "the feeling that everything is 'empty' to the very core." For Sundararajan, *kong* is negative affect that paradoxically is cultivated for its capability to positively transform a person. We follow her lead here, taking emptiness firstly as an emotion, not a theological idea. But it is a complex emotion, and when it occurs it often is ornamented with religious ideas.[7] Love can be experienced similarly. And shame.

As in Buddhism, emptiness has a long tradition in Christianity, reaching back to classics such as Saint Augustine's *Confessions*, and before that into a primitive Christianity shaped by Neoplatonic philosophy.[8] Nineteenth- and twentieth-century Protestant theologians such as Friedrich Schleiermacher and Rudolf Otto, the former accentuating a "feeling of absolute dependence" and the latter a feeling of "emptiness and nothingness" as the core of Christian spirituality, were familiar with the reports of medieval mystics such as Meister Eckhart and Saint John of the Cross (and Otto with Buddhists, whose notions of emptiness he compared to Meister Eckhart's).[9] Like their contemporaries, they were able to draw on a deep vocabulary about emptiness and nothingness in their writing. One of their influences, the German Eckhart (c. 1260–1327), wrote at length about the feeling of emptiness, about the "God beyond God," God as Absolute Unity, the Void, and the profound emotional states experienced in the mystic's search for God. The sixteenth-century Spanish mystic Saint John of the Cross likewise created a rich vocabulary for speaking about the experience of emptiness and its centrality to Christian spirituality. In *Dark Night of the Soul* (1585), he described the soul's journey to God and the trials experienced along the way. In that journey, it is "the mark of the spirit (that has been purged and annihilated with respect to all particular affections and all particularized knowledge) that, remaining in emptiness and darkness, it takes pleasure in no particular thing, but is capable of embracing all things in their totality." The experience of "aridness and emptiness," repeatedly referenced by the Spaniard, forced upon the soul recognition of its baseness and wretchedness. The feeling of emptiness, however, was also desire, a desperate yearning for union with God. It was a complex emotion, a feeling, as Sanjuanian scholar Laura L. Garcia observes, that "what we need in order to be united with God is to be empty of ourselves." Such was the conclusion also of the nineteenth-century Bowdoin College philosopher and psychologist Thomas C. Upham, a devout follower of Wesleyan holiness, who drew inspiration from (and authored a book about) Saint Catharine of Genoa, whom he quoted: "No matter whether he be man or angel, no being can be any thing in God until he has become nothing in himself. When the emptiness of the creature is filled with the fullness of God, then . . . God dwells in the creature."[10]

The experiences of emptiness and of fullness often were linked for religious persons such as Saint Catharine and, before her, Augustine, who anticipated how one day God "wilt destroy this emptiness with an amazing fullness," a hopeful expectation of "that time when I pass from the pinch of emptiness to the contentment of fullness." That time, as well as the means by which emptiness became fullness, and even the experience itself of emptiness-becoming-fullness, were thought to be hidden from full human comprehension. According to Eckhart, Saint John, and many other mystics, such feeling was indescribable, beyond what words could manage, and it was paradoxical. In that vein, the thirteenth-century stigmatic Blessed Angela of Foligno, futilely reaching to capture in language something of her feeling, referred to the "indescribable abyss of delights and illuminations." Professions of indescribability, however, did not keep the American religious press and religion writers from ongoing commentary on the theme, nor from earnest citation of medieval mystics, nor from seeking to educate about something that was imagined as beyond words. It did not keep the Mennonite *Herald of Truth*, located in Chicago, from republishing in 1880 an extract from Thomas à Kempis under the title "The Emptiness of Mere Human Knowledge," as a way into discussing the matter more fully.[11]

Calvin's Legacy

In *Everything and Nothing*, a rumination about Shakespeare's extraordinarily productive career, Jorge Luis Borges wrote: "There was no one in him: behind his face (which even through the bad paintings of those times resembles no other) and his words, which were copious, fantastic and stormy, there was only a bit of coldness, a dream dreamt by no one." From boyhood, writes Borges, Shakespeare had sensed "this emptiness." That depiction of Shakespeare is suggestive of the language about emptiness in the Puritanism that coalesced during Shakespeare's lifetime. Catherine Gimelli Martin, observing the Puritans' antipathy to "self-esteem," remarks that "not only did they link it to spiritual pride, but they considered even 'self-confidence' the equivalent of *self-conceitedness* and *self-fullness*, the diametric opposite of the self-emptiness that directed their 'utter dependence' on God." The Puritan mystic Francis Rous, as Jerald C. Brauer wrote, "shared several elements of classical Western Christian mysticism." Rous, a politically active Presbyterian (and later Independent) and a member of Cromwell's council of state after 1653, "stands firmly within the mystical tradition when he argues for the necessity of purging the total person in preparation for a heavenly visitation: only the pure in heart can see God, and one must be empty before one can be full." Only a minority of Puritans were as deeply mystical in their devotions as Rous, but, as Brauer points out, that "mystical dimension of piety is very strongly present within the evangelical tradition of Puritanism." As such, it influenced the construction of Puritan spiritual lives in New England as well as Old England. Thomas Hooker, a former fellow of Emmanuel College, Cambridge, which was a breeding ground for Puritans, came to Massachusetts and eventually decamped from there to Hartford, where he is remembered as "the Father of Connecticut." He is also remembered for preaching that "you must be empty if ever Christ will fill you." The Puritan cultivation of emptiness in expectation of being filled became an important component in the development of Christianity in America.[12]

In the fledgling communities of New England, Puritans kept records of their feelings of emptiness. One collection of those records is the book of conversion accounts of congregants in Rev. Thomas Shepard's First Church in Cambridge, Massachusetts. In the 1630s–40s, a succession of persons came before the church to relate their stories of experiencing saving grace, with the expectation that having confessed to a crucial stage in their regeneration, they would be admitted to full communion in the church—a status important for social as well as moral advancement. Shepard, who was the son-in-law of Hooker, recounted in his autobiography his own experience "of a total emptiness" as a central part of his spirituality. His congregants in Cambridge, as Andrea Knutson has observed, likewise claimed "emptiness" in their confessions. The tone of a young male's testimony was typical: "I lived without God in the world. Mr. Hooker's sermons about sight of sin and sense of it did stir up prayer. But I returned to the vanity and carelessness of my life" until "I heard directions how to come to Christ: (1) Come empty and poor and answerable with sense of want of everything." The joining of a feeling of emptiness to desire, to the "sense of want" or the anticipation of being filled, is redolent in the relations of Shepard's confessors just as it is present in the writings of other Puritans in the seventeenth and eighteenth centuries. That is not to say that Puritans, and other Christians, in every instance expressed their "want of God" to fill them when they spoke of their feelings of emptiness. In some cases, they felt empty because of the death of a loved one, or in migrating they felt the loss of familiar environs. Even those experiences, however, often led them to eventual reflection on the emptiness of the world and the vanity of things, and to renewed expressions of desire to be filled by God.[13]

In *Spiritual Milk for Boston Babes*, published in the 1640s, the Massachusetts Puritan leader John Cotton offered the children of New Englanders a catechism he proffered as milk "drawn out of the breasts of both testaments for their souls' nourishment." One of the various doctrinal sips that Cotton urged upon young Christians began with a question: "What is your corrupt nature?" The answer: "My corrupt nature is empty of grace, bent unto sin and only unto sin." That highly theologized representation of emptiness, in keeping with Calvin's dictum that individuals "cannot seriously aspire to [God] before we begin to become displeased with ourselves," framed much other discussion about the feeling of emptiness. There were other ways in which emptiness was expressed in more complicated fashion, however. The poet Anne Bradstreet versified about how the feeling of emptiness itself could prompt improper pursuits, observing, "Sometimes vainglory is the only bait/Whereby my empty soul is lured and caught." Bradstreet meditated on the prospect of feeling filled and tried to imagine how her seemingly limitless desire to be filled could be satisfied by God. In her *Meditation LI* she acknowledged: "The eyes and eares are the inlets or doors of the soul, through which innumerable objects enter, yet is not that spacious room filled, neither doth it ever say it is enough . . . and which is most strang, the more it receivs, the more empty it finds it self, and sees an impossibility, ever to be filled, but by him in whom all fullness dwells."[14] The New England poet Edward Taylor, who has been characterized (together with Jonathan Edwards and Ralph Waldo Emerson) as having engaged in the "pursuit of emptiness to absolute repletion," added his own queries to Bradstreet's questions about the realization of emptiness. In a voice that "fluctuates between confidence and despair," Taylor magnified God by describing his own emptiness and unworthiness. In Taylor's verse, as the human is disclosed to be progressively more lowly, so God is made greater and accordingly more capable of rescuing—filling up—the lowly sinner. "I am to Christ more base than to a King/A Mite, Fly, Worm, Ant, Serpent, Divell is," declared Taylor. "I/Must needs admire, when I recall to minde,/That's Fullness, This it's emptiness." The mood that informs Taylor's writing was "both a reaching upward for meaning and a confession of meaninglessness." In that context, Taylor's writing itself can be understood as "an act of desiring," and its expression was distinctly gendered. As Belden Lane has noted, that writing often expressed the Puritans' tendency to adopt "feminine imagery to emphasize the emptiness and self-effacement they saw as prerequisite to being filled by God." Exceptions to that were in the form of jeremiads, which Puritans such as Michael Wigglesworth fashioned in such a way as to emphasize meaninglessness at the expense of hope, as in the despairing "A Song of Emptiness to Fill Up the Empty Pages Following."[15]

The profound relationship between feeling empty and feeling filled, the play between feelings of intense desire born of emptiness and feelings of satisfaction and joy, is evidenced in much Puritan reflection on spirituality, including the writing of the Northampton minister Jonathan Edwards. In notes made about 1740, Edwards reported that taking a walk through the woods for the purpose of prayer and contemplation, he had "a view, that for me was extraordinary, of the glory of the Son of God. . . . The person of Christ appeared ineffably excellent, with an excellency great enough to swallow up all thought and conception." During an hour of loud weeping, Edwards felt "emptied and annihilated, to be in the dust, and to be full of Christ alone." That feeling of being both empty and full was not the norm for Edwards, however powerful it was in the woods that day. More common was Edwards's voicing of his doubts about his status before God and his expressions of intense longing. But even in the experience of alienation from God, Edwards petitioned God to assist him in feeling empty, one indication of the complex interweaving of the feeling of emptiness and distance from God with the feeling of closeness and union with God. "God knows the wickedness of my heart and the great and sinful deficiencies and offenses which I have been guilty of in the course of my ministry at Northhampton," Edwards lamented in a letter to the Scottish pastor Thomas Gillespie in the summer of 1751. "I desire that God would discover them to me more and more, and that now he would effectually humble me and mortify my pride and self-confidence, and empty me entirely of myself, and make me to know how that I deserve to be cast away as an abominable branch."[16]

Part of the process of cultivating longing for God was, for Edwards, imagining his own emptiness. He professed, "I love to think of coming to Christ, to receive salvation of him, poor in spirit and quite empty of self." Like Taylor, he wished that he "might be nothing, and that God might be all" at the same time that he craved the "loveliness" of a "calm rapture" in which he was filled with the love of God and was perfectly sanctified.[17] In his instructional writings, such as the *Treatise concerning Religious Affections*, Edwards was clear that the "experience of joy is the Holy Ghost, self-emptiness, a spirit to exalt God above all," and he continued to name the perfections of God in contrast to the meanness, emptiness, and unworthiness of sinners. He also carried forward some of his personal ruminations to the conclusion that "the more grace they have, while in this state of imperfection, the more they see their imperfection and emptiness, and distance from what ought to be." Grace increased the feeling of emptiness as it grew in the heart of the Christian. Paradoxically, it also produced extraordinary visions of God.[18]

Edwards, however, for all of his imaginings and his efforts to articulate his feelings, was resolved that his feelings were in the end inexpressible. Discovering anew the excellency of the gospel one Saturday night in 1739, he typically reported that "it appeared sweet, beyond all expression, to follow Christ." Holiness made the soul bloom like a field of flowers, he wrote; it "brought an inexpressible purity, brightness, peacefulness and ravishment to the soul."[19] Throughout his writings, Edwards declared that the related feelings of emptiness and of being filled by God's love were beyond words. William J. Scheick has addressed this issue directly, proposing that Edwards believed in an "emptiness at the core of . . . human language." Scheick notes that "this void at the center of human language intimates the presence of a divine reality that cannot be said or named in *sciential* discourse but that can be affectively registered as 'mental sensation.'" As a result, for Edwards "the denotative reality of God can only be encountered as *sapiential* pure idea (affective knowledge initiated by special grace) because God's excellence is incomprehensible and therefore unimaginable."[20] Just as an apprehension of the holiness of God could not be put into words (a belief of some of Edwards's opponents as well),[21] so also was the related feeling of emptiness impossible to capture in language. Given the linguistic problem—one that emerges in virtually all religions and recently has come to be cast as a "words" versus "embodiedness" debate—the feelings of emptiness or of God's love in one respect were, finally, incommunicable for those who experienced them. To say they were "meaningless moments" captures something of their resistance to linguistic representation.[22] But as glimpsed in the reports of colonial New Englanders, and in the writings of other Christians before and after them in Europe and North America, those moments were profound emotional experiences, considered revelatory to those who had them, and they were repeatedly referenced as building blocks of Christian life and fundamental to belief. The question arises, however, how a person or a community creates identity when their core experience is an incommunicable emotion of emptiness and when their hope is to become progressively more empty.

The modernist American poet William Carlos Williams, author of an influential overview of American literature, wrote about the inner emptiness of Puritans and their Yankee descendants in New England and elsewhere. Written at a time when Puritan-bashing was an unofficial American sport, *In the American Grain* (1925) judged Puritans harshly. Embedded in Williams's criticism, nevertheless, was an observation about the Puritans that continues to resonate. Remarking on the Pilgrims, he asserted that they, "out of the intensity of their emptiness imagining they are full, deceive themselves. . . . The Pilgrims, they, the seed, instead of growing, looked black at a world and damning its perfections praised a zero in themselves." Meant by Williams as an indictment of the Puritans, it was in fact a judgment that Puritans might have embraced as at least partly true. They would not have admitted to directly praising that zero, but they would have admitted to recognizing it. In fact, they did praise it indirectly, inasmuch as they made the feeling of emptiness the centerpiece of their spiritual lives and conceptualized that experience as a sign of their progress in grace toward God, each step increasing the feeling of emptiness and at the same time bringing them closer to God. The English novelist and critic D. H. Lawrence, writing at the same time as Williams, drew similar conclusions about the Puritans. For Lawrence, Puritans were hollow. They came to America to escape Europe, carrying with them little but a sense of what they did not want to be. "They came largely to get away," said Lawrence. "Away from what? In the long run, away from themselves." Such a view concludes that Puritans brought little but their own emptiness—and ways of thinking about it—and they made that emptiness the center of the culture they fashioned in America. For Lawrence, that hollow center continued to direct the course of American culture as it subsequently developed over several centuries.[23]

Kinds of Emptiness

A few weeks before his death in 1892, the American poet and Quaker abolitionist John Greenleaf Whittier wrote his last poem, "To Oliver Wendell Holmes"; Holmes was a fellow Fireside Poet. Touching on memory, brotherhood, sorrow, and age, it ended with a reference to the "naked soul" being filled with divine love.

> The hour draws near, howe'er delayed and late,
> When at the Eternal Gate
> We leave the words and works we call our own,
> And lift void hands alone

For love to fill. Our nakedness of soul
Brings to that Gate no toll;
Giftless we come to Him, who all things gives,
And live because He lives.[24]

The notion that a naked or empty soul brings "no toll" to the heavenly gate was by the end of the nineteenth century deeply embedded in American Christian thinking about sin and salvation. Even as Gospel of Wealth and Social Gospel theological trends emerged, that thinking coalesced around several key ideas, including the notion that the world was a place of vanities, of empty pursuits and worthless achievements, and the idea that emptiness was good, an experience to be valued. Nineteenth-century American discussions of emptiness could have an assortment of referents, such as the worthlessness of human undertakings, sin, a sense of guilt, chronic depression, and, paradoxically, a feeling of fullness. Emptiness was negatively conceived when it was associated with mere earthly objects and flawed human aspiration or, in certain cases, when it occurred because of the loss of a loved one or in other circumstances that called for empathy with human suffering. But it also was valued as a feeling linked to longing for God. It was, simply, to be both rejected and cultivated, a view of emptiness that required thoughtfulness about immediate circumstances and context (e.g., feeling empty on a battlefield versus in a church). Nineteenth-century writers did not directly address the issue of good versus bad emptiness. With a few exceptions, they were too close to the issue to see it as we might. Sometimes, approaching it obliquely, diverse writers might evidence a shared sense of where emptiness shaded from its positive aspects to its negative. At other times writers simply disagreed about whether the feeling was to be embraced, set aside, or vigorously cultivated. Complicating the discussion was a Christian trust in the impossibility of words to fully express feelings of either emptiness or fullness.

American writers sometimes pictured emptiness—as a feeling, a practice, or a course of life—in an unfavorable light. In recommending the example of Lady Elizabeth Hastings (d. 1739), the daughter of the seventh earl of Huntingdon, who was known as an educational benefactor, an English essay republished in Philadelphia in 1767 contrasted her piety to "the emptiness and vanity of a life spent in the pursuit of worldly profit, ease, or pleasure." That condemnation of vanity and emptiness was familiar to colonial Americans because of their constant exposure to it in sermons and published writings. Americans habitually associated their feelings of emptiness with the vanity of earthly pursuits. Under the banner of religion and morality, feelings of emptiness blended with a sense of the hollowness of earthly achievement. That process took place across the social order and among both men and women. In many cases, the deeper the feeling of emptiness, the more sweeping the profession of the vanity of the world. The African abolitionist Olaudah Equiano (d. 1797), a former slave and convert to Methodism, said, "[I] thought that my state was worse than any man's; my mind was unaccountable disturbed; I often willed for death. . . . And being much concerned about the state of my soul . . . I became a burden to myself, and viewed all things around me as emptiness and vanity." The religious press during the nineteenth century reinforced and refined this thinking. The *New York Evangelist* explained in "The Emptiness of Human Glory" that even massive and commanding sculptured marble cathedrals were little more than "crumbling tombstones." A Philadelphia religious and literary magazine, in explaining the "emptiness of worldly fame" with references to Milton's *Paradise Regained*, reminded readers that Satan was "insatiable of glory." The itinerant preacher Lorenzo Dow prayed that "the Lord would teach [him] the emptiness of earthly enjoyments."[25]

Philosophy, sometimes a help to thinking about God and creation, might also be empty. Disciples of Christ leader Alexander Campbell was grateful to have learned that the opinions of men were "empty and vain." The Princeton professor Charles Hodge, author of carefully reasoned systematic theology, explained that philosophy was no substitute for Christianity, because it was "void" of truth, reality and power: "It was κενός (empty, vain) in all of those senses." Worship that tilted toward philosophical consideration of moral questions at the expense of biblically grounded doctrine was similarly suspect. Campbell, like the energetic Methodist Episcopal Church bishop Francis Asbury, complained about "empty worship" and "empty externals" of religion that were the institutional vestiges of humans' overestimation of themselves.[26] The *New York Evangelist* similarly opined that a certain philosophically informed sermon on morality had been "eloquent" and "beautiful" but that "we mistake if many who went away with admiration of the preacher on their lips, did not have a feeling of emptiness in their hearts." Such statements had been common since the seventeenth century, as proponents of "experiential religion" jousted with those who were concerned that formal ritual and institutional authority not be overwhelmed by performances of emotion. In many cases, the debate was rhetorical positioning for control of religious doctrine, and despite the adversarial portrayal of more "formal" religion as lacking in real spiritual substance,

Christians of virtually all stripes understood and responded to arguments that placed the feeling of emptiness at the center of spirituality. There were not many who thought, like the millennialist William Miller, that the whole world without exception—philosophy, formal worship, church buildings, social life, family affection, human achievement in general—was a place of "vain allurements and empty show." And it was rare for a religious commentator to write the emptiness out of all human endeavor in a bid to establish the credentials of a certain strain of belief. But there were degrees of difference in the way congregations and denominations framed the issue. Overall, pronouncements about emptiness and vanity were part of a larger framing of Christian life that focused, in differing degrees of intensity, on the longing for God. They illustrate, however, that the notion of "empty worship," for example, implied that there was a corresponding "inner fullness." Inner fullness in turn implied a more complex corresponding inner emptiness.[27]

Some writers explicitly related the emptiness and vanity of earthly undertakings to the holiness of God. Sister Saint Francis Xavier stated in her letters that "the more we see things of the earth, the more we discover their emptiness but the more we study God, the more perfections we find in him." Sarah Morey Hunt, of Chester County, Pennsylvania, concerned about young people, thought it best to "show them the beauty of holiness and the emptiness of the vanities of this world." The Catholic Elizabeth Sullivan Stuart praised a "lovely Christian" the day after the woman's burial, noting that "she spoke of the emptiness of the earth, the joy & peace in believing." The erudite Rev. Joseph Stevens Buckminster, Unitarian minister at the Brattle Street Church in Boston, was no strict Calvinist, shied from doctrines of human depravity, and helped to bring German biblical criticism to America. He nevertheless urged his congregation, "May God open your hearts to understand his scriptures! . . . Compared with the knowledge, which they contain, every other subject of human inquiry is vanity and emptiness. Politicks, philosophy, poetry . . . are the chattering and plays of children." The emptiness and vanity of the world could be seen in relief against the excellence of the gospel and the beauty of God. The vision of emptiness was shaped by a vision of holiness. The feeling of joy, peace, and fulfillment was informed by the feeling of emptiness, and vice versa.[28]

Sin, which was widely regarded as detachment from God, was sometimes specifically cast as emptiness of soul. The *Christian Examiner*, remarking on spiritual development leading to an awareness of God's love, preached that "this consciousness, however, comes through the awakened sense of emptiness, or sin, in the creature detached from its Creator. . . . Religion comes to awaken this sense of emptiness." Emptiness, while a precondition for being filled by God, was sometimes spoken of as a consciousness of personal sin, which was represented as guilt. The Protestant pietist Henry Alline, whose example the psychologist William James found illuminating, complained that he felt himself to be "the most guilty wretch on earth." He added, "I had now so great a sense of the vanity and emptiness of all things here below." Those guilty of sin would be punished by more feelings of emptiness in the afterlife. Hell, observed the *Christian Inquirer*, "may be that of literal fire, or it may not. It may be physical suffering or the pangs of conscience, the absence of love, and the sense of emptiness." To be drawn to God, accordingly, was to be drawn not only as an empty vessel but also as a sinner. Philadelphian Eliza Paul Gurney, in a diary entry at midcentury, wrote that persons are "invited to come with our emptiness to the fullness which is in Christ,—aye, and with the burthen of our guilt and transgression." Emptiness could be conceptualized as sin, consciousness of sin, worldly vanities, and a species of guilt.[29]

Americans characterized depression as a feeling of emptiness. In some cases such discussions were explicitly framed in religious language, while at other times they were not. Feelings of emptiness did not always have to be religious. Lyman Beecher wrote of his "great emptiness" following the death of his first wife Roxana, but he did not frame it as a religious matter, as he sometimes did other references to emptiness. Mary Maclane, the "Wild Woman of Butte" (Butte, Montana), told the readers of her best-selling 1901 memoir: "I have been tortured so long with the dull, dull misery of Nothingness!" and bewailed "the wracked nerves of my Nothingness," but she did not mention God, grace, or Christian prayer. Many of those who self-reported depression, whether or not they believed it to be related specifically to spiritual emptiness, looked to religion in trying to understand their suffering, however. The New York poet and literary socialite Anne Lynch Botta, a Roman Catholic, confessed, "I have, ever since I grew up, been subject to attacks of depression that, while they lasted, made life almost unendurable. A sudden realization of the emptiness, shortness, nothingness of life comes over me." At those times, she wrote, "I need preaching to, and praying for, badly." Lucy Larcom, a Massachusetts mill girl and the author of *A New England Girlhood* (1889), was a devout Congregationalist. At the age of thirty-seven, she grieved, "My whole life has lost the feeling of reality. . . . I know well enough the theory of life; what principles to sustain me; what great objects there are to live for; and still there remains the same emptiness." Personal circumstances in many cases played a central role in such reports of depression. Abigail Bailey, severely abused by her husband in eighteenth-century New Hampshire, wrote, "I behold emptiness and vanity in all things below the sun. . . . My heart is full of grief, and my eyes of tears. . . . I mourn also in spiritual desertion. My prayer seems to be shut out from God." In her letters to family and friends, Elizabeth Sullivan Stuart complained frequently about the "nothingness" of life, often alongside references to deaths and illnesses of persons, including of family members. "Lent treasures to point us to heaven," she wrote, "& teach us the nothingness of earth." A feeling of emptiness and nothingness often presented as a symptom of depression. Not all cases of depression included a sense of spiritual emptiness, however.[30]

When Christians thought about spiritual emptiness, they usually considered it in relation to spiritual fullness. They expressed their understandings of that relationship in a wide range of writings during the nineteenth and early twentieth centuries. One important aspect of that thinking was summarized by the Adventist visionary Ellen Gould, who advised her followers in *God's Amazing Grace* to "empty themselves of self." That recommendation to give up what social psychologist Roy F. Baumeister has termed "the burden of selfhood" was grounded in a cluster of ideas about the self that had informed American thinking and feeling since colonial times. Sacvan Bercovitch's claim that there is a "Puritan origin of the American self" seems extravagant four decades after he made it, not only because we recognize many other origins to religious and cultural life than we did in the 1970s, but because we are less sure of a single "self" and more willing to talk about multiple "selves." Bercovitch's insight about "the profound Puritan ambivalence towards selfhood" remains useful, however. The Puritan, said Bercovitch, was "driven by self-loathing to Christ and forced back to himself by recognition that his labors are an assertion of what he loathes," so that "the force of I-ness is transparent in the violent vocabulary of self-abhorrence." The feeling of emptiness that guided Puritans in their religious life, and that remained a central part of Christianity in America even as it mingled with other Christian backgrounds, existed, in a way similar to what Bercovitch described, in symbiotic relationship with the feeling of fullness. It was good to feel empty, and greater emptiness led to greater yearning. Greater yearning brought a person closer to God, so that to be empty was, at certain peak moments, to be full.[31]

Nineteenth-century Americans aspired to emptiness and urged its cultivation. Isabella Marshall Graham was strongly influenced by Dr. John Witherspoon and was cofounder of a widows' and children's relief organization with Elizabeth Bayley Seton (later a Catholic saint). She said, gratefully, "[God is] teaching me my ignorance, and more and more of my own emptiness; and I am satisfied with this, too, because my all is in him; I am complete in him." Hannah Hobbie, of New York, also active in benevolent societies, reported in her diary: "I thank him that I can this day see his love and goodness in giving me greater discoveries of the wickedness of my heart, of the emptiness of the world, and of the great power of sin and Satan to deceive." Such emptiness was highly prized by Mary Coombs Greenleaf, who died in Oklahoma as a missionary to the Chickasaw and who prayed, "Nor do I ever wish to feel less the value of the soul, and the emptiness of the earth, than I do know." Catharine Beecher, writing to her father, Lyman Beecher, in 1823, explained her own process of drawing closer to God as one of practiced emptiness. She pursued emptiness as a way of improving herself religiously: "It was by withdrawing my thoughts and attention from everything else, and by a continued exercise to continue that vacuity and emptiness of soul which is felt when there is nothing to stimulate or interest that I succeeded" in spiritual development.[32]

The idea that a feeling of emptiness was good because it increased longing for God informed the thinking of many nineteenth-century American Christians. The general theological principle that informed reflection on feeling empty was grounded in a view of the importance of the "empty vessel," a phrase often repeated in magazines, sermons, and diaries. The *Friends' Review* stated it with a characteristically Quaker take in an article titled "Self-Emptiness": "The fullness of God ever waits upon an empty vessel. But how difficult it is to get the poor, legal heart emptied of its legality, that it may be filled with Christ. . . . Here lies the root of the difficulty—we can never 'draw water from the wells of salvation,' until we come thither with empty vessels." By the same token, a soul that came to the well "full" was sent away "empty." In language that illustrates the complex interplay between understandings of empty and full and underscores some of the paradox in American Christian thinking about emptiness, Rev. Joseph Lathrop, the pastor of a church in Springfield, Massachusetts, explained that divine grace "teaches man his emptiness, weakness, and unworthiness; and excites in him earnest desires after pardon and sanctification. To them who improve this grace, more is given. But a soul full of itself, and relying on its own strength and holiness, will be sent empty away." For Lathrop, grace was needed to experience emptiness, but unless one was empty, one could not be filled with grace. The negotiated language that ministers and their congregations managed to construct to be able to speak simultaneously in absolutes and in pragmatics was highly complex and led to broader conclusions about language itself. The Hartford minister Horace Bushnell, as historian E. Brooks Holifield has pointed out, was at the forefront of that development. What was clear for most, regardless of wording, was that "emptiness and aspiration," as *Zion's Herald* put it, were conjoined.[33]

The feeling of emptiness was a feeling of appetite. Yearning accordingly intensified as one grew more empty. Weak interest in religion, explained one writer, was a problem traceable to a "feeling of overfulness." The solution was to "create a feeling of emptiness, an 'aching void' that will soon lead to a return of appetite." The *Christian Advocate and Journal* was more explicit in discussing appetite, drawing on elementary physics in suggesting the example of a vacuum. As guilt builds, "the soul goes forth to God with a sense of emptiness, craving to be filled with his fullness. Into such a vacuum the waters of life are sure to flow til it is filled quite to overflowing." Philip Schaff, who founded the American Society of Church History in 1888, surveyed the religious history of the ancient world and remarked that it appeared that "even unbelief, by producing a feeling of emptiness," played a role in the rise of Christianity when one recognized that there was "at the time of Christ, so much religious yearning, as we find, only waiting to be satisfied." Such longing for God was valued in the nineteenth century alongside its satisfaction. Emptiness was blessed. Deborah Porter, a minister's wife in Bangor, Maine, confessed her joyful emptiness thus: "Oh, can I ever forget the time when, and the place where, Infinite Fullness vouchsafed to notice and to bless exceeding emptiness?" The loss of self that Ellen G. White advised and that is redolent in experiences such as these was summed up in the conversion account of Sarah Pierpont Edwards, the wife of Jonathan Edwards. Her husband had written down her narrative of her conversion, and he included it in "Some Thoughts concerning the Present Revival of Religion" (1742) after stripping out references to her sex and placing it in the third-person voice. After her original account was published in Sereno Dwight's *Works of Jonathan Edwards* (1830), it became popular reading for men and women alike. She offered great detail about her emotions, and especially with regard to emptiness. Reprinted in magazines throughout the century, the following is from the Fourth of July issue of the *Circular* from 1870:

> This lively sense of the beauty and excellence of divine things, continued during the morning, accompanied with peculiar sweetness and delight. To my own imagination, my soul seemed to be gone out of me to God and Christ in heaven, and have very little relation to my body. God and Christ were so present in me and near me, that I seemed removed from myself. The spiritual beauty of the Father and the Savior, seemed to engross my whole mind; and it was the instinctive feeling of my heart, "Thou art, and there is none beside thee." I never felt such an entire emptiness of self-love, or any regard to my private, selfish interest of my own. It seemed to me that I had entirely done with myself.[34]

Christians sometimes conceived the feeling of emptiness as an impediment to their work of reform and evangelization and sometimes they considered it to be a prompt to their activities, energizing them for a mission of spreading the gospel. Lyman Beecher reported how his sense of emptiness had the latter effect: "If I ever felt my own emptiness and unworthiness, and insufficiency, or any earnestness of desire to consecrate all my powers to the service of God, it seems to me that I feel all of these things eminently now." The colonial pastor Thomas Smith of Portland, Maine, had written similarly about the way in which the vigorous work of spreading Christianity grew out of "realizing your own nothingness." Saint Mother Theodore Guerin, foundress of the Sisters of Providence of Saint Mary's-of-the-Woods, was more explicit: "But I derive my hope above all, from our utter incapacity, for it is always upon nothingness that God is pleased to rear his works." The *Friends' Review* reprinted and commented on writings of the English Quaker Stanley Pumphrey, emphasizing how he had believed that "sometimes when there is the most feeling of emptiness and desertion the Lord is really the most present and the most good is done." The Quaker abolitionist Angelina Grimke Weld, however, was less certain that a sense of one's nothingness was useful to the reform effort. Writing her sister Sarah in 1836, she admitted, "I sometimes feel frightened to think of how long I was standing idle in the market-place, and cannot help attributing it in a great measure to the doctrine of nothingness so constantly preached up in our society. . . . I believe it has produced its legitimate fruit of nothingness in reducing us to nothing."[35]

Angelina Grimke Weld's suspicion that there was too much emphasis on the feeling of nothingness or emptiness was part of a larger pattern of ambivalence about emotion generally. American Christians, for all of their attention to the emotional cluster of emptiness, longing, and joy, sometimes voiced doubts about relying on feeling to direct judgment and to organize one's life in accord with Christian belief. American Protestants debated the place of emotion in religion almost from the beginning of the settlement of New England, and Catholics brought with them a long history of disagreements about it. In the eighteenth century, Charles Chauncy and Jonathan Mayhew voiced their objections to religion that they believed was overly emotional; in the nineteenth century, the revivalist party led by Charles Grandison Finney debated the urban seaboard establishment, including other supporters of revival like Lyman Beecher; and in the twentieth century, differences between fundamentalists and Pentecostals, charismatics and traditionalists, were common. Proponents of emotion took it as a reliable sign of holiness that could be expected to issue in Christian virtue, while skeptics argued that it could not be trusted and that faith and doctrine were the pillars of the Christian life. Finney warned his followers to be on guard against underestimating emotion. His lecture "On Being Filled with the Spirit" explained: "If you do not have the Spirit, you will be very apt to stumble at those who have. You will doubt the propriety of their conduct. If they seem to feel a good deal more than yourself, you will be likely to call it animal feeling." Timothy Dwight of Yale, on the other hand, preached that "empty and useless emotions" were mere "enjoyment, intended to be found in toying and trifling, without a word exercised, or an attempt made, to become wise, virtuous, or useful." The Baptist minister and systematic theologian Augustus H. Strong (d. 1921), questioning Longfellow's notion that "religious feeling" was a most worthy emotional state, concluded sharply: "Longfellow was by nature and by education a Pelagian. The problem of moral order never seriously vexed him." Something of a middle ground, in this case articulated by the *Independent* in 1893, was a call "to put an end to the distortion of feeling which results from trying to reduce feeling to one single type," although the *Independent*, too, leaned away from "emotional religion" and toward "duty." In the midst of this ongoing discussion, American Christians of all stripes, followers of Beecher as well as of Finney, Pentecostals as well as fundamentalists, continued to report their feelings of emptiness. Those reports suggested that although the experience of emptiness could be shaded in various ways, as a core emotion it could be readily identified. It was, moreover, associated with theological ideas that most Christians could appreciate. Language, though, continued to be a problem. As a shared Quaker writing expressed it, "This depth of need . . . is beyond words." Another journal, the *Christian Advocate*, accentuated the other side of the experience: "*That your joy might be full* . . . . the experience is beyond words. Such joy 'only he who feels it knows.' . . . After all it is *full*, perfect."[36]

In surveying the various kinds of feelings of emptiness in American Christianity as they developed into the early twentieth century, it is possible to partially differentiate Catholic from Protestant approaches. For Protestantism rooted in Calvin's notions of depravity—and that means the majority of American Protestantism—there was ongoing focus on the need to empty oneself completely of the "self." As Calvinist ideas were softened by the influence of both pietism and the Enlightenment, there were fewer doctrinaire assertions about the world as a dung heap and human accomplishment as worthless. Emptiness and longing for God remained standard within Protestantism, but gradually the idea that joy in union with God, which was represented, for example, in Sarah Pierpont Edwards's narrative, became more a part of emptiness. Catholics, for their part, brought a tradition of conceptualizing spiritual life in connection with the "void," the emptiness and nothingness of Saint John of the Cross and others. The sixteenth-century Sanjuanist style of spirituality was by no means universal in American Catholicism and not even common, but it represented something of what was common, and that was the feeling of emptiness. Catholics differed from Protestants in their beliefs about what filled that emptiness. There were some who pursued visions of God and affective experiences of God's love, and in so doing were like the many Protestants who longed for that in revival or at prayer. More likely, Catholics sought to fill their emptiness with doctrine, devotion, and participation in the sacramental mysticism of the Church. The "mystical body of Christ" was a site for longing for God and the realization of God's love.

The question arises, To what extent did Protestantism and Catholicism in America share a mystical or quasi-mystical approach to thinking about the feeling of emptiness? American religious historian Leigh Eric Schmidt, in surveying the history of the category "mysticism" in religious and academic discourses, has pointed out how for liberal Protestantism in America, by the early twentieth century, "it was primarily a construct formed of lacking and loss, an emptied space of longing for 'a heightened, intensified way of life,' a search for 'an *undivided whole of experience*.'" That same definition might, in fact, apply to more conservative Protestantism in America, absent the word "mysticism." Conservative Protestantism was equally about lack and loss and emptied space for longing, and it had been for some time. There were other differences among the two groups that were important, but as far as emptiness was concerned, the two ends of the Protestant spectrum were not far apart. Included as well in that spectrum was the vast, sometimes liberal, "metaphysical religion" that Catherine L. Albanese has documented as a large part of the American religious landscape from colonial times up to the present. Remarking on the nineteenth-century drift of Catholic mysticism into Protestantism, she has described the overlap of the two as a crucially important part of the coalescence of "metaphysical religion": "With ironies abounding, mysticism—which for Anglo-American Protestants was code for Catholicism . . .—this mysticism crept back into culture. . . . The work of the new American proponents of metaphysics was one of religious imagination and they had been prepared for it not only by Catholic 'superstition.' . . . The new metaphysicians had been prepared, too, by the seventeenth-century English Puritan culture broadly disseminated throughout the United States."[37]

One set of signs of the way in which elements of Catholic mysticism flowed into a broader culture of American Christianity—a development that should not be overestimated but one that left noticeable traces—is the conversion accounts of those Protestants who became Catholic.[38] Many such accounts, according to Jenny Franchot, can be read as the reports of men and women responding to profound social changes, which created "pressures characteristically experienced as an emptiness within, an absence remedied only by the redemptive 'substance' of Catholic dogma." The feeling of emptiness on the part of converts, however, was neither solely a response to economic, demographic, and domestic upheaval, nor a process that enabled the consumption of Catholic dogma. The blending of Puritan spirituality, Catholic mysticism, Protestant theology, and Enlightenment ideals that Albanese has detailed created a frame for conversion to Catholicism that ensured it unfolded as a complicated process, and one that was rooted in centuries of discourses about spiritual emptiness and wholeness. Something of that complicated historical frame is suggested by Robert Orsi's discussion of twentieth-century Catholicism. Catholicism had an exceptionally well-developed and historically deep ideology of emptiness, and one that was illustrated with a host of examples drawn from the lives of saints and from the imaginations of Catholic writers. Catholics deployed the language and imagery of emptiness in many ways, but especially in relation to the experience of pain. Orsi notes that for Catholics, "pain purged and disciplined the ego, stripping it of pride and self-love; it disclosed the emptiness of the world." As that experience of emptiness deepened, the prospect of salvation improved. Pain could beget conversion. In Catholic hospitals, "nurses were encouraged to watch for opportunities on their rounds to help lapsed Catholics renew their faith, and even to convert non-Catholics in the promising circumstances of physical distress." Converts, in fact, found in Catholicism a well-articulated culture of emptiness only minimally joined to the dogma of Catholicism, but pervasive. It fostered the idea of the suffering person not only as empty but as holy, a notion easily understandable to Protestants. To be empty was to be holy, to be full. Cripples, Orsi points out, were "thus emptied of all but their holiness and innocence." Suffering, which was redolent in Protestant ideas of emptiness and longing, was foregrounded in Catholic thinking and tied to an elaborated conception of body.[39]

Nineteenth-century personal narratives of conversion to Catholicism inventory experiences that correspond closely to what is found in Protestant narratives. Isaac Hecker (d. 1888) came from a Methodist background in New York, spent time at the transcendentalist mecca of Brook Farm, and converted to Catholicism soon after leaving there in 1844. He founded the Paulist Fathers, a Catholic missionary society, in 1858. His diary entries between 1842 and 1845 are replete with references to sin, grace, and the Holy Spirit, which are topics that might equally be found in a Methodist narrative. He prayed to Jesus, "Give me a taste of Thy divine humility and detestation of this world and all its empty and vain things." After a week in the company of Orestes Brownson, who also converted to Catholicism, he confessed, "All seems mystical. Nothing is definite. I have no settled views or clear thoughts of my own. I speak and write as if it were without consciousness; . . . I am bereft of all that makes me feel personal. . . . This is to me inexplicable." Hecker characterized his own "cloud of darkness" in one instance as lacking even feeling; he wrote that he could "feel no sense of things. No joy. No reality. No emotion. No impulse, no positive something within or around me. No love, no delight, nothing, nothing, nothing." He described being reduced to pure suffering and need, praying, "My sense of nothingness makes me feel stronger That Thou art all and makes me feel the need of Thee and nothing else." Though not all converts dramatized their feeling of emptiness to the extent that Hecker did, even Brownson, who was exceptionally active as a reformer and as a national political spokesman, complained that "our philanthropists and world-reformers may become so engrossed in their plans that they do not experience that aching void within, that emptiness of all created things."[40]

Transcendentalists and other Protestants were drawn to that particular strand of Catholic mysticism detectable in Brownson and Hecker, often, as historian Amanda Porterfield has written, "through their appreciation of the esthetic quality of Catholicism." As she notes, "in their appreciation of Catholic mysticism, they were reaffirming even a more basic Protestant and Puritan commitment to the inspiration and transformative power of the Holy Spirit." The Bowdoin College professor Thomas C. Upham, a Congregationalist strongly influenced by the Scottish Common Sense philosophy and later by evangelist Phoebe Palmer's notion of sanctification, placed his insights about the spiritual life within his biography of a fifteenth-century Catholic mystic. In *The Life of Catharine Adorna . . . Together with Explanations and Remarks, Tending to Illustrate the Doctrine of Holiness*, Upham emphasized how the empty self, through the workings of the Holy Spirit, arrived at sanctification. Those influenced by his writing include the Protestant evangelist from Indiana Dougan Clark, whose *The Offices of the Holy Spirit* (1878) lauds Saint Catharine, alongside Thomas à Kempis and others, who were "filled with the Spirit."[41]

American discussion about the feeling of emptiness and yearning for God continued throughout the twentieth century, but most of the distinguishing features were in place by 1900 or so. Catholics such as the social activists Daniel Berrigan and Dorothy Day wrote about it in much the same terms as had authors from the previous century. Day edged discussion of emptiness into childhood, recalling her own experience as a child "afraid of God, of death, or eternity. As soon as I closed my eyes at night the blackness of death surrounded me. I believed and yet was afraid of nothingness." Berrigan recast the classic *Dark Night of the Soul* as *Dark Night of the Resistance*, linking the discussion of the pain of spiritual emptiness with the call for social engagement. Early and midcentury Protestant leaders as different as revivalist Billy Graham and the antifundamentalist Harry Emerson Fosdick spoke to their audiences about the emptiness and the longing for God, one explaining how to be born again and the other blending lessons from the Bible with insights drawn from history and psychology but with an emphasis on feeling and interiority. The Catholic monk Thomas Merton wrote at length about the experience of emptiness in works such as *Zen and the Birds of Appetite* (1968), as did the Yale philosopher Louis Dupré. Susan Taube and Thomas J. J. Altizer, among many others, placed the experience of emptiness at the center of theological inquiries into the "absence of God" in enterprises variously referred to as postmodern theology, apophatic theology, negative theology, and "Death of God" theology. Twentieth-century American writers of all sorts—poets, novelists, nonfiction authors—participated in what literary historian Richard J. Gray has called the twentieth century "American compulsion to confront the abyss of the self," as in Sylvia Plath's poem "Tulips" (1961):

> I am learning peacefulness, lying by myself quietly
> As the light lies on these white walls, this bed, these hands.
> I am nobody . . .
> I have given my name and my day-clothes up to the nurses
> And my history to the anesthetist and my body to the surgeons.
> . . . .
> And I have no face, I have wanted to efface myself.

Some Christians appealed to the Virgin Mary to fill their emptiness. Luis Montoya and Ricardo Archuleta, musicians in Cerro, New Mexico, in 1940, sang of the sadness of leaving church:

> What sadness I carry in my breast, upon giving you,
> Mother, my tender goodbye.
> When I leave you in the sanctuary
> I feel an emptiness in my heart.[42]

The message of emptiness is the core of many electronic ministries in the interactive, socially enabled media world of the early twenty-first century. Media preachers and commentators, like Puritan ministers in the seventeenth century, encourage confessions of feelings of emptiness, and in response they offer words of consolation and encouragement. None have been more successful in that enterprise than Pat Robertson's Christian Broadcasting Network (CBN), which solicits accounts of the suffering of those identifying themselves as empty and translates their stories into inspiring lessons for a broader audience. Robertson's Pentecostal Christianity, with its focus on the authority of feeling, frames an approach to evangelism that, ironically, has made emotion central to the life of the church even as the global reach of the CBN has ensured that members are geographically distant from each other. The feeling of emptiness, which for Robertson was a crucial part of his own spiritual seeking, occurs for many of his audience in circumstances that would appear to foster it. That is, part of the success of CBN has been its promotion of a message of emptiness to an audience that is itself empty of community in the sense of actual physical contact among its members.[43]

Robertson's own recounting of his feeling of emptiness is broadly instructive about the emotional side of American Christianity. He described how as an unsuccessful young businessman and casual churchgoer, "there was just this incredible emptiness in my heart and I was looking for something better. . . . And I didn't know what it was." The feeling of emptiness, in his case, was emotion that was only vaguely cognized. It was not defined by conscious yearning for God or by a compelling desire to experience union with God. It was a relatively unadorned emotion of emptiness. Robertson eventually became adept at inventing language to characterize the feeling as a spiritual state and to direct it to religious belief. That many-layered language about the feeling of emptiness subsequently organized for his followers their thinking about space, time, body, community, and other aspects of religious life in America.[44]

Americans have felt empty in many different settings, including after the death of a loved one or because of other personal losses, because of physical suffering, and in the context of their practice of Christianity. Catholics and Protestants alike have reported the pain of emptiness alongside the joy of emptiness, as they simultaneously have sought to deepen their feelings of emptiness, increase their sense of longing, and aspire to being filled by God. They have fashioned many different linguistic expressions—some highly complex—to describe their feelings of emptiness while insisting that language cannot communicate that experience. And they have cultivated emptiness through embodied religious practice, which has played a role in efforts to structure the experience cognitively. The feeling of emptiness, physically felt by those who report it, has deeply informed Christian devotional practices and the communities that invent, refine, and promote the bodily disciplines that define that practice.

I want to climb to you, foot by foot
Along the prayer ladder:
Dusky flower,
Gloom tree in the nerves,
And then my body rigged with magic,
Crying to fill that great invention, your
    emptiness,
Your tricky silences between the stars.
—Paul Zweig

2 Body

The Empty Body

The feeling of emptiness in Christianity in American history has a cognitive aspect. Americans, after all, write and talk about emptiness—and sometimes by referring to nothingness, hollowness, or the void, or through other such linguistic renderings of it. They describe emptiness in detail, clustering it with other emotions and with ideas drawn from familiar religious, philosophical, and social discourses. The relation between emotion and cognition is always complicated, a fact well evidenced by the pointed debates about it in academic journals—and in a vast history of philosophical investigations since antiquity. Some have wondered about the extent to which a feeling is shaped by the language and the ideological matrices that inform and condition people's lives. Other writers have asked how social realities and aesthetic traditions are involved in the cognizing of a biological state. Many who have studied emotion and cognition have pondered how the cultural resources for emotional expression, from the ornamentation of churches to the scripting of collective penitential practices, function as prompts to it, thereby in some fashion playing roles both in engendering it and in channeling and managing it. The feeling of emptiness in American Christianity poses an especially interesting case because emptiness is so thoroughly wrapped up in all of American culture. As a feeling it has been important to American social and political life, notions of gender and race, thinking about space and time, models of community, what we eat and how we dress, and a great many other aspects of American lives.

Among American Christians, emptiness is cultivated and given expression in ritual. It is cultivated above all through inventive stagings of the body and in physically scripted enactments of devotion. American Christians have borrowed, invented, and adapted a wide range of means to accomplish that, but the most important techniques and processes have to do with physical disciplines and collective performances. When Americans perform rituals to prompt the feeling of emptiness and to enable expression of it, the body plays a central role in the dramas that result. Such rituals cultivate the feeling of emptiness, but they also cognize it, physically representing it to both the performers and the observers in ways that enable its conceptual integration into broader repertoires of behavior and thought. These rituals accordingly advance the crucial social work of normatizing specific feelings,[1] fostering the coalescence of feeling rules that establish expectations for interpersonal encounters. At bottom, however, there is a complicated give-and-take between the engendering of feelings of emptiness and the defining of them in actions and words. "Emotions," writes Birgitt Röttger-Rössler, are "bio-cultural processes" and thus involve bodily states as well as culturally derived schematizing of feeling. Röttger-Rössler proposes that "on the one hand, rituals articulate and 'cognize' feelings; on the other, they 'embody' them by intensifying physiological arousal and thus the bodily perception of the enacted emotion." The American religious landscape is a good place to explore for that kind of ritual complexity. In the religious history of America, we can see something of what anthropologist John Leavitt is getting at when he writes that it is possible to study emotions "as experiences learned and expressed in the body in social interactions through the mediation of systems of signs, verbal and nonverbal." Most importantly, argues Leavitt, we must recognize that even when we investigate them as social phenomena, "emotions are *felt* in bodily experience, not just known or thought or appraised." Our approach to the body here resonates with such a view, focusing on the social and historical while recognizing that feeling is a key part of the religious lives of individual American Christians and that the feeling of emptiness, a bodily state, links those lives to a broader network of collective behaviors and historical events.[2]

In the West, among Buddhist cultures in Asia, and in some cultural settings elsewhere, the representation of emptiness is a rich and complex art. That complexity already is in evidence in ancient Middle Eastern literature and, for example, in the intertwined images of Sophocles's *Antigone*, wherein the house, the soul, and the body—and especially the womb—among other things, all are recognizable as interrelated emblems of emptiness. Americans, drawing on that deep background as mediated in English and European cultures, have deployed all sorts of images in making points about what emptiness feels like, where it comes from, and what futures it signals. One common representation of emptiness in American Christian writing (and elsewhere) has been the empty stomach, and around that image Americans have fashioned numerous lessons about appetite, desire, fulfillment, pleasure, and salvation. In nineteenth-century England, the popular *Memoirs of a Stomach* (1850), the life of a English gentleman told from the point of view of the stomach, suggested just how closely self and stomach could be coincided, and *The Philosophy of the Stomach* (1856), written, admittedly, to make believers out of atheists, explained what the stomach had to do with religious sensibility. In America, as in England, there was a preoccupation with the empty stomach in medical reports and announcements of research. A common symptom of illness in America from colonial times up through much of the twentieth century was, as a Philadelphia medical manual put it pointedly in 1866, "emptiness in stomach." That emptiness, mentioned in many manuals, often was associated with other states of the body that dressed the notion of emptiness itself to coordinate it with anxiety. *The Science of Therapeutics*, published in New York in 1872, discussed the symptoms of a case of infectious disease in somewhat mysterious terms: "Stomach: . . . Thirst, burning in the pit of the stomach, and an indescribable, empty, gnawing, sinking feeling." A homeopathic manual from a few years earlier advised the administration of ipecacuanha to remedy the "feeling of emptiness and flaccidity in the stomach . . . anxiety and fear of death." An inventory of treatable conditions composed in Germany and later published in America, the well-read *Treatise on the Effects of Coffee* (1875), simply listed the complaint as "Stomach, empty feeling."[3]

American Christians, like other Christians before them, thought about the empty stomach in relation not only to an "indescribable, empty, gnawing, sinking feeling," but to the soul. In many instances their reflections on that indeed led them to conclude that there was something "indescribable" about the empty soul. Sometimes, however, Americans wrote with confidence about how the lessons drawn from study of the stomach could be applied to the soul. Typical of that line of reasoning was the short piece "Soul Starvation," published in the *Christian Observer* in 1907. Borrowing from another source (as was common in religious publishing for most of the nation's history), the *Observer* explained, "'There is nothing like an empty stomach to quicken the desire to earn one's bread.' . . . An empty stomach means physical hunger and physical hunger is sharp." In the same sense, "An empty soul means hunger and hunger for God is overpowering." Such hunger, which "gnaws into [one's] soul," eventuates in "a frantic desire to fill the vast emptiness of the soul which God alone can fill." The lesson, in the end, is that Jesus is "the bread of life" and that "there is nothing like an empty soul to quicken the desire to be a child of God."[4]

The author of "Soul Starvation" warned against persons being deceived by thinking that worldly riches would ever fill the emptiness of the soul. Other religious writers of the early twentieth century likewise warned against the excesses of the Gilded Age, and likewise emphasized that the cure of the soul was to be distinguished from easing the suffering of the stomach. The Presbyterian minister and temperance advocate Theodore Cuyler argued that to "endeavor to satisfy hungry souls by filling an empty stomach" was religious "treason" unless it included "remedies for sin-sick and perishing souls." That idea, which in some form had been a part of American Christianity since the colonial era, took on particular importance in the context of the emergent "social gospel" of the time, but it also reflected ministerial hopes for the "next great revival" of soulful spirituality. Religious leaders, however, were realistic about their prospects in that endeavor, having known, from their reading of *Seed-Time and Harvest*, a tale of sensitive pastoring that was serialized in nineteenth-century periodicals, that "it is easier to fill an empty stomach with bread-and-butter and wine, than to fill an empty heart with hope and joy."[5]

Religious leaders occasionally thought about stomach and soul in ways that drew upon more complex theological and philosophical ideas, and especially so in discussing the relation between emptiness and fullness, embodied feeling and "abstract" thought. One of those leaders was Henry Ward Beecher. From his pulpit in Brooklyn Heights, Beecher delivered messages that helped to shape national attitudes about issues ranging from abolition to adultery. His discourses typically were precise and reduced complex notions to terms accessible to his audiences. In preaching about reason and faith in 1879, Beecher emphasized how emptiness was both a physical and an "abstract" reality. He unpacked that claim with reference to a kind of dialectics. He explained that the experience of material things, through the "process of reasoning," became "a higher kind of thought." But because there is "another tendency cooperating all the time with this," it was apparent that "thoughts and feelings" were subject to a process that "attempts to realize them . . . by actually embodying them in the forms of matter." As an example of this process, Beecher cited the cycle of evaporation and precipitation in the atmosphere. Clouds form as if from nothing, and "the contents of this great emptiness, that nevertheless is full although it seems empty," fall only to rise invisibly as vapors, so that "water and vapor are all the time interchanging and keeping up a grand circulation." Beecher pressed on: "And in the human soul a precisely analogous process is going on. We take matter and generalize it, and lift it into the regions of thought and feeling or emotion, according to the nature of matter," while at the same time we make physical the abstract or seemingly ineffable aspects of experience through a process that works "perpetually backward and forward as a shuttle does in a loom." So, there is a tendency to make "life invisible and immaterial" alongside "another tendency in man to give distinctness to abstract and unembodied things." For Beecher, the heart, eyes, and stomach accordingly tell us much about what is going on in the soul because religious ideas and feelings can be manifested in the body.[6]

Beecher's ideas about embodied feeling were part of a larger discussion of emotion that was about to come to a head with William James's theorizing in *What Is an Emotion?* (1884). Beecher's intellectual interests, although they overlapped in some places with James's, were, however, primarily shaped by his familiarity with previous American Protestant theologians. Both Beecher and his father, Lyman Beecher, had been influenced by the Connecticut minister Jonathan Edwards, the theologian of the eighteenth-century Great Awakening. Edwards, who as we have seen had edited his wife's conversion account of emptiness and fullness, set the terms for much subsequent Protestant reflection on longing for God and the discernment of moral truth. Edwards had entered an excerpt of Thomas Case's *The Morning Exercise Methodized* into his *Miscellanies* in the 1740s: "The full stomach of the proud Pharisee loathes the honeycomb of Christ's righteousness; whilst to the hungry appetite of the humbled sinner, the bitterest passions of a Saviour are exceedingly sweet." That notion of longing for God was standard among writers who exploited images of food and hunger in addressing the feeling of emptiness. But it was Edwards's writing about appetite and taste that helped to shape Protestant thinking about "bodily sensation" and the action of the Holy Spirit in the nineteenth and twentieth centuries. In the *Treatise concerning Religious Affections* (1746), Edwards proposed that "as a man of a rectified palate judges of particular morsels by his taste . . . a spiritual taste of the soul, mightily helps the soul in its reasonings on the word of God" because it removes the "prejudices of a depraved appetite." There was, said Edwards, a "harmony" between the taste of the soul and spiritual truth, so that certain feelings (such as "love of God or holy fear") resulted in a heightened awareness of scripture that made plain the "meaning" of those emotions. Such harmony was no different from the process by which "the particular state of the stomach and palate, tends to bring such particular meats and drinks to mind." Edwards thus expanded the notion of a hungry Christian longing for God as an empty stomach hungered for food to include the idea that hunger was directed by grace to objects suitable to its satisfaction. Spiritual taste guided the empty soul to God.[7]

Edwards's thinking, some of which was too subtle for later ministers to fully exploit in their writing and preaching, is echoed in much Christian moral thought in America, including in Catholic writers such as the Catholic convert Orestes Brownson. Brownson, writing a century after Edwards, criticized the sexually experimental American Fourierist who has "his appetites and affections depraved, his moral tastes vitiated, so that he craves and relishes the meat that perishes." Good meat or bad, as taste or the stomach or both discern, the point above all was the fact of the craving. The empty stomach craved food as the empty soul craved God.[8]

Stomach, Blood, Tears, and Tongue

Americans cultivated emptiness through devotional practice, through physical disciplines that brought forward the awareness of emptiness and helped to shape it as an experience. Such rituals of cultivation cognized feeling at the same time that they fostered it as embodied piety. Singing, praying, reading, speaking, auditing, and writing all have served as linguistic platforms for the cognitive framing of emotions, including emptiness. Fasting, bleeding, silence, and labor likewise contributed to the cognizing of feeling, through the role of those disciplines in somatically organizing the experience of emptiness. The religious framing of work, sexuality, and the enslaved body on the plantation reflected other ways in which the feeling of emptiness and the cognizing of that feeling were important aspects of Christianity in America.

Fasting has been a part of the religious life of Christians since the earliest communities of believers were formed. It has been taught for centuries as one aspect of a central triad of lay Catholic religious observance—fasting, prayer, and almsgiving—and has been present in a wide range of Protestant groups. Calvin agreed with Luther and Zwingli that fasting did not produce merit in the way that "Papists" supposed, but Calvin was explicit in his recommendation of it in *The Institutes of the Christian Religion* for its capability to focus and enhance prayer. He asserted that "with a full stomach our mind is not so lifted up to God that it can be drawn to prayer with a serious and ardent affection and persevere in it." Fasting, "as it is a sign of self-abasement," brought a better tenor to prayer. Historians of English Puritanism have emphasized that fasting was central to Puritan religious practice. Theodore Dwight Bozeman has argued that it was an "eminent expression" of Puritan religious sensibilities, and Raymond A. Mentzer has shown as well how French Reformed Protestants embraced fasting as an individual and collective exercise. These backgrounds all translated to America, where Protestants continued the practice, at times relegating it to a secondary role in the practice of piety and at other times—such as in the twenty-first century—enthusiastically voicing their advocacy of it.[9]

One of the *Lessons in Life* that novelist and editor Josiah Gilbert Holland offered to his readers in 1861 was the observation: "It is curious to see how much fullness and emptiness of the stomach have to do with moods." Subsequent academic writing about emotion and the stomach largely have concurred. Sociologist Julius Rubin, in describing the mood of religious melancholy among American Protestants, emphasized that fasting among them typically has been understood as an act of "radical self-denial" that prepared a person for God's grace. For Rubin, "fasting assisted the saint in becoming a selfless, empty vessel." Puritans and Congregationalists such as Cotton Mather, Samuel Sewall, David Brainerd, Jonathan Edwards, Jonathan Parsons, and Samuel Hopkins fasted in conjunction with praying in search of a similar result. Methodists accepted John Wesley's designation of fasting as an ordinance of God, and although not all practiced Friday fasting and abstinence, as American Methodist historian Jesse Lee pointed out in 1810, some Methodists, such as John Stewart, an African American lay missionary to American Indians, engaged in "frequent fasting" to the point of "debility." Rachel Stearns, a young Methodist woman, devoted entire days to fasting and prayer in the 1830s and, as historian Candy Gunther Brown has concluded, did so in connection with frequent storms of anxiety and incidents of physical self-mortification. Shakers anticipating visits from Holy

Mother Wisdom in 1840 fasted entire days or pledged to get by on bread and water for a week. The Protestant Episcopal Church kept a regular calendar of fast days, much as Catholics did. But the Church of God in Christ developed a much more ambitious schedule of fasting. Religious historian Anthea Butler emphasized that its "leaders held fasting in such esteem that the annual convocation of that church started out with a corporate fast of three days for all participants," the participants deeply invested in the belief that fasting and prayer "go together." Individuals fasted frequently and for extended periods of time. The late-twentieth-century Promise Keepers founder Bill McCartney, a self-described "born-again Catholic," prayed and fasted to know what God meant for him to do. That approach also is redolent in Mormonism, where fasting sometimes precedes the making of a major decision or embarking on an important task. Before blessing a person, a Mormon "Melchizedek Priesthood holder" often will prepare for the moment by fasting, as will the person who is to receive the blessing. Mormons typically fast as well in ritual preparation for ordination, baptism/confirmation, receiving temple rites, anticipating a mission, and for other occasions. Church presidents as far back as the beginnings of Mormonism have fasted and called for fasts, and at various times Thursdays and Sundays have been designated fast days. Joseph Smith's *History of the Church of Jesus Christ of Latter Day Saints* tellingly recommended "that thy fasting may be perfect, or in other words, that thy joy may be full." The spirit of such exercises was summarized by Elder Spencer Condie in a General Conference Address in 2002, where he observed, "A loving Heavenly Father has promised you through his prophet Isaiah that through sincere fasting, as you subdue your physical appetites, He will help you 'loose the bands of wickedness' and 'break every yoke.' Claim that promise through fasting. Our emptiness will provide more room for the fullness of the gospel. The hollowing precedes the hallowing."[10]

Catholics in America were well supplied with advice about religious fasting. The guidance offered by *The Golden Manual*, which taught Catholic devotion to nineteenth- and twentieth-century Anglophone audiences, identified more than one hundred days of fasting and abstinence annually and urged readers to approach those days with heightened feeling and a deep sense of devotion. Catholic manuals and devotional guides outlined an interlocked set of reasons why fasting was necessary, but most concurred with the explanation offered by an Anglican guide to Catholic piety: "Fasting is literally abstinence from food and drink; but in a secondary sense it includes all forms of self denial." A twenty-first-century American Catholic group, the Order of the Legion of Saint Michael, prefaced its recommendation of fasting by heralding its efficacy as a means of mortification, exhorting members to bear in mind that "mortification in its fundamental essence is *Self-sacrifice, Self-denial*, and *Self-discipline*. It is Morte—*death*—death to the self." Fasting made one hungry, both for food and for God. As much as it was a denial of self and the cultivation of emptiness, it was also an affirmation of the search for God. It was, if we can draw upon what Caroline Bynum has shown in her study of fasting among medieval women, a means of coming closer to God. It begat an increase in longing for God, as the Anglican William Dodd prayed in *The Nature and Necessity of Fasting* (1756): "My heart is empty and disengaged and longs for thee, my heart is entirely devoted to thee; enter O my God, possess it with thy gracious presence, and fill it with thy love." The more one fasted, the deeper the emptiness and the stronger the longing. And should longing lead to a taste of God (literally in the transubstantiated Eucharist, or otherwise), that only increased appetite. *The Golden Manual* versified:

> Celestial sweetness unalloyed
> Who eat thee hunger still;
> Who drink of thee still feel a void,
> Which naught but Thou can fill.[11]

The denial of self typically has been a part of fasting as a penitential practice in Catholicism. But the cultivation of emptiness in fasting also has served as a central aspect of the ritual search for God and as such often has been characterized as joyful endeavor. The *American Benedictine Review* in 1984 published an article by the monk Adalbert de Vogüé that explained how fasting is "the happiness of feeling one's spirit grow lighter and stronger . . . more apt to listen to God and to seek him." The U.S. Bishops Committee on Pastoral Practices in 2000 took a similar perspective, teaching that "fasting from food creates in us a greater openness to God's Spirit" and emphasizing that "for Christians, suffering and joy are not incompatible." Or, as Bynum has written about the self-imposed physical trials of medieval women, "the physicality into which the woman sinks is unspeakable suffering and unspeakable joy." In recent decades, the emphasis on joy alongside penitential suffering has grown. At the same time, historians of Christianity have been more willing to consider how the emptying of the body expresses religious aspiration (and not just a sense of wretchedness) and how fasting itself has been a sensuous exercise. The central point with regard to Christian piety, however, is that emptiness is good and in emptiness there is fullness. The *American National Preacher*, in "The Proper Method of Religious Fasting" (1831), lectured its readers to "imagine not that a mere feeling of emptiness, and even of importunate hunger, must necessarily mark the approach of mischief. So far from this, they are feelings which you often *need*, for your physical as well as moral benefit." A century and a half later, John Piper's *A Hunger for God: Desiring God through Fasting and Prayer* proposed that the feeling of emptiness was desire for God, and that fasting cultivated both.[12]

The empty stomach as cultivated emptiness and a partner to prayer is one manifestation of the emptied body. Another Christian practice associated with the emptying of the body is weeping. In America, this practice is obvious and there is no need to rehearse it here in any detail. Tears empty the body. They clean it, removing corruption, including the corrupted self. God fills the empty—but clean—soul with grace. The colonial New England poet Edward Taylor expressed it as such:

> Had not my Soule's, thy Conduit, Pipes stopt bin
> With mud, what Ravishment would'st thou Convay?
> Let Graces Golden Spade dig till the Spring
> Of tears arise, and cleare this filth away.
> Lord, let thy Spirit raise my sighings till
> These Pipes my soule do with thy sweetness fill.

Catholics and Protestants weep and pray, as do Mormons and members of a wide range of para-Christian groups. When Francis Asbury noted "weeping on all sides" at camp meetings, he spoke for virtually all who had ever been to a revival. The spectacle of mass weeping, thoughtfully analyzed as ritual performed to prompt emotion in historian William Christian's study of religion early modern Spain, has been known to almost all Christians in America, alongside their own personal shedding of tears. American religious periodical literature, sermons, religious books, theological arguments, funerals, Passion Week services, baptisms, prayers, and every kind of vernacular practice overflowed with tears. Tears, described by Jacques Derrida as "an essence of the eye," accompanied a feeling of "the emptiness at the heart of the world." Tears emptied the body, making it ready to be filled by God.[13]

Another way in which to empty the body—less recognized by historians than tears—was to drain it of blood. Unlike fasting, which could entirely empty the stomach, bloodletting evacuated only some of the blood, but the performance of bloodletting, even in a limited way, was a prompt to the feeling of emptiness and a cognizing of it. Bloodletting—the willing opening of a vein for the purpose of removing blood from the body—was practiced for medical reasons, but the enactment of bleeding that took place in the chair of a barber-surgeon, in the doctor's office, the kitchen, the prayer room, or elsewhere overlapped with Christian ideas about bleeding as a devotional exercise.

Just as fasting emptied the stomach of food, so did bloodletting empty the body of blood. *The Pious Guide to Prayer and Devotion* (1808), like other manuals, associated fasting with the purposeful loss of blood, in this case with the self-imposed torments of Saint Aloyisius: "His disciplines were frequent and bloody; his fasts almost continual." That association of fasting with bloodletting has been studied in detail by behavioral researchers in recent decades, and a consensus has emerged that eating disorders often are part of a larger behavioral repertoire that includes self-cutting. It is not unusual for anorexics and bulimics to cut themselves, including deliberate venipuncture (as distinguished from epidermal cutting) undertaken to bleed the body, to empty it of its contents in the same way that the bulimic ingests emetics in order to purge the body by vomiting. A recent study of habitual female self-mutilators concluded that the typical female who suffers from the condition strongly evidences eating disorders and that "skin cutting is her usual practice."[14]

Skin-cutting and bloodletting have a biblical history—the man in Gadara possessed by an unclean spirit who roamed the mountains "cutting himself with stones" (Mark 5:5, KJV)—and that history is joined to a rich tradition of bloodletting rooted in Greek and Arab treatments of illnesses. In medieval Europe (and in medieval Asia),[15] deliberate personal bloodletting, or auto-exsanguination, was of great social and cultural significance and carried religious connotations. Men and women in religious orders for centuries made bloodletting a part of their annual calendar, with four occasions observed according to season and additional instances as required beyond those. Phlebotomy, Angela Montford has written, was "a part of the routine of religious life" among monks and nuns. There were differences: The Rule of the Order of the Humiliati, for example, proposed that members be bloodlet three times a year, but it left some choice in the matter to each person, while the Dominican Constitution mandated four bleedings a year and did not allow for personal choice. What mattered, as medievalist M. K. K. Yearl has noted, was how "the primary requirement for periodic bloodletting was arguably that it fit into a strict *regimen spiritualis*," that is, how it was a part of the liturgical calendar but also a matter of "spiritual prophylaxis." It was sometimes accompanied by chanting by members of the community, as the vein was opened and blood drained, although the staging varied with time and place. Some performances of the ritual, as one historical study of bloodletting has concluded, had vague "religious overtones," while in other settings it directly overlapped with liturgical exercises. In any event, in the wider context of blood mysticism in Christianity, blood as a core symbol of the Christian mythos rarely could be introduced into any aspect of religious life without bearing into that setting an abundance of prompts to think about mortality, salvation, emptiness, and fullness.[16]

The evacuation of blood from the body through religious disciplining has been presented in centuries of hagiographies as a commonplace of saintly devotion. The suffering saint, promoted as a model of piety through storytelling and written biographical accounts, is a bleeder. As historian Richard Kieckhefer has shown, medieval ascetic practice often imitated the Passion of Christ, so that devout men and women inflicted wounds on themselves in order to bleed as Christ did. The fourteenth-century nun Elspeth von Oye strapped to her back a cross of nails and struck herself with a flail, leaving bloody gashes in her skin. David S. Tinsley notes that she took "up her cross and her flail at the behest of God, who demands further bloodletting in *auditio* after *auditio*." According to Elspeth, that bloodletting empties her, making her a vessel ready to receive God, who informs her that it is precisely through the blood that drains from her that his own essence is given to her. Taking the voice of God, she writes: "Your cross, in which I see forever the image of my son, is a vessel dripping with bodily essence through which I pour the divine power of my essence into your soul." The *unio sanguinolenta*, as Tinsley notes, is a process in which Elspeth's blood is exchanged for the blood of Jesus. The Dominican Ita von Hohenfels likewise sought union with God in blood, walking a path of mortification (rather dramatically described) that would have been recognizable to twenty-first-century psychology researchers: "She took on the most strict regimen with much waking and night-long prayers and extraordinary discipline to the degree that she cut into her own flesh with knives until she reached the bone so that her flesh hung from her body and the blood ran so from her that it was noticed wherever she went. . . . So then she took up iron nails and no matter how much she scarred her flesh and how much she carved herself, she never thought it was enough, or that she was serving God as well as others had done."[17]

The German mystic Blessed Henry Suso (1300–1366) wrote an account of his own sufferings, but in the third person. He indicates exhilaration in self-cutting and bloodletting and a sense of purgation that came with his discipline. One day, writing tool in hand, "he set to work, and thrust the style into the flesh above his heart, drawing it backwards and forwards, up and down, until he had inscribed the name of Jesus upon his heart. The blood flowed plenteously out of his flesh from the sharp stabs, and ran down over his body." Not content, he secretly had fabricated an undergarment "into which a hundred and fifty brass nails, pointed and sharp, were driven, and the points of the nails were always turned towards the flesh.... In this he used to sleep at night." The Dominican Suso was familiar with the *via triplica*, a sequence of stages constituting spiritual practice that was progressively articulated in writings from Augustine to Meister Eckart and Saint John of the Cross. The first of those stages, upon which all progress rested, was the *via purgativa* or, in Orthodoxy, *catharsis*, a purging. For Suso, bloodletting was such a purge, an emptying that brought him closer to God. His remarks on the "time of the bloodletting" reflect both his own state of mind and the religious tenor of seasonal bloodletting in the order: "He made it a practice for a long time, when he was bled, to turn in spirit to God under the Cross, and, lifting up his wounded arm, to say, with an inward sigh:—Ah, Friend of my heart!"[18]

Catholics in America did not make a practice of whipping themselves bloody. But Catholics in America revered those who did, and in the nineteenth and twentieth centuries Catholics were particularly interested in blood, bleeding, and the stigmata. They believed that blood on the hands, feet, head, and abdomen of pious Catholics was a sign, like that given to Saint Francis of Assisi, of the Five Wounds of Jesus and the presence of God. Catholic sacramental life emphasized the power of the blood of Jesus (and especially so after Vatican II made the chalice of consecrated wine regularly available at communion). That emphasis enabled the smooth integration of bleeding as self-denial into the larger cultus. Historian of Catholicism Paula Kane has pointed out how in the late nineteenth and early twentieth centuries, the "mysticism of the Passion" of Jesus became more popular, as did devotion to the cult of the Sacred Heart of Jesus, which began in the seventeenth century but reemerged in a new version. At the same time, the "victim soul" became a larger part of Catholic devotional culture. "Victim souls" were persons who endured great physical suffering as part of a scheme of redemption for sinners in need of saving. Disproportionately women, some Catholics declared themselves ready to become a victim soul, imposing upon themselves severe hardships, including self-flagellation and other bloodletting practices. Some experienced the stigmata, including Europeans Theresa Neuman, Louise Lateau, Gemma Galgani, Padre Pio, Teresa Higginson, Marthe Robin, and, in the United States, Rose Ferron (1902–1936). The Passion of Jesus, the Sacred Heart, the bleeding out of wounds, and the drawing of blood through self-cutting were part of a core concern in Catholicism for blood, and especially the draining of blood from the body. Catholic holy cards, widely distributed, fostered popular interest in such things. The celebration of bloody suffering on certain feast days, the production of devotional literature addressing the bloody ordeals of victim souls, the presentation of bleeding victims as models of piety, and the pilgrimages to the towns of stigmatics, all reflect the pious emphasis on bloodletting. To be sick or bleeding, in a hospital bed or elsewhere, was to empty the body and prepare it for the influx of grace—all, as we have seen, a part of what Robert Orsi has discussed as ritual suffering in Catholicism. Additionally, Catholics' sufferings that involved bleeding from wounds that were not self-inflicted or sufferings that resulted from other physical debilities, came to be appreciated as an exercise in "offering it up." Widely practiced by American Catholics for much of the twentieth century, such devotional suffering was experienced as an emptying of the body at the same time it was understood to provide capital for what was conceived of as a "treasury of merit" to which all of the faithful contributed and that was debited to ransom endangered souls.[19]

Protestants in America developed a way of thinking about blood that differed in some ways from what Catholics believed. Protestants did not celebrate stigmatics and victim souls, or focus on the Sacred Heart of Jesus. Nevertheless, Protestants over the course of the nineteenth and twentieth centuries developed their own intense interest in bloodletting, and especially in the bloody Passion of Jesus. When traditionalist Catholic Mel Gibson's controversial *The Passion of the Christ* opened on two thousand movie screens on Ash Wednesday, 2004, it was described by critics as a celebration of "relentless bloodletting"—and that was after six minutes of bloodletting scenes were deleted from the final version. Evangelical Protestant groups organized "training rallies" in advance of the release to plan ways to build evangelizing campaigns around the movie. Churches bought copies of Christian guidelines to the movie to distribute to moviegoers. Protestant evangelical groups as well as some Catholics organized bus brigades to take people to the movie, collaborated with Gibson's marketing people in setting up the film as an occasion to demonstrate religious devotion, and arranged for exclusive showings in their churches. The movie consequently grossed hundreds of millions of dollars.[20]

Protestant interest in the early-twenty-first-century cinema of religious blood can be analyzed within the frame of the popular nineteenth-century American medical practice of bloodletting and the subsequent development of transfusion (as we shall see shortly). Bloodletting long has been associated with religion, with Christianity and other religions. Included especially visibly were the Aztecs, about whom contemporary historian of religion David Carrasco has written. Even *Medicine, Magic, and Religion*, published in New York in 1927, observed that "in many parts of the world the letting of blood by means of incisions or scarifications form part of a religious ritual." Americans, for their part, developed a deeper awareness of that relation beginning about the time that the Philadelphia physician Benjamin Rush inaugurated his campaign to cure disease by bloodletting in the late eighteenth century. As we have seen, monks and nuns in medieval and early modern Europe made religious occasions of bloodlettings, and there is a similar tenor to the thinking of Rush and others in America. Historian John Kloos has outlined how Rush imagined bloodletting as a component of the larger scheme of inculcation of Christian morality in the American populace. That sensibility had something to do with the notion of emptiness, of draining the body of poisons, an idea that had deep religious resonance. In *The Theory and Practice of Bloodletting* (1915), the American doctor Heinrich Stern insisted that his readers grasp that "this book, it must not be forgotten, does not deal with something that is to be added to the body, but with something that is to be withdrawn from it." Historian of medicine Susan E. Lederer, writing a century later, summarized that view: "Before 1900, most physicians and patients worried more about too much blood than too little; their efforts were directed at removing the excess blood." American Protestants usually did not construct the letting of their own blood as religious events. However, given the larger background of bloodletting in Western medical practice and the deep reverence for the spilled blood of Jesus in Christianity, it is important to recognize some kinds of bloodletting as episodes in the ongoing development of a larger complex of ideas about emptying the body of blood.[21]

One way of understanding bloodletting as a religious exercise for both Protestants and Catholics is to consider the slaughter of the Civil War. Historian Harry S. Stout has argued that during the Civil War, when "America was incarnating a millennial nationalism as the primal religious faith," bloodshed took on a strongly religious character as the central component of "the creation of a full-blown nondenominational civil religion." To empty the body of blood in battle was to seal a national compact with God. "In time," writes Stout, "all battlefield fatalities on both sides of the conflict were termed martyrs," so that the war was "transformed, in effect, into a moral crusade with religious foundations for which martyrs would willingly sacrifice themselves on their nations' altars." The blood sacrifice that occurred during the war, argues Stout, was a religious event, part of a civil religion with strong Christian undertones. It was dramatically articulated by theologians such as the Protestant minister Horace Bushnell, whose patriotism "perceived in bloodshed something mystically religious and moral." Drew Gilpin Faust has offered a similar perspective on the war—and an unflinching view of the extent of the bloodshed—while remarking as well on how it framed jeremiad-themed writing about atonement. Her view and Stout's both overlap with the opinion of Henry B. Smith of Union Theological Seminary, who summarized in 1867 some of the key points of such thinking about blood, emphasizing that "national unity" had been purchased at a great price, a terrible "sacrifice of blood." Smith explained that "in such sacrifice, which is a part of the inmost and vital law of Christianity itself, we have learned lessons which have rebuked our pride and vainglory." The wartime sacrifice of blood was an emptying of blood from the body required by Providence and indeed the law of Christianity, an atonement and an act of pious self-sacrifice all at once, which emptied the self of its pride, served as punishment for sin, and cemented a national covenant with God.[22]

The blending of themes of atonement with self-sacrifice in the Civil War era is a process visible as well in instances when white Christians shed the blood of African Americans. Historian Donald G. Mathews recently has addressed the substitutionary aspect of such bloodletting in "The Southern Rite of Human Sacrifice," a detailed analysis of the "blood sacrifice" that "is at the core of southern white fundamental Protestantism. Blood sacrifice is the connection between the purpose of white supremacists, the purity signified in segregation, the magnificence of God's wrath, and the permission granted the culture through the wrath of 'justified' Christians to sacrifice black men on the cross of white solidarity." Mathews observes how "the message of sin, guilt, and punishment" was widespread among southern Christians whose religious practice and everyday lives overflowed with occasions upon which to "cry 'guilt,' to teach guilt, to instill guilt: to make the offending soul shudder at the enormity of his/her guilt." That such guilt demanded judgment and punishment was deeply ingrained in white southern thinking about sin, salvation, and social order. As Mathews observes, "The feelings that sustained the credibility of the incredible doctrine of penal satisfaction had afflicted generations of white Southerners by the twentieth century. Even tepid or rebellious believers learned that religion was punishment." The mob that tortured to death a black man accused of assault, murder, rape, or other crimes made a perverse example of such justice; the sacrifice of the victim, according to Mathews, was experienced by whites as atonement for the sins of the community. But that victim at the same time, in being thrust into the role of scapegoat, served not only as the object of penal action but as a person with whom others identified. Indeed, as Kenneth Burke and René Girard have argued in their analyses of the mimetic character of scapegoating, a central part of the process is the identification of the members of the community with the scapegoat. In the South that meant identifying with the African American victim as he or she was drained of blood by tortures before being killed. The "alternate admiration and abuse of the victim" of lynching, as Orlando Patterson has written, was an aspect of a process in which observers both identified with and distanced themselves from the victim. To participate in a ritual of human sacrifice in the South was not the same as opening one's own vein, bleeding stigmatically, or dying on the battlefield. It was, however, a ritual with many layers, one of which was the prompting of members of the lynch mob to identify with the bloodied victim, at least for a time during the process of sacrifice.[23]

Because Christian notions about emptiness were intertwined with ideas about fullness, thinking about bleeding the body eventually was joined to ideas about filling it with new blood. The development of transfusion out of bloodletting, making use of ideas of emptiness and fullness, not only provided a substantial advance in therapy but proved for Protestants to be an effective way of thinking about self and salvation. Blood transfusions were attempted in the seventeenth and eighteenth centuries in Europe but did not become a consistently effective course of therapy until the twentieth century, after the discovery of blood groups by the Viennese doctor Karl Landsteiner in 1901 and the refinement of transfusing techniques. The first transfusions in America took place in New Orleans, where the racially charged atmosphere complicated the process in the 1850s. By the time transfusions were making their way into standard—rather than "heroic"—medical practice in the early twentieth century, Protestants (and probably other Christians) had had time to think about the process in connection with religious ideas of emptiness and fullness.[24]

Protestant writers emphasized that old blood had to be drained before the saving new blood of Jesus could be admitted to the body. Thus, to some extent, they extended the medieval notion of the *unio sanguinolenta*. The Congregationalist minister Henry Clay Trumbull explained in *The Blood Covenant* in 1898 that treating disease first of all was a matter of emptying the body: "In the leper, the very blood itself—the life—was death smitten. The only hope of a cure was purging out the old blood, by means of an inflowing current of new blood, which was new life." In a section titled "Blood Transfusion," Trumbull expanded upon "death itself being purged out of the veins by inflowing life." Because "new blood is new life," the blood of Jesus entered a person in a process involving the purging of old blood. Trumbull concluded: "So also with the sin-leprous nature. [One's] old life must be purged out, by the incoming of a new life; of such a life as only the Son of God can supply." The writers of *Popular Science* agreed with that estimate of the process of transfusion, having already asserted in 1889: "Take for instance, the transfusion of blood. . . . Take the bad blood out of a man and put new blood into him, and you draw off his diseases and infirmities and put new life into him." The mid-twentieth-century Protestant magazine *HIS* made the same point more economically: "Old Blood. Tired Blood. New Blood. But most important, Christ's blood, which makes old blood new." The African American religious movement leader Father Divine had another equally concise overview: "The very blood in your veins will not be the same."[25]

The relation between the feeling of emptiness and the feeling of fullness for American Christians is, as we have seen, decidedly dialectical. The body is emptied and filled in a reciprocal process, and sometimes a greater emptying brings a greater sense of fullness. Protestant thinking about blood purging and blood infusion reflects that complex dynamic. Old blood is purged by new blood. The body is emptied and filled at nearly the same time. It is transfused. A century after the development of transfusion, Protestant writers Philip Yancey and Paul Brand articulated one kind of Protestant thinking about the blood of Jesus in this way: "As I ponder the ancient symbolism behind the word 'blood' in the Christian religion, especially as suggested in Jesus's statements, I keep returning to the modern procedure of blood transfusion. Obviously, Jesus and the biblical authors did not envision a Red Cross blood supply depot when they used the word. And yet out of my experience blood transfusion has emerged as a kind of summary image of the Christian symbol." The American evangelist Billy Graham thought likewise, again emphasizing the emptying of the body as a prelude to the inflow of blood. Graham preached in the folksy style of his predecessor Billy Sunday that "God does not offer Band-Aids when you are bleeding to death, but He gave a life-saving transfusion, the blood of His Son." Such statements can be tracked back as far as Victorian England, when the Vicar of Leeds, Walter Farquhar Hook, exulted: "O wonderful transfusion of the blood of Christ, from the Head into the members, from his natural into his mystical body, from the side of Jesus Christ into the Christian's heart." That image was also credited to Rev. Lyman Abbott of the Plymouth Church in Brooklyn, in a *New York Observer and Chronicle* column that criticized him for his overreliance on it. It scolded Abbott for supposing that the Atonement was just a "voluntary transfusion of blood from a healthy person into the veins of a diseased person." Because Abbott "look[ed] upon sin as disease merely," which is "substituted" with Christ's blood, and did not acknowledge the deep corruption of the old blood, he missed the mark in understanding the full nature of the transformation of the soul through that transfusion.[26]

The idea of transfusion nevertheless caught on. The controversial Methodist bishop E. R. Hendrix in Kansas City warned that "there must be a transfusion of blood to save the race," but he turned that phrase in a way that identified the love of God with the blood of Jesus: "Love alone can do that, the love of God shed abroad in the heart by the Holy Ghost that is given unto us." That association of the blood of Jesus with the Holy Ghost in fact overlapped with Catholic thinking. In 1915 the *American Catholic Quarterly Review*, in the course of discussing the Passion of Christ and the Blood of the Lamb, proposed that "moreover, a transfusion of the whole Body and Blood of the Lamb of God into the communicant through his open mouth" takes place when a person receives the bread and drinks from the chalice. Catholics also understood blood as defined by the 1898 article "The HOLY GHOST—the Lifeblood of the Mystical Body of Christ." For most Protestants, the process did not involve the consecrated elements; the Holy Ghost was more important in understanding transfusion. A Protestant discussion in 2011, *The Holy Ghost: He Is the Blood of Jesus*, described how the redeeming death of Jesus "allows the individual to receive a type of spiritual 'blood-transfusion' via the Holy Ghost. This transfusion allows our natural human blood to be fused and cleansed with the Blood of Jesus." The devotional writer M. R. DeHaan likewise invoked the Holy Spirit in treating the topic of "'transfusion' by the Holy Spirit," in a Protestant devotional book on the subject, *Chemistry of the Blood* (1984).[27]

The focus on transfusion, and the particular understanding of transfusion as a process involving both emptying and filling, was important for Protestants and to some extent for Catholics. But instances remained in which bloodletting itself was the central image of religious devotion. The Penitentes of New Mexico have long engaged in what has been called, somewhat patronizingly, the "theatricalization of blood" in annual public performances of religious bloodletting. And there is the case of Moravians and their attention to the "side-hole" of Jesus and their emotionally rich practice of bloodletting, especially in early America. Jane T. Merritt has demonstrated how the Moravians "brought a sensual and emotional quality to their worship of Christ's wounds and blood" and how that sensibility was conveyed to American Indians in the eighteenth century. One of the Moravians' "most common medical procedures to reestablish the humoral balance of an individual was bloodletting. They performed bleeding operations with the same kind of reverence they felt for the wounds of Christ." American Indians took from their contact with Moravians a complex of religious ideas and feelings about bloodletting, in a manner that might or might not have been intended by the Moravians. Moravians might not have been fully aware of the cultural gravity of their own bloodletting events, and they might not have expected American Indians to find those events so important. Nevertheless, Indian embrace of ritualized bleeding as a part of Christian praxis can be gauged by the fact that bloodletting became so popular among Indians during the mid-eighteenth-century Indian Great Awakening in Pennsylvania that Moravians eventually were forced to limit the practice.[28]

For most American Christians, images of a body emptying itself of blood, and of new blood entering, are an important part of a complex and at times ambiguous experience of embodied emptiness. That many report feeling it should lead us to inquire about how physical experiences such as bleeding are related to the experience of gazing upon a body being bled, or at an image of a bleeding person, or feeling something inside the body that cannot be recognized by others. Saint Gertrude wrote in the thirteenth century how her experience of emptiness was "as though my bones were being emptied of all the marrow . . . so that nothing was felt to exist in all my substance." She nevertheless was clear that her experiences were entirely interior, that her bloodletting and emptying were felt in her heart rather than displayed on her skin. That sensibility was also present in American Christians such as Ann Willson, who in 1827 wrote her friend about how "heart answers to heart in deep feeling. A secret transfusion, or silent reciprocation." Bleeding, cultural critic Julia Kristeva has proposed, signals the "erasing of differences" and the undermining of identity as boundaries dissolve. Americans such as Ann Willson expressed their feeling of emptiness in language about bleeding and transfusion that suggested such an undermining of self. Although some American Christians practiced self-denial in their own bleeding, like Willson they more commonly felt it internally. The process of cognizing the feeling of emptiness included the invention of imagery that fostered that feeling of bleeding and linked it with theological ideas about self, identity, transformation, and the erasure of boundary.[29]

Bleeding and fasting are similar to religious silence. The practice of silence is a form of self-denial that has served to cultivate the feeling of emptiness in American Christians. As we think about how silence begets the feeling of emptiness, we can consider how psychological research in the wake of Charles Darwin and William James has shown that bodily postures and states purposely adopted by persons can lead directly to their feeling certain emotions. One kind of research involves discovered correlations between facial expressions and emotions: where persons are instructed to smile, they report positive affect, and when instructed to frown, negative affect. Religious disciplining of the body, as a means to cultivate certain emotions, operates similarly. Religious commentators frequently have read the correlation from the other side, namely, that a certain internal state leads to certain bodily expressions. Love of Jesus produces the stigmata. A feeling of awe of God leads to fasting. Or, as the *Rules of the Congregation* (1871) of Notre Dame, Indiana, explained: "A soul strongly impressed with the thought and conviction of the emptiness of the world, in which her nobler aspirations cannot be satisfied, feels the necessity of silence." But silence as a discipline undertaken in the interest of cultivating feeling was also recognized by Christian writers. As such it was frequently mentioned together with fasting and some other disciplines, and even sometimes referenced the blood of Jesus.[30]

Silence and fasting often are linked in Catholic devotional commentaries and guides; one twentieth-century proponent advised a fast "to control our speech." The models for silence include Jesus, whose silence as an infant as well as during his Passion was recognized and commended in America by *St. Vincent's Manual* (1856) and by *The Ursuline Manual* (1857), the latter chiding: "The silence of Jesus is a miracle of meekness—have you imitated it, when undeservedly or even justly reproved?" Mary, Saint Joseph, and Mary Magdalen likewise were presented as exemplars of silence for their behavior at the foot of the cross, the "Litany of St. Joseph" lauding Joseph's "pattern of silence and resignation." John Cassian and Saint Benedict made silence an important part of Christian practice—The Rule of Saint Benedict stipulated, "Therefore, due to the great importance of silence itself, perfect disciples should rarely be granted permission to speak." Saint Bernard, William of Saint Thierry, and Saint John of the Cross, among others, also prized it, and members of religious orders as well as individuals took vows of silence. Those who did not take vows were urged to practice silence after Mass, after confession, on certain dates of the liturgical calendar, and during novenas and other special devotions.[31]

Silence was a form of self-denial. Silence, like fasting and blood devotions, was a performance of emptiness and a prompt to self-negation. Lawrence Cunningham, describing the importance of silence in *The Catholic Experience* (1985), explained that "silence indicates the absence of God . . . God as absence." That observation might hold equally for Orthodox congregations in America, where silence has always been a central part of religious practice. It was, for the Trappist monk Thomas Merton (son of a woman whose religious community, the Quakers, engaged in silent worship), "silent emptiness" and as such a practice that, as one Merton scholar has written, "serves to narrow the distance between man and God." The Danish theologian Søren Kierkegaard proposed that silence was the epitome of prayer, and Catholic writing about silence evidences a similar understanding. Catholic silence is a devotional practice that provokes the feeling of emptiness—the voice is gone, no one is there—but at the same time, it has manifested as deep prayer, closeness to God, and the experience of fullness.[32]

Catholic worship services throughout American history have placed a premium upon silence in public worship (interspersed with music, singing, and collective prayer), even after Vatican II made provisions for greater involvement of lay voices in services. Protestants historically have been less likely to adopt silence as a ritual form. There have been exceptions, however. Some Protestant groups have a tradition of silence in worship and even in social relations, and to an extent greater than in Catholic or Orthodox liturgies. The Society of Friends is well known for its meeting-house gatherings during which persons sometimes do not speak for long periods of time. They gather and sit silently waiting for inspiration to speak, which can take the form of a prayer, a story, a song, or other forms. Quakers practice silence in expectation that it will lead to profound contact with God. As President Benjamin Harrison, in delivering a speech on the occasion of his fifty-eighth birthday, observed of a Quaker meeting, "silence there is apt to be broken by the moving of the spirit." Old Order Amish worship, which is held biweekly in homes, includes the reading of scripture, singing, and sermons. Services begin in silence and return to silence periodically throughout the meeting. Amish conversions tend to be silent. The historian John A. Hostetler has pointed out how Amish life is deeply infused with the Anabaptist notion of *Gelassenheit*, which can be understood as "conquest of selfishness," "inner surrender," and "silence of the soul." The point of silence for such Protestants is the same as for Catholics, summarized by a charismatic Catholic in the late twentieth century as such: "The aim of silence in religious practice . . . is to be blank—to be nothing—empty." There must be, she said, "an emptying of yourself . . . an emptying of yourself and an inpouring of God." Or, as a writer for the *Journal of Religion*, noting that reciprocal relationship in Christian liturgy, argued in 1924: "It is a silence which is not empty."[33]

The linking of silence to the "inpouring of God"—whether through Amish or Quaker worship waiting on the "spirit" or in Catholic devotions of various sorts—underscores the dialectics of empty/full in the Christian practice of silence. It frames, for example, a view of Protestant Pentecostalism that allows us to see the relation of Pentecostal worship to the experience of emptiness. Just as in the case of fasting, where the emptiness of the stomach was tied to the fullness of joy in an experience of God, silence has been associated with the joyful voicing of prayer. Kieran Flanagan, in a study of silence in Christian liturgy, has argued that because "silence is the absence of speech or movement, it serves to invert these explicit elements and to point to their implicit opposites." Silence "is about passing over a boundary," and as a form it is "necessarily 'tensive' and always characterized by some inadequacy. Silence enables the mysterious to be felt, but is also mysterious in what it effects." That perspective helps us to see what Alan Davies means when he proposes that "Pentecostals and Quakers have different methods for reaching the same solution, that of waiting on the Holy Spirit, Pentecostals through inspired noisiness, Quakers through silent waiting." Silence, understood in such a way, is prayer in the same way that those who fast name their practice as "prayer," and those who bleed do likewise. The glossolalia or "noisiness" of Pentecostal worship (as well as personal prayer) expresses the feeling of emptiness in its reciprocal relationship with the experience of fullness. But the feeling of emptiness remains the starting point even for prayer, as a recent Catholic commentary on prayer explained: "In a sense, the *horror vacui* of physics holds here also. Just as air automatically fills up all vacuums, we become filled with God the more we become empty of ourselves. And becoming empty of ourselves is part of what happens to us when we reach towards encounter with Him. Put in more traditional language, we will always be heard if we pray." A nineteenth-century prayer for revival stated the matter similarly but with a slightly more activist notion of prayer: "Want is emptiness. Emptiness invites in God. When we want him he always comes. Thus prayer is the doorkeeper that opens the soul and lifts up the gates and lets the King of Glory in." That understanding of silence as a part of a process of prayer has reemerged among early-twenty-first-century Baptists and Methodists, who increasingly are drawn to silent, meditative worship.[34]

Work and Sex

In an article entitled "Labor as Worship," a proponent of Shaker life in 1871 wrote what many in America believed: "We strictly follow the example of Jesus, the Apostles and the Primitive Church, who established the principle, that work is Christian worship." The author, like others who addressed the subject, also remarked on the "honest labor" modeled by Jesus and Joseph, both carpenters, and urged his readers likewise to engage especially in "hand labor." Americans in the 1870s, however, had long since moved beyond exclusive embrace of the ideal of "hand labor." Factories, specialized skills, body-killing toil, and bureaucratic business structures, along with the shift from self-reliance to dependencies within economic cells, all changed the way people thought about "hand labor." Nevertheless, "honest labor" was still esteemed and continued to be so, making periodic comebacks—such as during the emblematic 1960s back-to-the-farm movement—over the next century and a half. Many Americans also remained comfortable with the notion that there was something religious in work. As *Justified by Work*, a recent ethnography about religion among working-class Chicago Catholics, demonstrates, there are many in the early twenty-first century who explicitly link their labor to religious ideals, conceptualizing their work as religious service performed for their own salvation and for that of others.[35]

In early Christianity work often was understood to be the practice of self-denial. George Ovitt Jr. has emphasized the "consistent view of the centrality of labor as a means of developing the spiritual self" through the Middle Ages. Manual labor was embraced by early Christians and by medieval monastic cultures, as well as by those who were religious but not monastic, as a source of spiritual sustenance. Saint Basil held that "work itself should be a power of praise and thanksgiving reverently rendered to God who has bestowed upon man the faculties of work and the means of exercising those faculties." Saint Augustine viewed work as an exercise in self-denial, seeing in it an activity mortifying the flesh that became an act of devotion. Monastic theorists such as Saint Benedict "favored manual labor, but always as a means to a spiritual end." David E. Linge has written about how the fourth-century Christian anchorite Evagrius of Pontus, a teacher of John Cassian, compared work to fasting: "Hunger, toil, and solitude are the means of extinguishing the flames of desire." The fifth-century *Rule of the Four Fathers*, recommending self-denial through manual labor, made work a means of subduing the individual will. Labor was conceptualized as an activity that emptied the body of energy and will, purified the soul by chastening the flesh, and was offered as devotion to God. In monasteries, those goals became intensified, so that, as Lynn White Jr. points out, "the monks insisted that *laborare est orare*, work is worship."[36]

In *The Protestant Ethic and the Spirit of Capitalism*, Max Weber argued that the religious roots of capitalism were to be found in the "inner-worldly asceticism" of early modern Protestants and especially English Puritans and their descendants. Weber's attempt to link the religious ethic to the early development of capitalism overreached, but his insight into the centrality of work to the religious life of Puritans remains crucial for understanding American religious history. Reformation theologians, while not in agreement about the role of work in salvation, generally concurred with Huldreich Zwingli that "in the things of this life the laborer is most like to God." Martin Luther's articulation of the idea of calling was an important component in the spiritual valorization of work, and especially of work that "seems very trivial and contemptible" but that is "as great and precious, not on account of your worthiness, but because it has its place within that jewel and holy treasure, the Word and Commandment of God." Puritans in New England practiced, as historian Steven Innes wrote, "an ethic of disciplined work and self-denial." Puritans' anxieties about idleness and a general "unprofitableness" in the use of time reinforced their dedication to work, and their investment of labor eventually paid them strong financial dividends. Nevertheless, as Perry Miller remarked, echoing Weber, Puritans managed to cleave to the covenant they believed God had made with them by remaining "ascetic in the midst of prosperity."[37]

Much has been written about the Weber thesis and about its usefulness for understanding the economic development of the United States. Economic historians, additionally, have pointed to the many other factors over the course of several centuries that have influenced the way in which

Americans have conceptualized work. The emergence of an economic liberalism in America that encouraged individual initiative and abetted the development of large manufacturing and business operations and worker specialization prompted, for example, thinking about labor that was less inclined to value it as an activity that enriched the soul. Americans nevertheless clung to the notion of work as devotional activity for much of the nineteenth century. That view to some extent continued to inform ideas about work in the twentieth century. It was a view strongly voiced by Thomas Carlyle, who in the mid-nineteenth century wrote in *Past and Present* (a book serialized and published repeatedly in America): "The latest Gospel in this world is, Know thy work and do it." For Carlyle, "a man perfects himself by working. . . . The blessed glow of Labour in him, is it not a purifying fire, wherein all poison is burnt up, and of sour smoke itself there is made bright blessed flame! . . . All true work is sacred." The editor of the *Christian Union*, Hamilton Wright Mabie, saw something similar in work when he wrote at the turn of the century that "Work is sacred therefor not only because it is the fruit of self-denial, patience and toil, but because it uncovers the soul of the worker." But alongside the view expressed by Mabie, and complementary to it in America, was a sense of work chiefly as sacrifice and self-denial, and the idea that work was sacred precisely for that reason. The Episcopal priest and Yale professor William Graham Sumner (d. 1910), one of the most outspoken proponents of that view, continually emphasized the moral course of "labor, patience, suffering, self-denial." So also did the Congregationalist minister Jacob Abbott, who wrote that work "requires exertion and self-denial."[38]

The model worker was Jesus. Writers often pointed out that he was a carpenter, but they also described the work of Jesus as holy labor. The work of Jesus admired by American Christians was activity that took place according to a divine plan for labor. The *Methodist Magazine and Quarterly Review* explained in 1830, "The whole system of Divine economy, both Jewish and Christian, is founded in a spirit of labor and self-denial." And by labor, such magazines meant what *Farm and Garden* referred to as "exhausting labor." A Presbyterian journal accordingly could offer the insight that "Jesus Christ is a perfect pattern of self-denial. The eternal God emptied himself of his glory. . . . See the heavy cross under which he groaned and staggered for us." The Catholic *Pilgrim of Our Lady of Martyrs* emphasized that "Christ practiced and preached self-denial. He bore all the hardships incident to a life of poverty and hard labor." The biblical text frequently marshaled to reinforce discussions of Jesus as a hard worker was the letter of Paul to the Philippians (Phil. 2:5–8, ESV), in which Jesus is said to have "emptied himself" of his glory so as to serve humanity. "Christ, who was rich," said Thomas Tiplady, "for our sakes became poor. He emptied himself that our lives might be filled. . . . He spent himself among the poor, sick, blind, and sinful." The reference to *kenosis* in the Pauline text in many cases was taken to mean the salvific sacrifice of Jesus in a cosmic sense, but it also was employed to support arguments about the need for self-denial and devotion to God through the performance of work. Ministers writing in religious journals in the nineteenth and twentieth centuries often compared their own work and the work of missionaries to the work of Jesus, using the phrase "holy labor" to define their role. In such instances, they again emphasized self-denial. A memorial for the colonial New England missionary John Eliot recounted "the absolute self-sacrifice which caused him to add to an arduous profession duties which could not fail to be attended by everything uncomfortable and hostile. . . . He emptied himself." The consensus was that self-denial through toil was a way of becoming empty. The challenges of that path were rarely underestimated: "Self-emptying—oh, what a struggle it means sometimes. But brother, do not let the struggle keep you from getting down before God. We cannot afford to attempt to do his work without constantly being in the self-emptied state." The *New York Evangelist* nevertheless warned, "How few understand the precept, 'go work today in my vineyard!' . . . They do not love the religion of toil, hardship and self-denial. Oh, how few of us are like him who 'became poor,' 'emptied himself.'"[39]

With Jesus as a model, and with a clergy that exemplified the life of "holy labor," American Christians went to work, bearing in mind that "labor is one of the greatest blessings that God has brought out of the primeval 'curse.'" Periodicals from the *Ohio Cultivator* to the *Christian Index*, African American newspapers such as the *People's Advocate* and the *Washington Bee*, and volumes of collected sermons discussed how "labor and sweat" brought persons closer to the example of the carpenter Jesus who "wiped the sweat from his brow" and "emptied his heart of all its lifeblood" for humanity. Labor was a discipline that emptied a person as sweat, like blood, left the body. Labor also certified a person's increase as moral, a message delivered by Henry Ward Beecher in *Seven Lectures to Young Men* (1844): "Work. Let your sweat-drops wash your gains from all dishonesty. . . . Wealth gathered by vanity shall be diminished, but wealth gathered by labor shall increase."[40]

Through the nineteenth century and into the twentieth, many Americans continued to view labor as a means to what the popular family publication *Christian Work* referred to as the "self-emptied mind to which the grace of God is welcome." But the burgeoning industrial economy was changing the lives of many, and Americans' view of work as labor that emptied the self to receive God's grace was changing with it. As James B. Gilbert pointed out in *Work without Salvation*, working long had been imagined as the pathway to the good life and a thriving, productive society. As the twentieth century began, some voiced skepticism about the moral value of work in a factory system predicated on specialization and laborers' performance of monotonous routines of meaningless tasks. The coalescence of such thinking dovetailed with the maturing of the idea of menial labor as emblematic of African Americans, whose role was to serve whites. Frederic Douglass and Martin Delany had criticized black males for their willingness to limit themselves to work as porters, barbers, ditch-diggers, shoe-shiners, and other such tasks. In the intensifying Jim Crow tenor of American society—in the decades preceding the second coming of the Klan in the 1920s—to perform menial labor was apt to be seen as a degradation associated with what Delany called "a *whole race of servants*." For the Unitarian clergyman Edward Everett Hale, author of *How They Lived in Hampton* (1888), there was a difference between work and labor, the latter being for dumb brutes. Hale supported the surge in the immigration of Irish people to America, reasoning that the Irish could perform such labor and free "Americans" for more rewarding work. The notion of honest, exhausting labor, such as a farmer might invest in his field, became confused, and with it the idea that a person should follow the path of Jesus as "servant" to others (also language from Paul's letter to the Philippians). Adding to the confusion was the emergent critique of wealth that began to ring from Christian pulpits in the latter part of the nineteenth century. In addition to theological programs such as the Social Gospel, which offered an alternative vision—a moderate "reengineering" of the socioeconomic order—ministers specifically scolded those whose "selfishness," as one Baptist minister wrote, threatened "the public good." *Appleton's* contrasted the "selfish desire for gain" with the work of the "hard sons of toil," and the *Catholic World* approved a Puritanesque program "to save and increase wealth indeed, though *not for self*." Such viewpoints, which have been well reported by American economic and labor historians for more than a century, lamented the degraded status of work, the dilution of its moral value.[41]

The notion of work as a way of emptying oneself and therefore making the soul ready for encounter with God did not disappear from American Christianity, however. Developments such as the Christian commune movement of the 1960s–70s and various revivified Christian labor advocacies—as exemplified by the mid-twentieth-century *Catholic Worker*—evidence the power of an earlier perspective on the religious value of work. That perspective also is seen in the lives of the twentieth-century miners profiled by Richard J. Callahan Jr. in *Work and Faith in Kentucky Coal Fields* (2009), a book that details the blending of the mountain Holiness religion of Appalachia with the everyday routines of coal-field labor.[42]

The idea of work as self-sacrifice and the trust that "honest labor" was a means by which to empty the self declined as certain kinds of work were associated with African Americans. At the same time, feminist criticisms of domesticity, government, the economic order, and religion were making headway into the culture of work and changing it. The Woman's Movement of the nineteenth century, as it spilled over into the twentieth century and gained momentum in the forms both of temperance crusades and of the campaign for female suffrage, was grounded in a rethinking of self-sacrifice. While many strands of thought were joined in the coalescence of feminism in the early twentieth century, the observation by Elizabeth Stanton, in her commentary in *The Woman's Bible* (1898), that "self-development is a higher duty than self-sacrifice" represents a key argument in changing ideas about work. For Stanton and many others, the domestic sphere did not provide an environment conducive for all women to develop themselves through work. Work, rather than consisting in self-sacrifice, was meant to be fulfilling. Work was not an emptying, but a filling up.[43]

In the twentieth century, the idea of work as self-emptying labor performed in anticipation of readying oneself for grace increasingly was supplemented by the idea that work is itself fulfilling. The way in which work fulfills, however, is not specifically because it brings riches, although many people made that a goal and achieved it. Rather, in a Christian ethics that made gradual inroads into the workplace, fulfillment in work comes from losing oneself in work. This point recently has been made by the Catholic philosopher Peter Simpson. Simpson has argued that "to give oneself in work is to do one's work with all those virtues that one learnt about in the catechism: be diligent and honest . . . exercise self-control . . . persevere . . . show fortitude." Failure to act in such a way as a worker is "to take oneself from work instead of giving oneself to work. Hence it is, in the end, to lose oneself *from* work rather than find oneself *in* work." In other words, work is a creative endeavor requiring discipline, focus, and commitment, and people who give themselves over to their work are fulfilled by it. That idea has deep roots but was progressively articulated in the latter part of the twentieth century during a period of cultural change involving a new wave of feminism ("equal pay for equal work"), the development of Affirmative Action, and alterations in thinking about welfare ("workfare"). It has been obvious especially in the viewpoint represented by the theory of "flow" in the performance of work. Proposed by the psychologist Mihaly Csikszentmihalyi in a series of influential books, "flow" refers to the process of losing oneself in one's work. Persons learn to limit distractions "so that they may lose themselves in the creative process." Flow is "being completely involved in an activity for its own sake. The ego falls away. Time flies." Such a state, characterized by a loss of self, or at least an awareness of self, results in a sense of fulfillment.[44]

While "flow" moved theory of work in a new direction, it also resonated well with earlier Christian thinking about work and both expressed and helped to cognize the feeling of emptiness that Christians report. In the decades after 1980, discussions of the religious aspect of work not only leaned toward the notion of fulfillment but also, reframing a late-nineteenth-century argument, took a positive view of the role of religion in business success. American religious writers had for generations recommended the phrase "laborare est orare" (to work is to pray) as a guide to Christian activity in the world. From the *Plumbers, Gas, and Steamfitters Journal* in 1911 to the *Rhode Island Schoolmaster* in 1859, and in many publications before and after those, the phrase was used to describe self-sacrifice and a population of hard workers who made the world "ring with prayers," that is, labor as prayer. At the end of the twentieth century, that phrase continued to organize thinking about work in a host of manuals and inspirational books that claimed a basis for their gospels of success in that same spirit of "laborare est orare." Whether it was *Christ-Centered Selling: A Scripturally Based Guide to Principled, Profitable Persuasion* (2007) or *Spiritual Capital: Wealth We Can Live By* (2004), or *Work, Love, Pray: Practical Wisdom for Young Professional Christian Women* (2011), the message concorded with the title of a book chapter by the popular American "spiritual writer" Thomas Moore: "To Work Is to Pray." That conceptualization expresses and builds upon the deeply rooted idea that Christian emptying of the self is reciprocally related to the experience of fullness.[45]

American Christian thinking about sexual desire, like that about work, has been grounded in discussion of emptiness, and that discussion, like some others bearing on religion and emptiness, takes as its point of departure the supposition of an analogous relationship between body and soul. In "The Hunger of the Soul" (1870), the influential Protestant theologian Horace Bushnell articulated that relationship and suggested its paradoxical nature. "The analogy of the soul is so close to that of the body," wrote Bushnell, "that it speaks of its hunger, its food, its fullness, and growth, and fatness, under the images it derives from the body." The hungry soul, separated from God, seeks to satisfy itself "by a work of double feeding put upon the body. We call it sensuality." Persons are driven by a "passion of want that they are totally unable to moderate," blindly attempting to satisfy themselves, to no avail. In the end, gorged on the pleasures of the senses, they end up "venting their impatience with life, with curses on its emptiness." Bushnell's point, in fact, was that persons who give themselves over to sensuality are both full and empty: they are so full of themselves, through their own basking in the pleasures of the flesh, that they feel empty of holiness. "The soul," Bushnell concludes, "without God, is empty." The solution, then, was to empty the soul of all things that are not holy, including abandoning the gluttony of the senses. In the complex reasoning of Christian thinking about emptiness, the soul that was empty of God had to be emptied of what filled it in place of God so that it could be filled with God. Accordingly, whether a person's feeling of emptiness was the result of being filled with the unholy or was a genuine holy emptiness joined to spiritual desire was a matter to which religious professionals gave much consideration in consultation with Christian laypersons.[46]

American Christians think about sex in connection with soul-polluting lust and, in more subtle ways, with food. In Christian history gluttony frequently is mentioned alongside lust, as in the Bible, in early Christian writings, in medieval theological treatises, and in a host of Catholic, Orthodox, and Protestant writings since the Reformation. Gluttony and lust likewise have made frequent joint appearances in literature, during the Renaissance and afterward. Early modern literary scholar Gary Taylor, in analyzing the joining of the two in Thomas Middleton's *The Bloody Banquet* (1609), concluded that "often in Renaissance drama and Christian polemic, food is foreplay and gluttony the usher to lust." For American Christians such as Rev. Sylvester Graham, lust was explicitly connected to eating. In his widely read and much-studied *A Lecture to Young Men on Chastity* (1848), an emotional plea for avoidance of masturbation, sexual contact, and "impure thoughts," Graham explained that diet was a precipitating factor in lust. A vegetarian who proscribed spicy food, alcohol, refined bread, and chemical additives, Graham detailed in case studies how food intake led to sexual lust. "The truth of the matter is simply this—a pure and well regulated vegetable diet serves to take away or prevent all morbid or preternatural sexual lust." Graham's theorizing went beyond that recommendation, however. He expressed his ideas in terms of the dangers of a body and soul that were improperly "filled." He explained that "prurience, or concupiscence" results when a person's "mind becomes filled with unclean images." That condition forecloses the option of being filled with anything else: "The continued prurience of his genital organs appeals almost incessantly to his brain, and drags his mental energies and operations into the polluted current of his tyrant passion; and his imagination is constantly filled with lewd and obscene images, so that he scarcely has the power to fix his thoughts, for any length of time, on other subjects."[47]

Graham's advice to young men represented two interrelated sets of ideas about lust that Christian writers deployed in their discussions of sexuality: lust was an appetite, like the appetite for food, and its danger lay especially in its filling a person so completely that no room was left for God. Noah Webster's *Dictionary* defined lust as "to have carnal desire; to desire eagerly the gratification of the carnal appetite." Joseph Worcester, Webster's competitor and Nathaniel Hawthorne's teacher, offered a similar meaning in his *Dictionary* in 1860: "Concupiscience, n. Carnal appetite; lust." The *Catholic Telegraph* similarly framed appetite in another common way, informing that, "amongst all sensual gratifications, lust and gluttony are the most violent." The *Catholic Encyclopedia* in 1913 said lust was "the inordinate craving for, or indulgence of, the carnal pleasure which is experienced in the human organs of generation."[48]

Passion filled a person. In some cases, that passion was romantic love, but even in that case, the dynamic was the same as with lust, because even love, in 1803, was "a passion which, when it seizes on the soul, shuts out every other object; it engrosses the whole attention and leaves no room for any other wish or desire." Religious leaders concerned about lust spoke about it in the same way. *The Pursuit of Holiness* (1870) framed the case in general terms on an exegesis of Luke 2:7, "There was no room for them in the inn" (KJV). The author observed first that "Christ may come to the door of the inn, desiring to take up his abode there; but if there is no room for him, he must be cradled in the manger outside." The culprit in such a scenario was self-will, which filled the soul and made it impossible for Christ to enter: "The soul must be empty of self-will before God can work in it." When "we fulfill the desires of the flesh and of the mind . . . Christ is shut out." That principle, as many American Christian writers before and after observed, held true regardless of the way in which "self-will" was manifested. Discourses on sexual lust, such as Graham's, adopted the model, as did, for example, the *Mercersburg Review*, which advised "a continuous crucifixion of the flesh, with the affections and lusts, only to give proper room, however, for the fruits of the Spirit." Condemnations of the "lust for money" reasoned similarly. Rev. George Shepard of Maine wrote that "lust of gain" so "engrosses the affections as to leave no room for the love of God." The *Young Lady's Mentor* (1851) preached that "the love of money is so literally the 'root of all evil' that there is no room in the heart where it dwells for any other growth, for anything lovely or excellent." The mid-nineteenth-century *Bankers Magazine*, in a piece titled "The Morals of Money," stated that "the passion for wealth . . . leaves no room for the love of nobler objects," so that a person, filled but empty, became "LOST, to God and to himself." In the late twentieth century, when the message "greed is good" came under particularly strong criticism, so also did pride reemerge as an attribute of the greedy person. Recovering a tradition familiar to Puritans, a book on Christian discipleship proposed that "we must ask God that the flesh in us—particularly our pride—may die. If we are proud, God cannot come to us. Pride is the worst form of the flesh, because it leaves no room in the heart for God."[49]

Puritans themselves were keenly aware of the dangers of lust. Thomas Shepard, Cotton Mather, and Jonathan Edwards in New England all warned against it, Edwards perhaps thousands of times, including through the mouth of David Brainerd, when Edwards cited Brainerd's message to his brother: "Oh my dear brother, flee fleshly lusts, and the enchanting amusements, as well as corrupt doctrine, of the present day, and strive to live to God. Take this as the last line from/Your affectionate dying brother." Edwards himself created a particularly striking image, among a great many sketches of the soul filled with lust: "A man, by gratifying his lusts in his imaginations and thoughts, may make his soul in the sight of God to be a hold of foul spirits, and like a cage of every unclean and hateful bird." Sex itself, as Edmund Morgan pointed out with reference to John Cotton's writing, was not intrinsically dangerous for Puritans, but only inasmuch as it interfered with the ability to focus one's life and thoughts on God. Puritans and their descendants continued to imagine lust as just that problem, however. Richard Godbeer recently has shown that even as sexual mores and roles in New England were becoming more diverse and shifting, lust still remained a primary concern. In New York and the Chesapeake, as John D'Emilio and Estelle B. Freeman have written, a more "genteel" model recognized lust but, in comparison to the New England way, did not put lust in the foreground of sexuality. Nevertheless, it is important to recognize that the conceptualizing of lust as a problem—it filled up a soul meant for God's grace—remained a central theme in discussions of lust from colonial times through the twentieth century. In 1965, when Billy Graham wrote in *World Aflame*, "We need a new heart that will not have lust and greed and hate in it," he was speaking a language about emptying the heart that virtually all American Christians could understand.[50]

When the revivalist Charles Finney warned that lust was a corrupt "state of the heart" that must be avoided, he was referring to both men and women. One complication of Christian thinking about lust and emptiness was the related view of women, and sometimes men, as "empty vessels," waiting to be filled with religion and civilization and, in the case of women, with whatever their fathers, husbands, or male associates thought useful. Women sometimes were called "the weaker vessel," a designation that implied much of the same. But the notion of "empty vessel" carried with it something more. Building on historian Nancy Cott's description of the nineteenth-century construction of women as "passionless" actors performing in a cult of domesticity, Barbara Welter thought that the mid-nineteenth-century American woman was "the hostage in the home" who at marriage "bestowed the greatest treasure upon her husband, and from that time on was completely dependent upon him, an empty vessel, without legal or emotional existence of her own." It is possible even to see the Antinomian proponent Anne Hutchinson, moreover, in a related way. One historian treated Hutchinson's rejection of patriarchy as an emptying process preliminary to being filled with the spirit, a development that enabled Hutchinson's religious self-understanding as "little more than a vehicle or empty vessel."[51]

American historians have amply illustrated the complex fashion in which religious ideas in various periods were blended with arguments having to do with male power and social tradition, and although those intertwinings have shifted from time to time, they remain important for understanding both gender history and religious history. For now, we will note that specifically religious notions of "empty vessel" did not overlap perfectly with other ideas having to do with social roles and power hierarchies. Hutchinson, for example, while emptying herself of loyalty to certain social traditions, viewed herself largely in religious terms. Nonreligious women in the nineteenth century, to view the issue from another angle, still could be seen as empty in terms of their role as "social" vessels. For now, I suggest just two things. First, there was a religious model for woman as an empty vessel. As religious writers observed, Mary "took her place at the feet of Jesus as an empty vessel that might be filled." Religious emptiness could overlap with social emptiness, but it did not have to do so. Second, and more importantly, it was possible to be empty and full at the same time—empty and vaguely desiring God, yet full and leaving no room for God. Such a notion played loosely with the master metaphor of emptiness/fullness but added texture to the discussion. *The American Catholic Quarterly Review* proposed how one could be empty and filled (but not with holiness) simultaneously:

> If one were to drop into the sea an empty vessel, say a bottle, the sea water would rush into it at once and fill it to its utmost capacity, would it not? But suppose the empty bottle, instead of being open, is tightly stopped up and sealed, then the whole ocean presses around it in vain; no sea-water will get into that empty vessel. . . . The Christian . . . if he be void of self, and of all worldly, inordinate affection, he will be filled to his utmost capacity with the divine element. . . . But if a Christian is stopped up against the inrush of God by self-complacency or filled with inordinate love of created things, no entrance can be made into him.[52]

In the twentieth century, sexual lust became less of a concern among Christians. However, awareness of it by no means evaporated and in fact remained undiminished in some Christian communities. Jazz Age sexual liberalism, the Women's Movement, sexual freedom advocacies in the 1960s–70s, and the universal availability of Internet prompts to lust made the century different from previous ones. For Christians, the most important development in the area of sexual behavior was the gradual "spiritualization" of marriage, a bit of irony that tended not only to naturalize (previously problematic) sexual relations between married partners but to encourage sexual play as Christian practice. The idea of marriage as a spiritual union was by no means invented in the twentieth century. Mormons, whose nineteenth-century polygamy prompted much comment on their "satyriasis," had conceptualized marriage as a spiritual union in which a man and a woman were sealed together for eternity. The experiment at Oneida and to a lesser extent Brook Farm likewise imagined such spiritual partnerships between men and women. Nathaniel Hawthorne and Sophia Peabody considered their married sex to have a religious character, she making a touching notebook entry about her body: "Before our marriage . . . I knew nothing of its capacities & the truly married alone can know what a wondrous instrument it is for purposes of the heart . . . because it is a spiritual joy." The *Catholic World* in 1893 suggested something similar in discussing Jesus's mother Mary at Cana: "She obtained the miracle of the water changed to wine not merely to satisfy the needs of an embarrassed wedding-party, but to show that Christian marriage changes the natural water of a carnal passion into the pure wine of a 'chaste love and spiritual delight.'" In the twentieth century, as Amy DeRogatis has shown, evangelical Protestants have been much more willing to speak about and explore sexual technique and to link that with "God's plan for humanity." Replacing the word *lust* with *libido*, evangelical sex manuals promoted the idea of personal fulfillment through sex. Terry Wier and Mark Carruth's *Holy Sex: God's Purpose and Plan for Our Sexuality* made the crucial distinction: "Fulfilling lustful desires is never enough to bring true satisfaction. What the couple needs is to learn to touch each other's spirits during sexual union. Even if they eventually become skilled enough to give each other the ultimate in physical stimulation, they still have not gone 'all the way'—to a joining not only of bodies and souls, but also of spirits." In the larger scheme of things, the inflow of grace to a born-again Christian becomes a sexual event, because "Born Again is a sexual term" and "God's word is like his spiritual sperm." Male and female both are empty vessels desiring to be filled in a sexual way.[53]

The *Holy Sex* turn toward a theory of sexual fulfillment among evangelical Protestants and especially Pentecostals began in the 1960s. Daniel K. Williams has pointed out how the magazine *Christian Life*, among others, broke ground for a revised approach to sex, but it was Bob Jones University graduate Tim LaHaye's *The Act of Marriage* in the 1970s that spelled out the terms of the new gospel of sexual fulfillment. Central to LaHaye's teachings was the claim that "the 'God-shaped vacuum' in the heart of every person can be satisfied by none other than God himself. Unless that God-shaped vacuum is filled by a personal relationship with God, human beings are condemned throughout their lives to an endless treadmill of activity in trying to fill it." LaHaye and his followers accordingly made the sexual act in marriage a means by which to be filled with Christ. In order to "fill that spiritual void within their lives," men and women opened themselves to each other and to God all at once. The union of a man and a woman was also a union with Christ. The celebration of marital sex was explained as both the pursuit of pleasure and the spiritual union with one's partner and God simultaneously. Such behavior required emptying the self both in advance and in ongoing fashion during the act of sex. *Thank God for Sex* noted, "In order to get maximum pleasure from sexual intercourse, you need to get your mind prepared. Mental preparation requires that you empty your mind." That bespoke the larger principle that what was required in sexual congress was the loss of self. "Great sex," said *Sexy Christians*, "transcends our natural self-centeredness and moves us to lose ourselves in the depths of a relationship with our spouse and our God." Sex "in some mysterious way . . . really does bind souls together," but in an equally mysterious way it bound them to God in a kind of spiritual-sexual trinity. *Intended for Pleasure: Sex Technique and Sexual Fulfillment in Christian Marriage* (1977) typified evangelical rethinking of sex in the 1970s in concluding: "Thus the properly and lovingly executed and mutually satisfying sexual union is God's way of demonstrating to us a spiritual truth. It speaks to us of the greatest love story ever told," namely, the sacrifice of Jesus, and represents how "the sexual relationship between two growing Christians can be intimate fellowship as well as delight." An overview published by an Anglican thirty-five years later represents the extension of that perspective to other Protestant groups in remarking similarly that "the abandonment of the self in the giving of oneself to another, one of the many rich possibilities of love-making, is exceeded only by God's self-abandonment on a cross, the complete giving over of Godself in self-surrender." Because, as the *Good Girls Guide to Great Sex* explained, Christian bodies were situated at "the intersection between the holy and sexual hunger," men and women were to lose themselves to each other, surrender to each other in a way that fostered their spiritual union and their union with God all at once. Protestant sex, it turns out, was an emptying of the self and a filling of it with God.[54]

Catholic officials, showing little official interest in Protestant reframing of sex, continued to warn against masturbation and officially reject birth control, and within that cloud of ideas, sexual pleasure remained an ambiguous and still vaguely suspect goal. The fact that over 80 percent of late-twentieth-century American Catholics rejected the Church's teaching on birth control said something about their actual practice of sex. Church leadership, however, did not retreat, instead reaffirming traditional mores grounded in the Pauline motto that "there is no longer male and female; for all of you are one in Jesus Christ" (Gal. 3:28, NRSV), a sidestepping of the central issue of gender and pleasure. There was much less of the Protestant-flavored esprit de corps, such as was expressed in *The Good Girl's Guide*: "Sex is even greater when you bring God into it. . . . So sex with God on our side means lots of surrender and lots of fun!"[55]

The Empty Colored Body

For much of American history, American Christians believed that the colored body needed emptying—on an extraordinary order—if it was to become Christian. Richard Henry Pratt, founder of the nonreservation Indian school in Carlisle, Pennsylvania, delivered that message in an address there in 1882, pointedly declaring, "All the Indian there is in the race should be dead. Kill the Indian in him, and save the man." Summoning support for his claim, he emphasized that Africans had been emptied of their beliefs and customs by the slave system, which, while "horrible" in one sense was also "the greatest blessing that ever came to the Negro race" because it forced Africans to acquire the English language and to learn to be hard-working, industrious, and moral. Slavery drove from the bodies of Africans their savage and superstitious traditions, preparing them—as a great many nineteenth-century writers observed—to become Christian. "We make a great mistake in feeding our civilization to the Indians," said Pratt in emphasizing the need to exterminate Indian culture, "instead of feeding the Indians to our civilization."[56]

The emptying of the captive body, as Saidiya V. Hartman has observed, is a matter of pleasure taken in the possession of property. Writing about slavery in nineteenth-century America, Hartman depicted the relationship between the emptying of the slave body and the aspirations of the master, as projected onto the slave: "The fungibility of the commodity makes the captive body an abstract and empty vessel vulnerable to the projection of others' feelings, ideas, desires, and values; and, as property, the dispossessed body of the enslaved is the surrogate for the master's body." The "beaten and mutilated body" of the slave, emptied of its content, is made ready to receive what is valuable. That course of preparation was well outlined in Christian theorizing about the slave body, and well practiced, as Presbyterian minister C. Vann Rensselaer wrote in 1858, when "the whip is placed in the hands of the master, and he may use it at his pleasure." Slaves' bodies were emptied of sweat in the fields and of blood at the whipping post, and they were kept empty of food as a means of disciplining them. If Hartman is right, the Christian master to some extent pleasurably disciplined himself in the process of sweating and bleeding his surrogate as he "fed" him to Christian civilization (a process that sometimes involved sacrificing the surrogate). Most importantly, in the overall view, slaves were emptied of what Pratt called "the race," namely their religious traditions and other cultural and linguistic identities. What historian Jon

Butler has called the African spiritual "holocaust" was an epic process of erasing race, in Pratt's sense. That frequently was expressed as an ongoing battle to drive out any form of "superstition" from black communities. Jane Singleton Marrinda, born in slavery in Hartford, North Carolina, in 1840, recalled, for example, how the mixing of herbs and roots on the plantation was criminalized, so "dat the Marsters took steps to drive it out by severe punishment to those that took part in any way." Religious practice in such cases was all but exterminated. Ideas were to be erased as well. Professor Robert Ryland, appointed by the white overseers of the First African Baptist Church in Richmond as its first preacher, reported that his mission of emptying slaves was to "preach *out* of their minds their dreams and fancies, their visions and revelations, and all their long cherished superstitions—and to preach *into* their minds a knowledge of the great facts of their religion [i.e., Christianity]."[57]

Christian missionaries, as Father Placide Tempels, a mid-twentieth-century Belgian missionary to the Congo, wrote, thought of the African as "an empty vessel requiring education on the spheres of religion and civilization in order to be rendered truly human." In America since the eighteenth century, much the same viewpoint predominated, with poor results according to critics such as American Muslim leader Wallace D. Muhammad, who asserted that "this world was putting foreign life into the empty vessel and the foreign life could not grow in a vessel that was foreign to it." Moreover, in the plantation system, overseers at the same time prosecuted a program of certifying that emptiness, draining blacks of physical life at the same time that they suppressed African beliefs. And even when empty Africans, additionally emptied of blood and culture under the whip, became Christian, their Christianity, as many observers reported, was itself sometimes empty. That was not a compliment to their longing for God, but rather an expression of suspicion that they were still too filled with Africa to truly embrace the Christian gospel. An African American in some cases could be empty and full at the same time, but as a perverse inversion of the empty/full white Christian. In the latter case, emptiness was next to godliness, while in the former it was a sign of the demonic.[58]

The dangers of the empty body (alongside the foulness of the soul empty of God) were most dramatically represented in stories about the walking dead or zombies, and those stories, while not absent from Anglophone literature, were widespread in African American populations in the American South and the Caribbean. In the twenty-first century, at a time when Americans express their feelings of emptiness to television and radio talk show hosts as a matter of course, it is no accident that they entertain themselves with a burgeoning literature and cinema about zombies, as well as zombie games, drills, jokes, and academic conferences. The African American newspaper *Rising Son* asked its readers in 1904 to consider the empty body as they would an empty house. "In like manner," said the paper, "what a difference between a body with a soul in wholehearted possession of all its functions, and a body from which the tenant has removed! It is the same body, and yet it is not the same at all." Such a question might point to a vague awareness of the double consciousness that W. E. B. DuBois was writing about at the time, or it might just reflect a sense of what had been lost in the forced relocation of Africans to the Americas. In either case, the strenuous effort to prepare Africans for the gospel by emptying them is detectable in the ironic survival of African ideas about the living dead, the hollowed body that walks but that was never filled by the Christian gospel.[59]

The Full Body

In an American Christian notion of happy endings, the truly empty body is the truly full body. It is empty of self and full of the spirit of God. For some, such a vision is complicated by race—can persons of color ever be empty enough of color to be filled by God? Indeed, can anyone, regardless of race, be truly emptied and truly filled? Such questions remained, even in the otherwise effusive *Friend's Review*, which published a concise statement about emptiness and fullness in 1864. "The fullness of God ever waits upon an empty vessel," declared the author of "Self-Emptiness." Warning that "this is difficult work," the article offered the vision of "the grand moral point of self-emptiness" as the reward for unceasing effort to empty oneself, affirming that "the more completely the sinner gets emptied of himself, the more settled his peace will be." But when is the self truly empty? How can one know that nothing remains hidden inside the vessel, that is, whether one is "still cleaving to some little bit of self . . . the very smallest possible atom of the creature, its state, its feelings . . . something or other of the creature kept in, which keeps Christ out"? Just as importantly, what does being full feel like?[60]

In an America where Christianity and consumer capitalism collaborate, there are many opportunities to feel full and many prompts to feel empty. As Jean Kilbourne has written, Americans suffer from "a sense of emptiness. Our capitalistic culture encourages this because *people who feel empty make great consumers*. The emptier we feel, the more likely we are to turn to products, especially potentially addictive products, to fill us up, to make us feel whole." Advertising creates demand for products by persuading consumers that they are at a loss, that they are missing something, that they are empty bodies to one extent or another. That message oddly intersects with a Christian notion of the desirability of emptiness, that to be empty is to lose the self and to make ready for God. It also resonates with the Christian notion of being worthy of being filled, of being ready and deserving. When Rev. Frederick J. Eikerenkoetter II ("Rev. Ike"), a mid-to-late-twentieth-century African American proponent of the Gospel of Prosperity, mixed his Christian self-help message with his insistence that persons were deserving to be filled with success—as measured in property—he was articulating the longing for identity, the sense of emptiness, the desire for fullness, and the pursuit of material success that are joined in American Christianity. "I identified with success and prosperity that I saw around me," said Rev. Ike in reporting his personal transition from poverty to wealth. "I identified with the riches I saw around me, and I saw myself as rich. I saw myself being, doing, and having all the good I desired. . . . I always identify with success and prosperity." Spiritual advancement was a matter of imagining oneself full and then becoming full, a process that would at the same time empty the self of a previous, unwanted identity. For Rev. Ike and his followers—like some nineteenth-century proponents of the Gospel of Wealth—the full body was a sign that the body was empty.[61]

They cannot scare me with their empty
spaces
Between stars—on stars where no human
race is.
I have it in me so much nearer home
To scare myself with my own desert places.
—Robert Frost

3

Space

Spatial Feeling

William James, known among religion scholars for his amenable approach to the subject of religion in *The Varieties of Religious Experience* (1902), was deeply interested in the matter of space and spatial perception throughout his writing career. It was the topic of his first published article, "The Spatial Quale" (1879), and it comprised the longest chapter in *The Principles of Psychology* (1890). He considered and reconsidered it in numerous articles and book chapters, all the while refining his thinking about it along empiricist lines. His discussions of it were built around what he called "the spatial feeling," a term he introduced in "The Spatial Quale." His earliest statements, though cast as anti-Kantian, flirted with what at the time was called intuitionism, the theory that persons are equipped as subjects with mental capabilities that help to order their experience. He wrote that the spatial quale—by which he meant vastness or voluminousness—was "an entirely peculiar kind of feeling, indescribable except in terms of itself . . . a specific quality of sensibility, *sui generis*." James, even though he was writing against the Kantian philosopher J. Elliott Cabot, shied away from asserting a fully empiricist approach. He maintained that spatial relations and spatial orders were part of "the sensible matrix, so to speak, of a unifying intuition, in which they lie embedded." Such language has been taken by some, including a critic a full century later, as a "relief" from James's "excessively heavy burden" of empiricism. But we also might see James as having developed his spatial thinking gradually, adding detail and force to an empirical philosophy through later writings. As Martin J. Farrell recently has argued, the spatial feeling as James articulated it in greater detail in *Principles* took a harder empirical edge, grounded more clearly in the primacy of experience. James, argued Farrell, abandoned talk of "an inner state that has to transcend itself" (the problem with common-sense theories, according to James) in favor of "'felt transitions' between one bit of experience and another."[1]

James was attacked for his empiricist views about "spatial feeling" even before he had refined them in a more decidedly empiricist direction. Philosophers and theologians who had invested in Kantian arguments about a priori categories of knowing and, in the case of theologians, who had used those arguments to advance Christian intellectual agendas, protested. Typical was the criticism leveled by Rev. J. Frederic Dutton in *The Unitarian Review* (by no means a radically conservative journal) in 1891, just after publication of the *Principles*. Referring to James's book, Dutton complained that "a long chapter in the second volume is devoted to the discussion of how we sense space. Here is a work . . . spoiled by a false philosophy, or rather by the effort to teach philosophy where no philosophy as yet exists." For Dutton, philosophy "teaches that there are certain primary concepts, categories, or forms of thought—call them what you will—which inhere in the very nature of thought itself and of the soul itself, and without which the universe would be to us unmeaning, a chaos." Dutton made explicit the religious leanings of his argument in detailing the importance of those "thought forms," asserting that "we find them first within the mind; they are discovered to us as essentially spiritual." When joined to sensations, then, they "compel us to recognize an infinite other-self, whose appearance is Nature, whose reality is God." All experience, Dutton added, "comes before us first in the form of feeling. From the spiritual element in experience arises . . . the basis of all religion."[2]

Dutton's debate with James about spatial feeling suggests the extent to which American Christians in the late nineteenth century were invested in the idea that one knew space by feeling it and that such a feeling was at its core spiritual. That idea had deep roots in Anglo-American theologies, and it continued to inform American Christian thinking even after public reception of James's ideas became more welcoming. As early as 1721, the young Jonathan Edwards had declared: "I had as good speak plain: I have already said as much as that space is God," and though he subsequently labored to refine and arguably alter that view, his youthful immaterialism was shared by others who in their own ways imagined that absolute, eternal, infinite space was ontologically partnered with religious affections. The intuition of space and the feeling of God remained joined in much Protestant theologizing. The Scottish Common Sense philosopher at Princeton James McCosh moved the intuitionist argument forward in 1866 with *The Intuitions of the Mind Inductively Investigated*, and Baptist theologian Augustus Strong likewise kept much Protestant discussion about space within those confines in the first part of the twentieth century. "We prefer the view," wrote Strong, drawing on predecessors, "that 'Space . . . is a form of intuition and not a mode of existence.'" Charles Beecher's *Spiritual Manifestations* (1879) contained a discussion of space in which he asserted, "Time and space are objective realities, or, perhaps we should say, necessary forms of thought; but the sense or feeling of them may vary. We cannot admit the possibility of a mind . . . without the sense of succession and extension." The point was made more explicitly by Congregational pastor Edwin Victor Bigelow in 1891. In asking, "How arises the sensation of an object occupying space?" Bigelow rejected Locke's empirical approach and recommended the view that "spatial impressions are the simplest acts of the soul." That perspective mimicked the view of the English Catholic writer Rev. Stephen Eyre Jarvis, who approved the idea that the "Human Soul" had an innate "feeling of space, which is still retained after death as the foundation of her activity as a feeling principle."[3]

Religious publications sometimes urged their readers, as did the *Christian Union*, to simply "feel the exhilarations of space" during a walk in nature. Often, when discussing the feeling of space, writers accented the mysterious or even mystical in space, a style with roots deep in colonial American sermonics. The Boston Congregationalist pastor Benjamin Colman, for example, had urged his congregation in 1742 to consider how "space is so mysterious and inexplicable a Thing in nature," that when we read the "open Volume of nature" we can only see God and "adore him in his Incomprehensibleness." Some also upheld the notion of the soul itself as empty space. Mather Byles, preaching in 1732, had taken pains to explain to his auditors that the soul of Adam after the fall was left "desolate and empty" and that where it "was once filled full of God, now has in it a vast Casm. . . . Our souls feel something wanting . . . and they try to fill up the empty Space, with every thing they can lay their Hands on." The Rev. Jonathan Brace of Connecticut, preaching more than a century later, put a finer point on the idea of Adam's empty soul, arguing that God placed humans in an empty landscape to encourage their striving toward holiness. "God," he said, "has, mercifully to us, made the things of earth insufficient and empty. . . . He disturbs our rest here, that we may seek rest elsewhere; 'makes earth appear to us like a desert, that our eyes may be raised to the glories of heaven." The ongoing American Christian depiction of the land as desert is an expression of that sense of emptiness and its role in turning the soul to God.[4]

Deserts

Puritans in early New England imagined the landscape of North America as a desert. It was for them a dark wilderness, a void, an empty space. It was an empty beginning, imagined along the lines of what John Locke later wrote in his *Second Treatise on Government*: "In the beginning, all the world was America." They imagined it as they imagined their souls, empty and wanting. In the case of the soul, grace was required, holiness that flowed from regeneration and a realignment of the soul with God. The land, the geographical space of North America, full of sin and evil, was a constant remonstrance to Puritans about the state of their souls, a mirror of their souls, conceptualized in much the same way as the religiously constructed notion of the soul itself. The land was to be filled also with grace, but that grace would be mediated through the machinery of colonization, through the westward procession of Christian civilization, as Puritans dreamed that. Puritans felt the land, the geographic space that was to be rendered Christian, just as they felt their empty souls reaching for God. They proceeded in the linked enterprises of colonization and regeneration in similar ways, complaining loudly about the emptiness and desolation of both soul and space, and at the same time understanding that such emptiness was a part of God's plan to fill both. They embodied what the twentieth-century theologian Thomas J. J. Altizer called the "Christian nostalgia for the garden of paradise," applied both to the land and to the soul, "a nostalgia which is clearly a longing for timelessness, and a longing for spacelessness as well, a spacelessness and timelessness which are the full opposites of the full actuality of space and time. Such a longing is a longing for the reversal of that actuality." Puritans looked straight through the native inhabitants of New England and saw an empty land, one that certainly bore little resemblance to their English familiars, but also was shaped as place by their engagement with it, in the way that Michel de Certeau has expressively outlined that process in his essay on the city, as a space crisscrossed and layered by the human activity that makes it place. Puritans engaged the land, as literary historian Rob Wilson has written, as "vast space as well as by a kind of self-willed emptiness towards this New World landscape." Puritans made an empty place to match their empty souls.[5]

The attitudes of Puritans and their immediate descendants toward the wilderness have been remarked upon by many historians, from groundbreaking interpretations by Perry Miller, Alan Heimert, and Richard Slotkin, to more recent studies by scholars who have adopted an "environmental" approach to New England history. Much recent scholarship has been infused with critical sensibilities honed through reflection on power, force, and accommodation in colonial and postcolonial settings, which is to say that scholarship has come a long way from Perry Miller's channeling of his Puritan subjects in describing American history in 1956 as "the massive narrative of the European movement of European culture into the vacant wilderness of America." Much of this scholarship, both early and later, in any event has taken seriously what Douglas McKnight has described in writing about Puritans and space: "Again, a dark void was not just the external metaphor for the wilderness of America but also for the internal condition of 'man.'" We have seen how David Brainerd at the end of his life concluded that "the world is a vast empty space." Puritans, and many Christians after them, made that point with particular attention to North America.[6]

Richard Slotkin has described how the earliest settlers in New England "emphasized the virtual emptiness of the land." Typical was early New Englander William Bradford, who reported: "The place they [the Pilgrims] had thoughts on was some of those vast and unpeopled countries of America, which are fruitful and fit for habitation, being devoid of all civil inhabitants, where there are only savage and brutish men which range up and down, little otherwise than the wild beasts of the same." Slotkin has argued that such views of the New World were part of a theology of purification, in which persons were subjected to trials (often violent) and were thought through virtue to emerge from them regenerated. That certainly was one of themes of Bunyan's *Pilgrim's Progress*, a book that influenced Puritans and others in their thinking about life's sufferings. The crucial point, however, is that Puritans and other Christians in America envisaged geographic space as they did their souls. Because emptiness was central to their self-understanding of Christians, because the feeling of emptiness was central to their Christian identity, space itself would be empty.[7]

Since Perry Miller titled his classic book *Errand into the Wilderness* (1956), those who have studied the Puritans and their literary descendants generally have adopted the term *wilderness* to describe what worried the Puritans, and attracted them as well. The word *desert*, sometimes in colonial writing *desart*, was almost as common and served better to carry forward some of the key aspects of the Puritan spatial imagination, including notions of empty, desolate, barren, and vast. Edward Johnson's *A History of New England* (1654), based upon the author's residency in New England since 1636, referred to the land as "this desart Wilderness." It was a "barren desart," a "howling desart," a "dismall Desart," and a "desolate desart." Cotton Mather explained that "the first planters of these colonies" were chosen by God for "a Voluntary Exile in a Squalid, horrid, *American* Desart." In that desert, Mather noted elsewhere, lived men who were more like animals, who were to be hunted down as in 1704 when Mather reported of the military missions "into the Desert, in places almost inaccessible, if possible, to find those bloody Rebels in their obscure recesses under a covert of a vast hideous Wilderness (their manner of living there being much like that of the Wild Beasts of the same)." The political and social implications of empty space were, minimally, that those who inhabited it were dismissed as beasts. But emptiness, as much as it was a challenge, a mystery to be feared, also invited filling-in. The venerable Puritan pastor Solomon Stoddard explained the concept in his ambiguously titled *An Answer to Some Cases of Conscience Respecting the Country* (1722). In a series of questions and answers, somewhat in the style of a catechism, Stoddard queried: "Did we any wrong to the Indians in buying their land at a small price?" His answer was forthright: "A. 1. There was some part of the land that was not purchased, neither was there need that it should; it was *vacuum domicilium*; and so might be possessed by virtue of God's grant to Mankind, Gen. 1.28. . . . When Abraham came into the Land of *Canaan*, he made use of vacant Land as he pleased: so did Isaac and Jacob." The famous observer of emergent Americanness Alexis de Tocqueville absorbed from his American informants essentially the same story a century later. He reported in *Democracy in America* (1835): "Although the vast country I have been describing was inhabited by many indigenous tribes, it may justly be said, at the time of its discovery by Europeans, to have formed one great desert. The Indians occupied without possessing it."[8]

There were dissonant voices here and there. Scott Simmon has pointed out how Nathaniel Hawthorne in *The Scarlet Letter* (1850) reframed the desert as a reprieve from the oppressive moralism of the Puritans "by recognizing that the Indian might remain in the 'desert' to the extent that the race serves to represent for whites what is missing from the constrained Puritan imagination." He notes that Hawthorne writes of Hester Prynne that her "intellect and heart had their home, as it were, in desert places, where she roamed as freely as the wild Indian in his woods." Her amenability to the "desert" after all might have been read more as a matter of a Christian ideal than either Simmon or Hawthorne recognized, but the point remains that at least in terms of conceptualizations of the desert, there were some who leaned toward seeing the desert as possibility, who vocalized it as a precondition for Christian fullness. It is empty space as the literary critic John Wall noted in respect of Heidegger: "The emptiness of space, far from being a deficiency, is a bringing-forth."[9]

What is clear for much of the history of European exploration and settlement of North America is that the boundary between white space and Indian space was vague, temporary, and, over the course of time, a retreating line. The Georgia land office articulated as much in an enactment in 1783 when it published legal notice regarding "all warrants heretofore (that is to say since the Revolution) obtained for vacant land, and surveys that have been made, in consequence of such warrants, within the present temporary boundary line between the white inhabitants of this state and the Indians." It was enacted that "the present temporary boundary line" is "hereby declared to be null and void, to all intents and purposes, as though such surveys or lines had never been made." The notion of "vacant land" redolent in such enactments was widespread and was applied not only to Indian boundaries but to urban boundaries as well. A short treatise on space and law suggestively titled *An Explanation of the Map of the City and Liberties of Philadelphia* in 1774 described property ownership and boundaries in the city with frequent reference to vacant land as itself a boundary, separating one "property" from another. Likewise, the laws of the province of South Carolina in 1736 recorded Act 572: "An Act for the better and more certain Regulating and Adjusting the meets and Boundaries of Queen Street . . . and for appropriating such waste or vacant land as shall be found on the North Side of the said Street." Spaces such as those described in legal publications were vacant because, in the words of geographer Robert David Sack, they "contained" no "things," including people. In *Human Territoriality: Its Theory and History*, Sack argues that "things need space to exist," and "when the things to be contained are not present, the territory is conceptually 'empty.'" The empty space of the American desert, then, was difficult both to experience and to imagine, precisely because it was an empty container, because it lacked things. At the same time, it could be imagined, and even, perhaps, experienced, and especially so when its posited vacantness corresponded to a cultivated Christian sense of emptiness, a profound feeling that informed belief and bodily practice. The empty space of the desert in colonial America, like later American deserts, was, like all colonial space, discourse. Colonial literature historian John Noyes has written of Namibia, "Empty space is a written space"; boundaries, spatial relations, transformations, passages: all are "writings which determine the spatiality of the colony." Puritans and their descendants made empty space in writing—including maps—and they drew on their Christian experience in doing so. They imagined the landscape as they felt their souls. The land, in its natural features, its social, racial, and political geographies, and its placemaking processes, offered them opportunities to enrich their beliefs about the good Christian life, the denial of self, and the salvific expectation of being filled.[10]

The desert described by colonial Christians reemerged in American writing in the nineteenth century. Its revival was cast in dramatic terms, and its quality of emptiness was greatly enlarged. Thomas Jefferson, in the *Description of Louisiana* sent to Congress in 1803, reported that the boundaries of that territory were "involved in some obscurity" and that "many of the present establishments are separated from each other by immense and trackless deserts." He emphasized that "one extraordinary fact, relative to salt, must not be omitted. There exists, about one thousand miles up the Missouri, and not far from that river, a *salt mountain*. . . . The Mountain is said to be one hundred and eighty miles long, and forty-five in width, composed of solid rock salt, without any trees, or even shrubs on it." A few years later, Lieutenant Zebulon M. Pike reported on his travels westward. He was deeply impressed with the "sandy, sterile desert" he explored, writing that "these vast plains of the western hemisphere may become in time as celebrated as the sandy deserts of Africa; for I saw in my route, in various places, tracts of many leagues where the wind had thrown up the sand in all the fanciful form of the ocean's rolling wave, and on which not a speck of vegetable matter existed." The myth of the desert east of the Rockies began to coalesce with the exploration of Major Stephen H. Long, who set out with a small party for the Yellowstone River. As Richard H. Dillon demonstrated, that expedition, which employed William A. Swift as its geographer, was responsible for embedding the designation Great American Desert in the minds of easterners. Swift's map (known as the Long Map) indicated the perception of the waste and desolation of the region across its middle: "Great American Desert." As Dillon showed, that *Map of the Arkansa and Other Territories of the United States* (1820) was widely copied by mapmakers and was instrumental in creating the myth of the Great American Desert, a Sahara in North America. The trope was picked up by most of those who storied the West, such as Timothy Flint for his *History and Geography of the Mississippi Valley* (1833), which bespoke a country that "may be likened to the Great Sahara of the African deserts." Francis Parkman's *Oregon Trail* (1847) painted the details of "the 'great American desert,'—those barren wastes, the haunts of the buffalo and the Indian, where the very shadow of civilization lies a hundred leagues behind" the traveler. Parkman warned his readers that anyone planning to visit the region "need not think to enter at once upon the paradise of his imagination." In fact, the great desert, a great emptiness, *was* one paradise of the imagination for Christians, inasmuch as it was constructed in conjunction with the Christian hope of being filled. Other popularizers followed, including the outspoken and dramatically inclined Horace Greeley, editor of the *New York Tribune*. In his *An Overland Journey from New York to San Francisco in the Summer of 1859* (1860), Greeley described his experience of the region in language that doubled up on the idea of emptiness, invoking an image of bodily purgation as well as of barren waste: "Of grass there is little, and that little of miserable quality—either a scanty furze or coarse alkaline sort of rush, less fit for food than physic."[11]

Americans everywhere embraced the myth of the great American desert. Senator Richard Mentor Johnson's trade report in 1825 offhandedly mentioned "the great American desert, extending to the Rocky Mountains." Between then and 1900, the desert became a richer myth, and the myth was utilized for various purposes. The desert expanded geographically as well. While places such as Wyoming and Colorado remained the epitome of the desert—the missionary Rev. W. E. Hamilton reflected in 1876 that the "most desolate portion . . . lies along the vast desert plains" of those territories—those who traveled westward variously expanded it to include California, "a vast unexplored desert," the Southwest, "a vast desert that stretches westward . . . nearly to the shore of the Pacific," and the "vast desert and mountain region" from the Cordilleras of New Mexico again to the Pacific. When

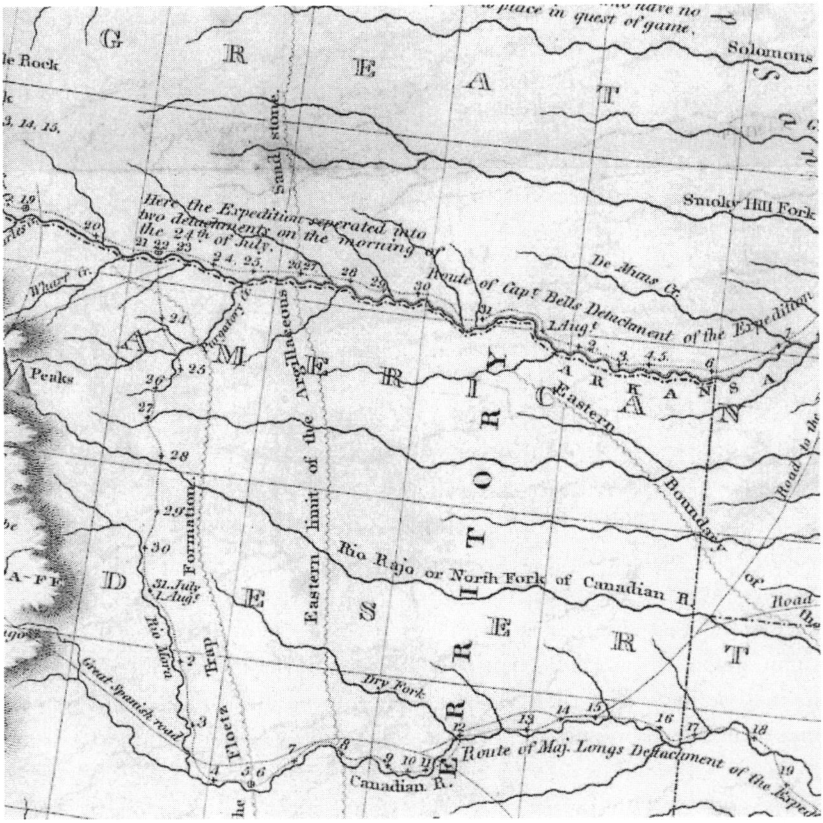

Figure 3.1 Stephen H. Long, "Country Drained by the Mississippi Western Section" in *Account of An Expedition From Pittsburgh to the Rocky Mountains* . . . . (Philadelphia: Cary and Lea, 1823). With "GREAT AMERICAN DESERT" written across it, Long's map of the trans-Mississippi set the terms for how Americans would imagine the Great Plains for most of the nineteenth century. Long's sense of the emptiness of the place also is expressed in his reference to American Indians (themselves often perceived as empty) in a comment at the top of the map section: "The Great Desert is frequented by roving bands of Indians who have no fixed places of residence but roam from place to place in quest of game." Reprinted with permission of the David Rumsey Map Collection, www.davidrumsey.com.

Charles Rhoads wrote in *The Friend: A Religious and Literary Journal* in 1891 that the "great American Desert" extended for hundreds of miles into the mountains and that "the whole scene reminded one of the dust storms encountered by travellers on the Sahara," he was articulating a belief already well in circulation in most middle-class American reading (and writing) communities. In 1899, when the American biographer Hamlin Garland, writing about his travel on the "route to the Golden River," was using "the Big Prairie" to refer to the northernmost parts of the region, it was still "a land so sullen, so silent. It was an empty land. . . . It would serve well as the representation of the ancient Horseman's conception of hell." After 1900, some still imagined the desert as "the Great Emptiness." Some of those were Europeans who had absorbed the idea from their reading about America. H. G. Wells's first book, begun at the age of twelve, was *The Desert Daisy*. In 1906, echoing the judgment of another European observer in the previous century, he wrote that American cities were "mere scratchings on a virgin surface. An empty wilderness manifest[ed] itself" in what was "still an unsettled land."[12]

American Christians felt the Great American Desert—through their reading, except for the few travelers who ventured there—as barrenness, sterilty, void. Increasingly, as the idea of the American desert became more popular, as the myth grew, Christians spoke at once of their spiritual predicaments and the emptiness of the desert. The notion of desert developed by Puritans in conjunction with their own sense of emptiness (and their guilt over that) had been drawn partly from Old Testament accounts of Moses leading the Jews through the desert to the promised land. The Winthropian idea of the "city on the hill" was grounded in that image and took shape as a controlling metaphor for Puritan spiritual and social life. In the nineteenth century, those ideas were forcefully reiterated in Americans' references to the desert west of the Mississippi. Americans felt the desert of their spiritual lives as they felt the desert of the plains.

"The mind," said the *Methodist Review* in 1891, even for ministers, can seem "a dry, dead, empty desert in which nothing could ever grow." More importantly, the soul could become a desert. In a chapter entitled "Deserts" in his *The Soul in Suffering* (1919), psychiatrist Robert Sproul Carroll of Asheville, North Carolina, explained that "we each learn to know the solitudes of life, for as though ordained, our path certainly comes to the desert places." Once in the desert, then, the "smother of the emptiness of loneliness now throws us back upon our own soul for the answer to our need." Sometimes that desert was immediately recognizable, but sometimes it was in retrospect that Christians recognized the desert that their spiritual life had been. A "Mr. H." gave testimony at a "faith meeting" in Boston in 1873 that illustrated how that could happen: "I make no claims to perfection. I only claim that Jesus has done a work in me compared with which my whole past experience seems like a desert." The point for Christians was to feel the desert and to soldier on, as pilgrims seeking an oasis. The *Friend's Intelligencer* pointed out that "our world is a spiritual *Sahara*, a vast desert full of pilgrims that are way-worn and weary." Christian writing, while recognizing the depth of the feeling of emptiness, also preached that such was God's plan to draw persons to grace. Lebanon, Indiana, pastor Rev. A. W. Cash wrote about "Soul-Thirst" in 1914 in such a way. Referencing the Gospel of John, he averred that "the inspired prophet had prophesied of a time when the soul of man would be 'like the desert.'" In the case of the woman of Samaria at Jacob's well, God "opened up in her soul and heart a thirst" that prepared her to receive "water springing up into everlasting life." The desert, then, was both a symbol of the feeling of spiritual emptiness before God and a sign of promise, and both of those were redolent in its vastness. In 1902, a visitor to the West related this experience: "You feel your smallness here, your utter helplessness in the face of the great impassive, elemental things of nature. . . . You feel God, and you never forget." Said the visitor, some persons speak of "the 'dreary' desert, the 'hopeless,' the 'cheerless" desert. But the desert deserves none of these adjectives. . . . The desert of the arid land is eternally hopeful, smiling, strong, rejoicing in itself." When the Presbyterian social reformer Mrs. Joanna Bethune, known as "the mother of Sabbath-schools in America," lamented in 1827, "I am like an owl in the desert—a pelican in the wilderness. I feel empty of everything. . . . Come, then, Lord, take complete possession of my heart," she was expressing herself in an image drawn from a biblical text (Ps. 102:6). At the same time, she was illustrating the aptness of an image that had deep resonance for Americans who felt the Great American Desert with their own souls. The Rev. George B. Ide of Springfield, Massachusetts, made the explicit connection in preaching about the Gospel of John: "An immigrant is journeying across the Great American Desert. . . . He is perishing with thirst. Nothing is visible wherever he looks but the blazing sky above, and the hot, arid, waste around, brown with drought, or white with drifting salt." With "brain on fire," the man "drags himself forward, battling with death," feeling "the horrors of the dry and burning desert." The feeling of hopelessness turns to hope and then to joy, however: "But God has opened a Fountain. . . . The waters of Salvation welling forth from the Mercy-seat above, have desended in copious floods to refresh and bless the earth."[13]

Toward the end of the nineteenth century, some writers noted the extent to which the myth of the Great American Desert had sunk in among Americans, and they criticized its power to sway thinking. In "The 'Great American Desert'—There is None," published in the *Magazine of Western*

History in 1885, the author complained that "nothing crept over the youthful mind in the schoolroom or confronted daring pioneers on the westward growth of the nation, as the great American desert. It took position in North America much as the Sahara did in Africa, and the two claimed about equal space and importance on our childhood maps." The "imagined desert" is a "delusion," said the author. Ray Stannard Baker added early in the next century that "the desert was no desert. It was a cramped and mendicant imagination and a weak faith in humanity that first called it a desert." Such statements, optimistic about the rewards of westward migration, represented another side of an American mentality about frontier and expansion. That mentality has been well described by Richard Slotkin, Henry Nash Smith, Patricia Limerick, and Mary Lawlor and, more explicitly from the perspective of spatial theory, by Husan L. Hsu in his analysis of "spatial feeling" in *Geography and the Production of Space in Nineteenth-Century American Literature*. In terms of the history of Christianity in America, what was especially relevant was the notion of an empty desert made into Eden. Indeed, the Christian idea of emptiness, which was entirely bound up with the notion of fullness, could not have been conjoined with the myth of the Great American Desert unless there was hope for the empty desert to be filled.[14]

In 1857, *Zion's Herald and Wesleyan Journal* published "God's Plan in Geography," a pithy overview of the imagined Christian future of the American West: "We know that civilization has marched from east to west, from Asia to Europe, and even across the Atlantic to the new world—growing and expanding in its course. We can see what has been developed in Asia and in Europe, and may predict something for America." For *Chautauquan* writer Edwin Earle Sparks, soon to be the president of Pennsylvania State University, that meant that the West was to be redeemed through irrigation brought by the "frontier"—those settlers on the leading edge of migration. "The stimulating influence of the frontier," said Sparks in 1902, "shall be to redeem the vast tract lying void in the mid-continent, to blot from the map the 'great American desert' stretched athwart the path of the people." Boston University faculty member Frank Parsons thought likewise, describing in 1901 "an army of wealth-creators" who would make the desert bloom like Eden: "East of the Rockies stretches that vast expanse known as the American desert—a very considerable portion, if not the entire area, of which region can be transformed into a garden-spot by the making of great reservoirs." Many back east, and down east, opined regarding what had happened and prognosticated about what was to be. Because of the steamboat, said an analyst in Maine, "the great empty land of the west has been filling up with people." Cy Warman, author of *The Story of the Railroads*, had his own theory involving steel rails. But the *Congregationalist* in 1900 was less interested in the how than in the fact that "the vast desert region in our Western states, which for so long was, and by many still is, assumed to be practically uninhabitable, really is capable of becoming, and here and there already has become, a new Garden of Eden."[15]

Such effusiveness was nothing new to Americans. Even as the myth of the Great American Desert was just colaescing, American writers were pointing out how colonial predictions of the American future already were coming true. Nathaniel Ames's mid-eighteenth-century reflections on the American prospect, republished in 1825 under the title "Prophecy Fulfilled," deployed the typical argument that civilization moved from east to west. Ames continued: "As the celestial light of the gospel was directed here by the finger of God, it will doubtless finally drive the long night of heathenish darkness from America:—so arts and sciences will change the face of nature in their tour from hence over the Appalachian mountains to the western ocean: and as they march through the vast desert, the residence of wild beasts will be broken up; instead of which the stones and trees will dance together at the music of Orpheus." In an interconnected strand of imagining, from 1753 to 1825, to 1900, and in years before and after, the promise was obvious. But beneath the hopefulness was a strong sense of the challenges. American Christians continued to feel the emptiness of the desert. The *Congregationalist*'s enthusiasm for the project of blooming the desert was drawn as much from feeling its foreboding emptiness and dangerous barrenness as from reports of advances in irrigation technology. When the *Congregationalist* said that some persons still regarded it as uninhabitable, it was expressing the survival of a belief in the necessary precondition for any exhultation about Eden. The desert was worth preserving for the feelings it prompted and the feelings it expressed. Perhaps more prophetic than readers realized at the time, another writer, thinking more darkly about the West at the same time that the *Congregationalist* was sketching paradise, voiced concern about the shifting geography: "The *Spectator* is yet to be convinced that with the disappearance of the 'Great American Desert' and its vast 'unexplored regions' serious loss has not been sustained."[16]

One way to think about how Americans have constructed "empty" geographic space is to appreciate how they have prized the limitlessness of that space. At the same time, American embrace of the notion of the limitlessness of space has undermined the coalescence of collective identity because cultural emblems signifying power, ways of knowing, values, and relationalities cannot be embedded in a territory entirely unmarked by boundaries.[17] Religious historian David Chidester, remarking on the relation between conceptualizations of space and the possibilities for "meaning," has written: "The entire field of American religion and popular culture, its machinery of production, patterns of consumption, and sacred artifacts, is poised between the extremes of possibility and authenticity." One might find "American space empty of meaning because it could mean anything." The lure of the possible always has been closely tied to spatial thinking in America, and the religious picturing of an American future always has been defined in spatial terms. When the editors of American poet Joaquin Miller's "The Ship in the Desert" published that long poem in a collection of Miller's work in 1878, they gushed that the "design of the poem—the book contains one only—is to portray the vastness, the almost *boundlessness* of 'the great American desert,'—the regions between the Mississippi River and the Rocky Mountains. 'An infinite sense of room.'" That is similar to the turn given to the American desert by the French observer Jean Baudrillard in his travelogue-cum-critical-essay *Amérique* (1986), although in Baudrillard's case, that boundlessness was, by the late twentieth century (at the least), a cultivated posturing, and not intrinsically worthy of commendation. Reflecting on his hasty American road trip, Baudrillard pronounced America as a whole to be an empty, silent, desert always full of possibility and thus "everywhere, preserving insignificance." Speedy freeway travel, he declared, was the constantly repeated "rite that initiates us into emptiness." American culture was empty, invisible, an absence signified by freeway billboards, a void through which people sped, smiling and hollow. "Americans may have no identity," wrote Baudrillard, "but they do have wonderful teeth." Such is the America lamented by sociologist Robert Bellah in 1975 in his estimation that civil religion in America was "an empty and broken shell" and that the "present spiritual condition of America" was so feeble that the "main drift of American society is to the edge of the abyss."[18]

One man's abyss is another man's salvation. A recurring theme in the devotional literature of Christianity in America has been the cultivation of emptiness, and that emptiness often is associated in Christian writing with the desert. The desert, presented as a spiritual proving ground involving emptiness, longing, solitude, and remaking, represents, as the Dutch-born American priest Henri Nouwen wrote in 1981, "the furnace of transformation." Rev. Kent Ira Goff recently detailed that image in his chapter "Emptiness as a Space for God." For Goff, emptiness is "a kind of a spiritual homing instinct, a 'God-shaped vacuum,'" to be experienced as spiritual possibility: "Ask: What's the invitation in the emptiness?" Anne Graham Lotz, the daughter of evangelist Billy Graham, likewise urges her readers to recognize that "he finds us on the desert road . . . the place of emptiness and spiritual dryness. . . . I've looked toward the desert of what seemed like emptiness and dryness and weakness, and I've glimpsed his glory in the cloud." God finds persons in the desert, as Louisiana revival preacher Tommy Tenney says, because "he is trying to use your emptiness to openly display his fullness." Or, in the simpler language cherished by many Christians, the desert is where one is "born again." Allan W. Jones, the dean of Grace Cathedral in San Francisco, explained the idea in *Soul Making: The Desert Way of Spirituality* this way: "Thus the desert of which I speak is a desert of the spirit: a place of silence, waiting, and temptation. It is also a place of revelation, conversion, and transformation. A true revelation is a very disturbing event. . . . It involves being 'made over,' being made new, being 'born again.'" It should be plain, then, as pastor R. Kent Hughes, of Wheaton, Illinois, writes, that "the key to the Spirit-filled Christian life is found in a paradox: cultivating an attitude of perpetual emptiness brings with it a perpetual fullness." The American desert of Baudrillard, inauthentic and plastic, is the desert of American Christianity as well: empty but full of possibility. It is the Christian America of the "Holy Land Experience" in Orlando, Florida, a "living-museum" populated by actors representing ancient personages and made to appear to be a place far away in both time and space—exactly the sort of American desert Baudrillard described. It is also the same desert that invites Christians to get in touch with their emptiness so that they can be filled by God, born again.[19]

Mormons crossed the desert and settled the scarce verdant strips of land in the Great Basin, a space called by Wallace Stegner "a dead land, though a very rich one." They pilgrimaged through emptiness and settled in a place where they were able to bring forth from "dead" land a rich communal society. They did so emboldened by revelations given to church leaders, such as that of November 3, 1831, in Hiram, Ohio, where church members learned that in "the barren deserts there shall come forth pools of living water & the parched ground shall no longer be a thirsty land & they shall bring forth their rich treasures." In emptiness there was possibility, or, in the words of a Mormon hymn: "In the desert are fountains continually springing,/The heavenly music of Zion is ringing."[20]

Social Space

American Christians imagined themselves as the overseers of a manifest destiny, a divinely ordained imperial project of dominating North American indigenes and establishing a Christian social order across the continent from east to west. The imagined empty spaces of the West—when in fact the land was not empty at all—were building blocks in the vaunted project of manifest destiny, and those imagined empty spaces also were reflections and projections of a historically deep Christian sensibility about the state of the soul, the process of personal regeneration, and the progress of collective salvation leading to the Kingdom of God. There was much imagined society in the intellectual and emotional technologies of manifest destiny, along the lines sketched by Edward Said in his observations on "imagined geography" and Benedict Anderson in discussing "imagined communities." That is, Americans felt space in ways that enabled them to authenticate their power, authority, and colonial agendas, drawing upon and refining their Christianity in the process. They practiced what cultural geographer Derek Gregory has called "the will-to-power disguised as the will-to-map."[21]

Communities are not just imagined, however. People form social collectives based on shared occupation of space—and of much smaller spaces than the great American West—where they live in face-to-face contact with each other. When Frederic Jameson writes that "our daily life, our psychic experiences, our cultural languages, are dominated by categories of space," he has in mind, I think, something of the cultural sedimentation of place through the daily life of walking, talking, buying, selling, thinking, and feeling as those activities unfold within space, a la Certeau's description of "walking in the city." In order to appreciate how the marking and management of space is involved in the representation and cultivation of the feeling of emptiness, we can consider a few examples of such place-making activity within local religious communities.[22]

The feeling of emptiness collaborates with literary and material tropes of empty space in local Christian settings in America. In the interest of better understanding that dynamic, let us think for a moment about the social system, the social *space*, to be precise, within which this happens. It is important to acknowledge that social groups define themselves in relation to others. Specifically, groups define themselves by saying *what they are not* as much as by saying what they are. If we are to believe the German social-systems theorist Niklas Luhmann, a leading advocate of the notion of social system, difference is prior to identity. That is to say—and this is the core of Luhmann's "difference" theory—one distinguishes a table from other objects before one indicates what it is (Luhmann adds, paradoxically, that distinction presupposes itself). His grand theory is contestable, but his point is that social groups create and maintain collective identity by defining themselves in relation to other groups, and especially by saying *what they are not*. They push off from other groups in defining themselves.[23] We could extend that approach by stating that groups sometimes behave as if they lack a clear collective self-understanding; that is, they lack a fully formed core identity that they can marshal in a positive fashion against a field of other groups. They accordingly define themselves in relation to other groups, define themselves negatively, by differentiating—in some cases to a great degree—from other groups. Identity is built through such negative definition. The twentieth-century American theorist of social conflict Lewis Coser described that mode of thinking in *The Functions of Social Conflict*, an extended mediation of the social-conflict theories of Georg Simmel: "A group defines itself by struggling with other groups." For Coser, and some others, "negative reference groups"—in other words, groups that can be used as foils—are crucial in "the creation and integration of new groups." Sociologist of religion Martin Reisebrodt observes more pointedly regarding the making of Christian communities that Christianity "constitutes itself in relation to other religious practices and beliefs."[24]

I invoke the body of scholarship represented by Luhmann and others in proposing that religious communities in America have created identities for themselves by pushing off against other groups. In taking that perspective, it is helpful to visualize the process spatially as a kind of tessellation, similar to what we see in works of art such as M. C. Escher's "Lizards" (1942). In Escher's depiction, the lizards are defined negatively as well as positively. They completely surround each other and in so doing determine the boundaries that define them. The line marking one is also the line marking another. Most importantly, the definition of a lizard can be seen to be accomplished entirely by the patterning that arises through the shape given it by others. Religious communities are never entirely constructed as social groups exclusively through negative definition, but there are times when negative definition plays the critical role in their self-understanding. To be more precise, for religious groups in America, the process of establishing collective identity has been at least as much a matter of negative definition as it has been a seemingly extraordinary maturation of a kernel of self-understanding, of a quiddity elaborated within the group before being projected externally. In short, many religious communities developed self-

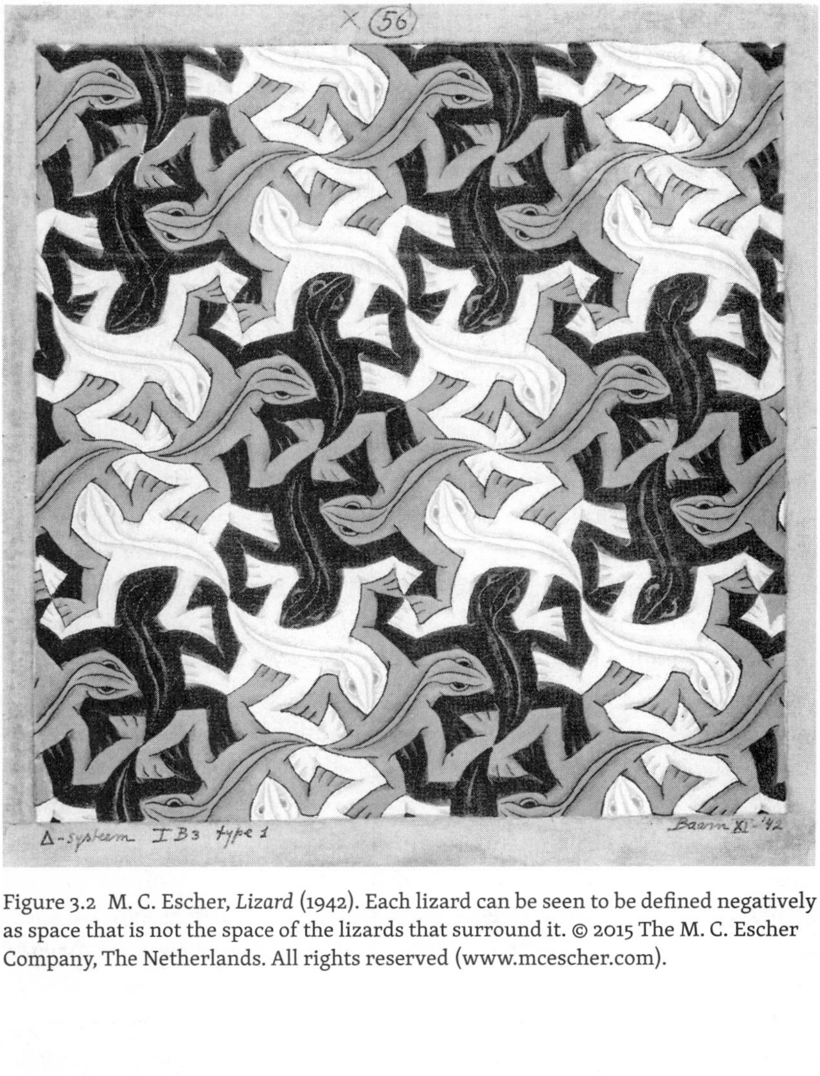

Figure 3.2 M. C. Escher, *Lizard* (1942). Each lizard can be seen to be defined negatively as space that is not the space of the lizards that surround it. © 2015 The M. C. Escher Company, The Netherlands. All rights reserved (www.mcescher.com).

understandings as social groups by a process of negative definition as much as or more so than by a reasoned extension of in-group articles of faith. They behaved out of a sense of lack alongside a sense of inspired mission.

America has provided a rich environment for such a process of community development. In a religiously plural society, the opportunities available to a group for deepening collective self-understanding are high because of the broad possibility of encounter with other groups. There are more groups to encounter and push off from. Those encounters, moreover, are spatially framed. Again, a central tenet in the thinking of scholars working in human geography is that social groups define themselves through their occupation of space. The more competition there is for space, the more contact there will be between groups. Scarcity of space means competition for space, which means more engagement and debate among social groups that occupy that space.

In nineteenth-century America, contact and competition between social groups increased markedly. Religious groups, like ethnic and racial groups, and economic classes contended more determinedly for space. The closing of the frontier in the late nineteenth century profoundly affected the American imagination of space and especially undermined the notion that "empty space" was freely available to groups that chose to distance themselves from the growing commotion of urbanization and industrialization (as Mormons did in the mid-nineteenth century). At the same time, immigration greatly increased, adding millions of religiously diverse new Americans to city space-scapes and prompting the drawing of sharper and clearer boundaries between groups. The city increasingly came to represent what was modern about America, all of the problems as well as the promise of modernity, and the notion of empty space became a less compelling myth—but it did not disappear completely. We can glimpse something of the spatial responses of religious communities after 1900 in considering three events: (1) the Catholic effort made in urban settings to differentiate spatially; (2) the removal to the suburbs of Protestant communities that pushed off from others by crossing city boundaries; and (3) the rejection of spatial categories by fundamentalists who sought both to reform the world and to escape from it. In observing how such groups marked spatial boundaries, moved them, strengthened them, and relaxed them, we learn something not only about emptiness but about how groups constructed identities.

Late-nineteenth- and early-twentieth-century Catholic communities in American cities were hyperaware of differences between themselves and other denominations (and, to some extent, aware of differences among Catholic congregations themselves—Irish, Italian, Polish, and other ethnicities—and differences of class or, most simply, neighborhood). Nineteenth-century American Catholic history is overflowing with incidences of Catholics proclaiming the ways in which they were not like Protestants or other non-Catholic groups. A vigorous campaign of defining themselves through differentiation characterized much Catholic rhetoric of the nineteenth century (and of some of the twentieth century as well). At the same time, as Robert Orsi and others have shown, Catholics vigorously "represented" themselves in all manner of public stagings of religious community—such as the *festa* in Italian Harlem. Such events contributed to fashioning a public face for Catholicism, but encounter with other groups and ongoing efforts to define through differentiation continued. In the bounded urban spaces where congregations dramatically encountered one another, the constant process of building and maintaining the components of collective identity by pushing off from other groups fostered an atmosphere of concern about the consequences of "negative definition." Was American Catholicism, finally, identifiable just as an inventory of things that it claimed it was not? And was such negative definition capable of sustaining a collective sense of belonging and purpose? One response to that question was to claim to be, as writers of the time termed it, "Americanist." That meant relaxing some of the program of differentiation and finding ways to join Roman Catholic traditions with American democratic ideals that were thought to be embedded in most Protestant denominations. Another response was to retrench and carry forward the fight against opponents, identifying those opponents more clearly and by degrees fashioning a collective American Catholic persona distinct from them. The latter response, which won out with support from Rome, brought its own problems, however, including the worry that group identity was hollow; that is, so much of the Catholic effort was spent in distinguishing itself from other groups that it risked appearing less spiritually and ritually substantial, even "empty" as many of its critics of the time (including those on the inside) characterized it. As political pundits periodically remind us, when you unrelentingly communicate that you are not your opponent, that you differ from your opponent, you progressively lose the opportunity to define yourself positively. The Catholic response to that worry had several spatial referents, including the *horror vacui*, or the fear of emptiness, that characterized some Catholic church decoration in the late nineteenth and first part of the twentieth centuries. In a broader sense, it was a reflection of concern about emptiness within the group, a concern about the lack of coherent collective self-understanding.[25]

The *New York Times* architecture critic Herbert Muschamp, looking back over a century of American architecture in 2000, observed, "*Horror vacui*—fear of emptiness—is the driving force in contemporary American taste," having developed steady momentum from the late nineteenth century onward. Long established in Latin American Catholic baroque churches, *horror vacui* as decoration meant that the interior of the church and often the exterior were filled to bursting with items emblematic of the faith of the community. Side altars, stained glass, elaborate archways and pillars, dramatic sculpture, detailed carvings, ceiling ornamentation, images of Jesus and the saints, flourishes of color and light, complex delineation of space—all such features, layered on top of one another, represented the battle against emptiness—which was, in another phrasing, a struggle to assert identity. The baroque style that came to be associated with *horror vacui* emerged in early modern Europe as the Catholic Church was asserting itself against Lutheran and Reformed critics. In America, the same process of self-defense/self-assertion took place anew as Catholic immigrants settled in cities and formed neighborhood congregations. Baroque was the language of the material culture that many embraced. It was characterized by play between feelings of emptiness and of fullness, along the lines sketched by literary critic Christine Buci-Glucksmann, who, critically building on Walter Benjamin's notion of mutability and fragmentarity in the baroque aesthetic, has argued that the baroque aesthetic in literature arises at a moment within Christianity in which *jouissance* and the feeling of melancholy play the two leading roles. The baroque is "an excavation of an absence." It is a "madness of seeing" in which plenitude and emptiness are simultaneously pitched, a drama where emotion arises from a sense that "the world is at once valued and devalued." Or, in the words of Mexican novelist Carlos Fuentes: "The baroque, language of abundance, is also the language of insufficiency." In the material culture of public worship, the case is similar.[26]

Baroque Revival churches appeared in American cities with greater frequency in the latter part of the nineteenth and early twentieth centuries, at a time when the shifting urban demographics and spatial rethinking described above were well under way. Baroque Revival in general had begun to gain in popularity about the time of the Civil War, when it appeared alongside Romanesque, Neoclassic, Gothic, Greek Revival, Georgian, and Italianate styles. The influence of the English architect Nicholas Hawksmoor (d. 1736) was visible in those churches of the late nineteenth century (as it was in earlier American churches). In the early twentieth century, the influence of Latin American Catholic baroque churches likewise was important in some regions, and especially after the favorable reception of Bertram Grosvenor Goodhue's eclectic colonial-style buildings at the 1915–16 Panama-California Exposition in San Diego. The style reached the peak of its implementation just around the turn of the century, and it can be clearly seen, for example, in immigrant-rich New York City. The Church of Saint Francis Xavier (1882), the Saint Nicholas Russian Orthodox Cathedral (1901), the Saint Jean Baptiste Church (1910–14), the Saint Jerome's Roman Catholic Church (1900), and the Most Holy Redeemer Catholic Church (1870s), among other houses of worship (and many residential and civic buildings) impressively incorporated the baroque aesthetic. It was present in other cities as well, but in few more strikingly than in Buffalo, where Our Lady of Victory Basilica and National Shrine was completed in the mid-1920s.[27]

A particularly good example of Baroque Revival in New York at this time is the Roman Catholic Church of Saint Ignatius, located at Park Avenue and Eighty-Fourth Street in New York City, which was dedicated in 1898. Its interior is elaborately ornamented, with varied, layered patternings of color and light, exotic European and African marbles, intricately carved pilasters and wainscoting, sumptuous iconography and statuary, and extravagant ritual appliances. Overall, it exemplifies the expression of *horror vacui*, the fear of emptiness. It also serves as an illustrative counterpoint to the late-twentieth-century trend toward Protestant megachurches that, through their construction as enormous seating galleries, likewise expressed a fear of emptiness, not by overfilling the interior with inert material culture but by regularly packing it with a great many heavily recruited Christian human bodies.

While some urban Catholic congregations in the early twentieth century, pushing off from other social groups, worshipped in churches filled to bursting with artifacts reminding them of who they were, other religious communities took a different approach to modernity. Another response to the tessellation of urban space—the deep and detailed marking of space that helped to set the stage for a negative framing of collective identity—was the hegira to the suburbs that took place during the late nineteenth and early twentieth centuries. One example of this is the religious relocations that took place in those years along the Philadelphia Main Line, a string of affluent towns—Ardmore, Radnor, Glenside, Bryn Mawr, and others—that sprang up along the main rail line westward out of Philadelphia.

The rich who fled the city of Philadelphia to fashion exclusive suburban retreats—and especially Episcopalian enclaves—left behind a city that was a hodgepodge of many different groups increasingly vying for space. Suburban historian Margaret Marsh describes social space in Philadelphia at the end of the nineteenth century in this way: "The dispersal of the urban population to Philadelphia's outer city first became significant during the 1880s. Until that time, most Philadelphians lived in a small urban sector," which, notes Marsh, "was remarkably heterogeneous; rich, poor, and modestly prosperous citizens all shared the same small urban space. Even

Figure 3.3 Church of St. Ignatius Loyola, New York, NY (main aisle, 1999). The extraordinary baroque detail throughout St. Ignatius Church in New York is seen from the center aisle leading to the altar. The baroque representation of *horror vacui*, a fear of emptiness, is represented throughout the church. Reprinted with permission of the Church of St. Ignatius Loyola. Photograph by Laurie Lambrecht.

the most fashionable residential district was still located in the heart of the city." Most of the elite families of the city continued to reside in their neighborhoods along Chestnut, Walnut, Spruce, and Pine streets through the 1880s. Black Philadelphians occupied space immediately to their south, and middle- and lower-income native whites, along with immigrants

Figure 3.4 Church of St. Ignatius Loyola, New York, NY (side aisle, 1999). The elaborate carved marble, inlays, detailed windows, decorations, woodwork, and plays of light and color fill the space of the church. Reprinted with permission of the Church of St. Ignatius Loyola. Photograph by Laurie Lambrecht.

from Ireland, Germany, and elsewhere, lived in neighborhoods scattered throughout the city. As Marsh points out: "People of moderate means were interspersed with the wealthy. Luxurious townhouses fronted the major thoroughfares while small cramped row houses jammed the back alleys and side streets." In short, through the 1880s, there was ongoing and intensify-

Figure 3.5 Church of St. Ignatius Loyola, New York, NY (baptistry, 1999). The baptistry, with a dome of Tiffany jewel glass and curved walls, is filled with art and architectural detail. Reprinted with permission of the Church of St. Ignatius Loyola. Photograph by Laurie Lambrecht.

ing competition for space among all the various groups—religious, ethnic, class, occupational, and so forth—that made up the society of the city. In the 1880s, some started moving out.[28]

Before those changes of the 1880s took place, the Episcopal rector Phillips Brooks, reflecting in 1881 on his relocation from Philadelphia to Boston

Figure 3.6 Church of St. Ignatius Loyola, New York, NY (sacristy door, 1999). The elaborately detailed door to the sacristy depicts saints (added 1920s). Reprinted with permission of the Church of St. Ignatius Loyola. Photograph by Laurie Lambrecht.

some years earlier (1869), observed that there had been just enough debate among the city's religious groups in the 1860s to keep congregations lively and on their toes. "Philadelphia is a city where the Episcopal Church is thoroughly at home. Side by side with the gentler Puritanism of that sunnier clime, the Quakerism which quarreled and protested, but always quarreled and protested peacefully, the Church of England had lived and flourished in colonial days, and handed down a well-established church which sprang of her veins at the Revolution. It was the temperate zone of religious life with all its quiet richness." The city in the second half of the nineteenth century presumably became a less "temperate" place for the Episcopalian congregations. The period 1870 to 1905 was, as Deborah Mathias Gough has written, a "gloomy situation" for Episcopal churches such as Christ Church, which survived shrinking budgets, neighborhood arguments, and internal differences, but just barely so. Less lucky were Saint Paul's and the Church of the Mediator, which closed; Saint James, the Church of the Ascension, the Church of the Atonement, and Calvary Monumental, which moved; and St Luke's, which merged with the Church of the Epiphany. The urban Episcopal churches in Old Philadelphia, Rittenhouse Square, and West Philadelphia lost an average of 30 percent of their membership between 1900 and 1940. The churches along the Main Line—Redeemer, Good Shepherd, Saint Asaph's, Saint Martin's, and Saint David's, grew by 189 percent during that same period. All told, the number of Episcopal communicants on the Main Line grew by a factor of 27 from 1860 to 1940, prompting historian Digby Baltzell to observe of the Main Line that by 1940 the "fashionable suburban churches became the center of upper class Episcopalianism." The suburban historian Robert Fishman has argued in *Bourgeois Utopias* that the origin of London suburbs was closely tied to evangelical religion and its growing concern for "the family." In America, religion also played a role as suburbs—and especially elite communities such as the Main Line towns, among others—were founded or enlarged in the later part of the nineteenth and beginning of the twentieth centuries.[29]

Certainly class was involved in the instance of the Main Line. Those suburbs coalesced around the hallmark features of country clubs, cricket fields, polo grounds, parks, and manicured lawns and gardens. But the exodus of Philadelphia Episcopalians to the suburbs should be understood as a combination of several factors. Episcopalians left an urban environment in which they had to continuously and energetically maintain boundaries by articulating what they were and were not. For Episcopalians, the process of differentiating finally came to mean explicit spatial distancing, a pushing off from other groups in the form of opening a spatial gulf between themselves and others. That performance of distancing was in part a pilgrimage to the suburbs in an attempt to recover something of the mythic "emptiness" of American space as opposed to the city, which was filled with immigrants, sin, corruption, dirt, and danger. It was an effort to reclaim the American imaginary of pristine "empty space," fantasized as something prior to the closing of the frontier, the arrival of immigrant masses, and the deep tessellation of the religious landscape of the city. As suburban historian John R. Stilgoe writes, the American suburb was both attractive and puzzling in its flirtation with the "utter rawness" of emptiness. Upper-class Episcopal suburbs such as those just west of Philadelphia accordingly took shape, in spatial terms, as the pursuit of emptiness, of empty space—rather than the fear of emptiness, the *horror vacui*. Their growth was one side of the same religious coin.[30]

One final example of a spatial strategy of response to American modernity can be glimpsed in the rise of fundamentalism. Fundamentalism is often discussed as a protest against modernity. It was, as historians such as Margaret Bendroth and Thekla Joiner and sociologists Rhys Williams, Christian Smith, and Martin Reisebrodt recently have emphasized, an urban phenomenon in its early-twentieth-century origins. It took shape as a protest against the science that challenged belief in the supernatural, against cultural pluralism in the industrialized city, and, as Reisebrodt writes, against "structural pluralism in that life is divided into private and public spheres." The collected pamphlets on a wide range of topics published in four volumes by the Bible Institute of Los Angeles in 1910–15 as *The Fundamentals* were not systematic theology but rather a continuous series of protests, alongside copious references to the enemies of truth, the Bible, and revelation, and assertions about what a good Christian *is not*. The first half of volume 4, for example, opened with a dozen chapters, each describing something that the true Christian was not: for example, a true Christian was not a Darwinist, an evolutionist, a socialist, a Jehovah's Witness ("Millennial Dawnist"), a Mormon, an Eddyist, a person of the world, a spiritualist, a Sabbath-breaker, or a Satanist. Elsewhere fundamentalist writers and preachers condemned Romanism, secularism, Unitarianism, and a great many other groups and "isms." With its primary strength in the Baptist and Presbyterian denominations, fundamentalism emerged in the urban North but quickly became associated with the South. Its lack of a standard, coherent theology ensured that it would remain a cross-denominational movement—and the lack likewise ensured that its critics would complain that it was an intellectually shallow campaign against other groups, the *Christian Century* in 1922 referring to the "creedless" Baptist fundamentalists. In short, Christian fundamentalism (which could be defined eventually to include later twentieth-century Lefebvrian Catholicism alongside the Protestant groups) was a protest movement against modernity that, in its beginnings, conformed closely to the sociological model of collective identity as a process grounded in differentiation and lack of internal resources—its so-called "creedlessness" (a term that exaggerates but also brings forward a key element of the social constitution of the group). Reisebrodt accordingly notes that "the fundamentalist self-perception derived unavoidably from its characterization of the enemy," a view seconded by sociologist Christian Smith.[31]

Fundamentalists wished to be both in the world and out of it. Baptist fundamentalists, especially, tended to be premillennialists. The Presbyterian wing was divided between pre- and postmillennialists. But the overall tenor of fundamentalism was, as Reisebrodt has observed, a matter of "oscillation" between a religious nationalism that sought fundamentalist reform in American life and an anticipation of the end of the world. In the words of Rhys Williams, fundamentalism was "'in' the emerging industrial city but not quite 'of' it."[32] That posture was reflected in the fundamentalist penchant for staging public performances of "old-time" religion in the interstices between the socially marked spaces of the city. Fundamentalism as it took shape as a program of protest against modernity did not fit the map of bounded religious spaces that organized the city. Fundamentalism fell into the cracks, or more precisely, it represented itself from within the interstices between the marked territories. Revivalism, as many American historians have argued, historically has favored liminal settings—parks or fields, city corners, the woods by the river, hastily assembled warehouselike tabernacles, the beach, and so forth. The fundamentalists of the early twentieth century who rejected the world rejected its spatial logics, but because they wanted to remain in the world, they were forced to find space to gather. When we look at their revival settings, we can see something of their complex relationship with other religious groups in society and, moreover, with American society as a whole.

One illustration of the spatial imagination of revivalists is the Billy Sunday campaign in Chicago in 1918. That revival took place in a wooden tabernacle—a temporary structure built just for the revival—on the edge of the city, at the lakefront, in relatively nondescript urban space. Streetcar lines were laid to transport people to it. Billy Sunday did not wish to have the warehouselike tabernacle look like a church, because according to him, "[The churches] have fallen down on their job. . . . So far as the mass of people is concerned churches repel rather than attract. . . . There is nothing about any of it to suggest the church or any of its surroundings." In short, as Thekla Joiner has concluded in her study of turn-of-the-century revi-

Figure 3.7 Billy Sunday revival tabernacle. From *Chicago Daily News*, March 15, 1918. The tabernacle for the Billy Sunday revival in Chicago in 1918 was built in liminal space on the Chicago waterfront, the edge where the water and the city meet, away from neighborhoods and ambiguously related to the city's public life. Photograph: Chicago History Museum. Glass negative, DN-0070057. Photographer: *Chicago Daily News*.

valism in Chicago, the tabernacle was a "zealously created liminal space." Such space expressed a feeling of emptiness in a way that differed from the examples of urban Catholic baroque churches or the migrations of Protestants seeking the empty spaces of the suburbs. In fundamentalism's implicit refusal to either stay and fight (at Saint Ignatius) or to retreat (to the Main Line), its urban revival site spoke even more clearly about the worldview of its leaders and presumably many of its participants. The profound spatial emptiness of the geography of such a fundamentalist revival gathering—liminality read here as "nowhere," as a tabula rasa—signals a deep sense of personal and collective emptiness.[33] The highly polemical preaching and publishing of fundamentalists appears in such a context as an exceptionally determined effort to define group belonging out of emptiness by identifying opponents.[34]

For these Catholics, Episcopalians, and Fundamentalists, spatial strategies were influenced by the feeling of emptiness, inflected differently in each case. Reading the geographic spaces of their respective Christianities, we can glimpse not only something of that feeling, but something of the ways in which they defined themselves as groups of believers, how they drew boundaries, and, especially, the degree to which they relied upon other groups as foils for their own self-understanding.

Gendered Space

Charles Hambricke-Stowe, in writing about Puritan devotional disciplines in early New England, emphasized that Puritans considered "secret prayer" undertaken in the "closet" to be imperative to devotional life. Widely practiced in early America, in the middle colonies and the South as well as in the Northeast, prayer offered in solitude remained the backbone of Protestant piety in America. American Roman Catholics, as historian Colleen McDannell has shown, although not as engaged in family religion until the twentieth century, also embraced the performance of private devotions. They did not develop the tradition of the prayer closet as did Protestants, however. Americans Protestants cultivated closet prayer throughout the seventeenth and eighteenth centuries as an indispensible exercise, drawing on the writing of American spiritual guides such as Cotton Mather and Jonathan Edwards and the memoirs of women such as Mrs. Abigail Abbot Bailey, who reported that in the "much time . . . spent upon [her] knees in [her] closet" she had experienced deep and complex feelings. "I, a feeble worm," she wrote, "learned an important lesson upon the emptiness of the creature." Guides to piety such as the minor devotional classic by Samuel Merivale (d. 1771), *Daily Devotions for the Closet*, published for the first time in America in 1808, sharpened the Protestant focus on the closet in the nineteenth century.[35]

Middle-class white Protestants (and some of lower and higher status) experimented with different kinds of spaces for their closets. For some, it was a corner of a family room occupied late in the evening, or an outbuilding. More commonly, the closet was something like that described by Rev. Asa Bullard in 1888, who wrote of his practice as a youth: "In seeking a place for retirement for my secret devotions, I thought of a large closet out of the spare chamber. That closet was the place where my mother kept her blankets, comforters and various kinds of bedclothes. It was large, and without a window. When the door was shut, it was total darkness." Upon entering the closet, said the *Methodist Review* in 1831, "give seven or eight minutes to reading and meditation; and then, with a mind thus composed, with affections thus rekindled, 'pour out your heart before God' and commune with Him 'who seeth in secret'" another eight or nine minutes. Many Protestants reported spending more than fifteen minutes; some remained on their knees for hours.[36]

The closet was a private space shut off from the rest of the house, which itself was imagined as a refuge from the world. As McDannell observes, architectural pattern-book creators "conceived of the home as a refuge from the work-world of the city." The home, the *New York Observer* enthused, was "a refuge from the world, the flesh, and the devil." In rural areas, the home likewise was imagined as a haven, as "a loving retreat from the outer cares and vexations of life," where, as the *Indiana Farmer's Guide* said, we emulate the disciples of Jesus when we retire to the closet: "We recall how Jesus told his disciples that when they sought him in prayer they should enter their closets and pray in secret." Other nineteenth- and twentieth-century writers emphasized that the closet was "the 'inner chamber' to shut out the world," so far removed from the familiar that it "is exactly like a cell in the desert."[37]

Within the closet, Christians emptied themselves. In 1843 the *Baptist Missionary Magazine* published an article with the title "Sentiments to Be Pondered Over by the Christian in the Solitude of the Closet," which admonished: "*Christ requires all, and the surrender of less than all is not Christianity.*" Early in the next century the *Congregationalist*'s long-running section "Closet and Altar" reiterated the point that had been made unceasingly, in an article entitled "Self-Surrender," stressing that it was only by the "free surrender of the heart" that closet piety would prove fructifying. The same column at other times recommended a prayer to enable persons in that enterprise: "I bless thee that thou art thyself and has bindered me from being myself." The point of closet devotions was to empty the self, a theme repeated constantly in "Closet and Altar." Closet prayers suggested by the magazine over the years included phrasings such as "Let my emptiness and dryness, like a barren and thirsty land, thirst for thee." Christians trained in closet prayer knew their "emptiness," and they understood with "Closet and Altar" the reasons for cultivating that emptiness: "The true fast is the making of an emptiness about the soul that the higher fulness may fill it." As the popular English preacher C. H. Spurgeon wrote in his *Daily Readings for the Family or the Closet* (published in New York in 1867), "the most healthy state of a Christian is to be always empty in self," and closet prayer was the recommended way to ensure that health. The closet was a place of soul-fasting, silence, the desert. For the *Gospel Herald*, the closet in fact held within it another, deeper closet; thus the *Herald* urged that "we should pray from the closet of our hearts." The house was a refuge from the rumble of the world. The closet was a refuge from the buzz of the home. The heart was a refuge from the silent desert of the closet. Christians escaped to emptiness only to search for more profound emptiness. That search had a strong spatial aspect. It was, somewhat paradoxically, a search for a place of emptiness, undertaken as the cultivation of feeling. As the *Western Literary Miscellany* explained, prayer itself was best when "unuttered or unexpressed." In "'the secret place,' when we have 'entered our closet and shut the door,' the world is shut out" and all that is left are "things to be felt, not seen or heard." For such Christians in the closet, prayer was a feeling of emptiness, of empty space.[38]

The closet was gendered feminine. As the inner sanctum of the house, we might expect it to be gendered in the same way that a house is gendered. The gender of the house, where it takes place, is not so easy to determine, however. Anthropologists Setha M. Low and Denise Lawrence-Zúŋiga, while noting that houses typically are gendered female, caution that such is not always the case, and Doreen S. Massey likewise has warned against overstating the feminine gendering of the home. We can note with Deborah Clark that the empty house is often gendered female in American fiction, as, for example, in William Faulkner's writing (*Sanctuary*, published in 1931), but it may not be accurate to claim that the American home, as a class, is gendered female. More useful would be to consider emptiness, femininity, the home, and the closet together and to refine the analysis by focusing on how actors define things by a technique of stating what they are not. As Erica Longfellow has pointed out, the notions of privacy and the private in seventeenth-century England were "simply the negative of public; secrecy or separation from that which is open, available, or pertaining to the community or nation as a whole." Later on, in America in the 1890s, that conceptualization began to change as a "right to privacy" argument coalesced. But the idea of the private, of the closet, in particular, as a space defined by what it was not is helpful in understanding the gendering of that space.[39]

Scholars have written much about womanhood and the domestic sphere in American history and especially in the nineteenth century. One assumption underlying much of that writing is that because women spent so much time in the home, vis-à-vis a male (husband, son, brother, father) who presumably worked outside of the home, there is a kind of feminity that attaches to the home. If Certeau is right that place is made by the activities of those who inhabit it, it is reasonable to conclude that households structured in such fashion accordingly will embody something female. But place-making is a complex process full of contradiction and recursion, thick with politics and seeded with sites of power (e.g., the marital bed, the workshop, the kitchen, the clothes closet), and any analysis of the movement of persons in and through a house rests as much on understanding claims to power, authority, and identity in the home as in plotting the chronologies of the inhabitants' occupation of its spaces. Ruth Madigan and Moira Munro's English suburban houses and Pierre Bourdieu's Kabyle house are cases in point—those spaces are highly complex and gendered in unexpected ways. We should be cognizant of the claims of many American historians about the connection of womanhood with domesticity and the home (especially in the period up to 1900). But we can venture a broader understanding of gendered space in the home by bearing in mind as well the historical importance specifically of emptiness both to the construction of femininity and to religion. Like Faulkner, we should think about emptiness, women, and the home together. The space and situation—the occasions of its use—are multilayered.[40]

To understand the home as a refuge from the world, and the closet as a place where the cares of the home in turn are left behind, is to define both home and closet negatively, that is, by what they are not. The closet, especially, is defined by what is left outside of it, including the self, which is denied or, as Christians said, surrendered. The closet is a place where men act as women. They open their hearts, weep, and express their deepest feelings, but most importantly, through that performance they present themselves as empty vessels to be filled. Like Judith Sutpen in Faulkner's *Absalom, Absalom!*, who "was just the blank shape, the empty vessel," men in the closet were conceptualized as engaged in a process of losing self, becoming empty vessels ready to be filled by God. The notion of woman as empty has a long history, from Aristotle up to the early twenty-first century, when Roman Catholic writer Katrina J. Zeno, in discussing "The Empty Place," emphasized as Aristotle had that female emptiness was indicated by the genitals: "Only women are created with an empty space within. . . . We make a gift of self so that others can receive the gift of self, their very life." As Luce Irigaray and others have argued, the construction of woman grounded in such a view of the female anatomy consequently proffers a figure who "resists all adequate definition," that is, *positive* definition as distinguished from inventorying what is absent. Borrowing Claire Pajackowska's evocative term (made in a discussion of whiteness), woman is "an absent centre." She is constructed as a lack, or, as Cynthia A. Freeland has written, "as an empty gap, a space, nothing—or to put it in this context, as an empty place." In the closet men and women both were expected to feel empty, and thus to become themselves "empty places."[41]

Women were not constructed solely as empty vessels. There was possibility in nineteenth- and twentieth-century notions of womanhood for additional female selves, and in certain contexts those other selves eclipsed the figure of the empty woman. And men certainly were not aspiring exclusively to emptiness in their practice of Christianity. As I have argued elsewhere, in the Protestant practice of prayer, boldness was important for both men and women alongside passivity and meekness.[42] In terms of the spatial framing of Christian piety, however, it is obvious that a concept such as "emptiness" had immediate powerful resonance. As American Christians envisioned the soul, the land, their neighborhoods, their homes and closets, and space itself, they brought a sensibility about empty space to their imaginings. They felt space when they turned their minds to all of those things, and they turned their minds to those things often.

> But now across an emptiness of time I see
>   you.
> —Robert Duncan

4

Time

Feeling Time

In order to appreciate fully the American Christian experience of the emptiness of time, we should try to understand how Americans felt time, sometimes as empty and sometimes as full, and, in certain fleeting moments, paradoxically as both. It is felt time that we are concerned with in this chapter, and there are important backgrounds regarding such feeling that we need to consider before we can directly address the expression of emptiness itself. We might begin by noting how the philosopher Eva Brann, in describing phenomenologist Edmund Husserl's study of time, characterized his central question as "why the explicit knowledge of time is so fugitive when the lived knowledge is so slippery-smooth." That insight offers welcome perspective on the ways in which American Christians have expressed their own sense of time in words and actions. There are matters of agreement and disagreement in their discussions of time, differences regarding duration, measurement, sequence, and the category of time itself; there are similarities as well, and not least in terms of the perception of time. American philosophers and theologians sometimes expressed understandings of time that corresponded with what many men and women said about their everyday lives. At other times, those same men and women represented their experiences of time in ways that challenged what academic and professional writers proposed. Christian faith guided many in their thinking about time, and that faith was expressed especially in the claim that time was felt by the soul.[1]

Americans often favored poetry in expressing their feelings about time. Poetry that had a mystical flavor was especially popular. *The Magnetism of the Bible* (1909), by the Scottish Presbyterian pastor Malcolm McPhail in Boston, incorporated into a discussion of time, salvation, and judgment an oft-repeated excerpt from Alfred Tennyson's "The Mystic": "Time flowing in the middle of the night,/And all things creeping to a day of doom." That language appealed to Christians whose sense of time was framed by concerns about death and afterlife, and it brought forward the felt experience of time as a profound spiritual moment and one vital to regeneration. Michael Wigglesworth, among many other colonial poets, had framed time in jeremiads such as *The Day of Doom* (1662), and ministers and academic writers frequently drew upon English poetry, including Shakespeare, in their discussions of time, the passing of time, and the end of time, in a fashion consonant with Wigglesworth's dramatization:

> For at midnight brake forth a Light,
> which turn'd the night to day,
> And speedily an hideous cry
> did all the world dismay.
> Sinners awake, their hearts do ake,
> trembling their loynes surprizeth;
> Amaz'd with fear, by what they hear,
> each one of them ariseth.[2]

American writers were forthright in insisting that the perception of time was a matter of feeling. Some upheld theories that allowed for subjective differences in what was felt. Others advanced theories about common feelings. Still others wrote about the harmony of individuals' feelings of time that emerged within a social contract about the measurement of time. Rev. Charles Beecher, whose spiritualist mysticism added a troublesome wrinkle to his Congregationalist orthodoxy, spoke for many in the mid-nineteenth century when he proposed that there was "a feeling of time" just as there was a feeling of space. Moreover, because "minds may differ widely in the *sense* of time," that is, because "the sense or feeling" of time may vary, it was important to appreciate how society made a "common measure of time" by gently reshaping into a shared scheme what "might *seem* to spirits." The prolific writer Denton Snider, a founding member of the Saint Louis Philosophical Society and author of Bible commentaries alongside criticism of Shakespeare, expressed some of his Hegelian leanings in his own thinking about time. Less interested in diverse experiences and eager to define a common sense of time, he detailed the "Cosmical Sense of Time." He ventured that the feeling was common for all and was defined especially by a feature that another religious writer, Mircea Eliade, installed as the centerpiece of his own theory of religion and time half a century later. Snider wrote in 1905: "The fundamental fact which Cosmical Feeling stirs in the soul is that the Universe is cyclical, eternally self-returning and therein like the soul itself." The African American newspaper *The Plaindealer* informed its readers in 1936, the year that Hollywood released *Reefer Madness*, that one of the more curious things about marijuana was how its use led to the "loss of any sense of time or space," a serious danger given that "common sense begins with a sense of time." The English physiologist Thomas Laycock, whose widely read *Mind and Brain* was published in New York in 1869, in writing about "the experience of time," likewise had noted that biology was involved in that experience, but he retained the crucial emphasis on something extrabiological. He remarked that the formation of cognitions about time developed from "a series of mental processes and teleorganic changes" and that it was through a processing sequence "of instinctive faculties and states of consciousness that the intuition of time first enters as an element of mental existence." Other writers took halting steps toward blending intuition with biology, but many openly resisted the temptation to scientifically verify anything at all about the sense of time. Typical were a group of Andover Seminary professors, who, in an open letter recommending the appointment to the faculty of Dr. Newman Smyth in 1882, explained that just because the phrase "eternal punishment" did not appear where one might expect to find it in the candidate's writing, there was no need for alarm: "If the phrase 'eternal punishment' is not used, it is because theologians have dogmatized over the phrase as though our intuition of eternity should be scientifically defined in terms derived from our experience of time." The Jewish philosopher Morris Raphael Cohen, an immigrant from Minsk who studied with Josiah Royce and William James, noted that "some hours do not feel as long as others, and as we get older, the hours and the years pass more quickly. If reality is identified with feeling, physical time is not real." That was a view many Christians could comprehend. When the *New Monthly Magazine* commented in 1822 that the "ordinary language of moralists respecting Time shows that we really know nothing respecting it," it meant to convey, in a way similar to the later Husserl, that the "explicit knowledge of time is so fugitive" and the "lived knowledge is so slippery-smooth." In asking, "Whence the prevalent feeling of the brevity of our life? Not assuredly from its comparison with any thing which is presented to our senses," it meant to confirm that, somehow, "we feel the past and future in each fragment of the instant." Americans in general felt what literary scholar Phillip Fisher calls "the shape and pace of time" in each instant, so that "wonder, anger, grief and fear reveal different ways that time is rushed, dilated, ordered, and used up." Biology, clock-measured hours, the ideas of dogmatists and moralists, the movement of heavenly bodies through the sky above, all were involved in the experience of time, but what was real was the feeling.[3]

In America, in the years before the advent of Kantian thinking about time—that is, during the seventeenth and eighteenth centuries—there was little effort made to philosophically parse the experience of time. Christian theologies largely sufficed for orienting people to time, and those theologies did so by establishing markers in the ground of sin, salvation, and redemption, a la Wigglesworth. Eventually, Kant's ideas took hold in America, and as they did, the discussion of time became more refined. Orestes Brownson, who both embraced and criticized Kant's writings, published a discussion of Kant in his *Review* in 1844, noting that "in point of fact, all thinking is intuition." The "intuition of time," said the *Review*, must precede the mark or measure of time. That is, "an event occurs. I can have intuition of it only by having an intuition of a determinate portion of time. This implies intuition of *a priori* time in general, and this last the *transcendental* intuition of time." The *Southern Quarterly Review* spoke likewise, vigorously affirming that since ideas of time and space "are absolutely intuitive elements of the mind itself, the total immateriality and immortality of the mind is put beyond contradiction or dispute." Time, indeed, was "a pure intuition of the mind." The most articulate American writer offering a systematic exposition of Kantian thought was the theologian Laurens P. Hickok, who argued that time was a "subjective intuition," or, more precisely, that "the primitive intuition gives the pure form of time in its indefiniteness." His protégé was

John Bascom, whose own students included the Social Gospel leader Washington Gladden and psychologist G. Stanley Hall, the eventual editor of the *American Journal of Religious Psychology and Education*. In *The Principles of Psychology* (1869), Bascom outlined a view deeply imbued with the theory of intuitionism, urging his readers at one point, "Feel your way, feel on and feel ever. . . . Feel space, feel time, feel number."[4]

For Christians, to know time by intuition was to know time with the soul. Brownson explained in 1844 that "perception is used exclusively of the external world, and intuition exclusively of the spiritual world." Using the example of the intuitive "form" of perception of God, Brownson declared that "under this form the soul sees and recognizes him; and experiences the *emotion*, which is the prominent feature in the phenomenon called the religious sentiment." That joining of intuition with soul and emotion defined the frame of mind most common among Christians in America for generations. Some years after the publication of William James's empirically oriented "The Perception of Time" in 1886, Rev. Johnston Estep Walter responded with *Nature and Cognition of Space and Time* (1914), in which he complained of James's theory: "But in these conceptions of cerebral process and mental process there is no recognition of a real permanent element—of a real permanent brain and a real permanent soul." James's theory about time was flawed in that it proposed "stream of consciousness as if entirely abstracted from the permanent soul." Such a view was in league with a Christian sense, as the *Methodist Quarterly Review* put it, of truths "revealed in the intuitions of the soul." The *Journal of Speculative Philosophy* had quoted Kant to its readership in 1877 on the point that "the soul is the organ of the internal sense," and that idea, complicit with ideas received from colonial American religious writers and as one that made sense to Christians of all stripes, remained a centerpiece of Christian notions of time. Time was felt in the soul. And it was thought crucial that Christians experience time in that way. The evangelical minister Frederick William Robertson of Brighton, England, whose sermons were published in New York in 1871, proposed language that worked for Americans in warning that "the man who has felt with his soul the significance of time will not be long in learning any lesson that this world has to teach him."[5]

For many writers, the feeling of time, the intuition of time, was described as an emotion. That understanding came via English writers who had drawn from Kant (sometimes in ways that missed some of the subtleties of Kantian argumentation) the theory that emotion and intuition were intertwined. The *Encyclopaedia Londinensis* in 1812 had explained that "the idea which arises in the mind in consequence of our *Internal Sense*, being affected by any emotion, passion, or action, in man, is an Internal Perception or Intuition." J. G. Macvicar followed two decades later with a discussion of "*Reason*, which consists in applying all the collateral ideas suggested by any one more remote idea in a train, to the essence of mind, with a view to discover which of them is accompanied with that particular state of sensibility or emotion named *Intuition*." By 1875, a broader theory linking the three central elements of religion, emotion, and intuition was common in England and America, in general along the lines defined by the *Contemporary Review*: "But for us now, religion is, we say, morality touched with emotion. And when morality is touched with emotion, it is equally religion. . . . And those in whom it appears thus touched with emotion are those who have most bent for it, most feeling. . . . Now such a bent, such a feeling, when it declares itself, we call an intuition."[6]

The soul's feeling of time was often expressed through reference to "spiritual time." William Henry Holcombe, physician to the Mississippi State Hospital, framed his comments regarding time in Christian language about regeneration and the "spiritual body." For Holcombe, "Spiritual time" measured "the progress towards perfection." E. R. Sproul, among other Christians who were reorganizing their ideas about revelation after the arrival in America of "higher criticism" of the Bible, relied upon the idea of "spiritual time" to make the numbers work in his harmonizing archaeological records with scriptural references to "weeks." His approach was given fuller play by S. D. Baldwin, president of Soule Female College in Murfreesboro, Tennessee, in 1875. Baldwin defined two kinds of time, "Full Time" and "Abbreviated Time." In grappling, like Sproul, with the problem of the prophecy of "seventy weeks" in Daniel 9:24–27, he offered the following rule of recalibration: "We reply, that the principle is this, that spiritual time is to be added to these weeks; that it is not expressed in them; and that the weeks are weeks of secular time. The weeks are, therefore, abbreviated weeks, and represent full time but do not express it." Such a turn of interpretation rested on an understanding of time that differentiated what was felt from what could be measured in a "secular" way. Spiritual time was felt time, not what was indicated by a clock face. That idea, according to communications researcher Ronald E. Lee, is what informed Martin Luther King Jr. in his crafting an argument for progress in civil rights in the "Letter from a Birmingham Jail," and King's letter found a reception among those whose feeling of spiritual time had been refined and affirmed in Christian prayer and worship. An important component of such practice, moreover, was the affective perception of eternity. Andrew Jackson Davis, a central figure in what historian Catherine Albanese has identified as a broad "metaphysical religion" in America, had valorized that perception in his definition of prayer, declaring that "prayer is the grand vehicle of the spiritual; time and space are absorbed in an infinite eternity." The Brooklyn organist and choirmaster R. Huntington Woodman, a representative of a Christianity more orthodox than Davis's, likewise enthused that "in the small assembly and in the great, is something, a sense of God's infiniteness within the soul of man, an intuition of eternity within the scope of time, that can be uttered in common worship through music alone." What is crucial for understanding the piety of Davis and Woodman, Brownson and King, and other American Christians, is that the feeling of eternity was a sense of timelessness, emptiness, and fullness, mixed in unequal and shifting proportions, depending on personal circumstances and historical settings. The feeling of eternity was a central aspect of the American Christian experience of time, a matter of both discontentment and yearning, what the *Continental Monthly* expressed in citing Schlegel: "Longing is man's intuition of eternity."[7]

Americans' remarks about their feelings of time, and especially of eternity, suggest complex ideation and at times paradoxical understandings of time—and sometimes the difficulty of even thinking about it. "Eternity!," said the *Massachusetts Missionary Magazine* in 1807. "What is it? Who can explain it? Who can comprehend it?" The Catholic *Our Paper* of the Massachusetts Reformatory at Concord groaned similarly almost a century later, and the *Catholic Pulpit* wondered, "What is eternity? The term, fellow-Christians, is one with which all are acquainted; the import has never yet been fathomed by mortal mind." Individuals felt it in different ways, at different times. In the nineteenth century Hannah Hobbie, like many, felt its gravity in reflecting on her salvation: "O how should a sense of the shortness of time, the unutterable worth of the soul, and the solemnity of eternity awaken us." Susan Allibone, a lifelong member of Saint Andrew's Episcopal Church in Philadelphia, likewise confessed, "I am sensible of feelings of solemnity I have seldom known before—perhaps eternity is near." For Virginian Elizabeth Lindsay Lomax, uplifting inspiration rather than solemnity was joined to a feeling of eternity: "This is truly a beautiful place, the sunsets beyond the Blue Ridge bring a sense of beauty and eternity that one never finds in a crowded city." Magazines offered the same range of perspective. The *Living Age* leaned more toward Lomax's vision in agreeing that "the eternal prospect" was a matter of "timeless bliss," while others expressed themselves simply by saying that they felt eternity. What the *Plaindealer* called "a sense of Time and Eternity" was what Rev. P. A. Nordell of Connecticut meant when he finished a translation of Old Testament Hebrew words about time by simply concluding that God "has put eternity in man's heart."[8]

But what did American Christians feel when they felt eternity? The most common imagistic rendering of the feeling of eternity was the feeling of being on an ocean. The *Lady's Book* in 1830 said of standing on the shore and witnessing the waves surge and retreat over and over again: "This is what may be called the feeling of eternity." Working the same theme, the Bloomington, Illinois, Methodist pastor Frank Crane in the early twentieth century recalled "the feeling produced by the ocean," reporting that "as day after day I sit upon the deck and watch each morning repeat the boundlessness of yesterday . . . I seem to feel eternity closing in upon me . . . so close I can feel its breath." The *New York Evangelist* shared with a large readership Ralph Waldo Emerson's description of the experience of the ebbing sea as a prompt to "feel the eternity of man" and elsewhere pictured eternity as the feeling of "one vast, boundless, shoreless, bottomless, topless ocean." Some attempts at describing feelings of time, more economical in their linguistics, were apt to be repeated. The feminist writer Winifred Kirkland, author of *The Joys of Being a Woman* (1918), characterized eternity as "a sea of timelessness," using language that was fundamental to Christians' feelings of time, and the *Methodist Review* urged that the Gospel of John be understood as "a vision out of time into eternity." Both phrases were common, and the latter was employed in many American communities to report the death of a person, a passing "out of time and into eternity." It represented a habit of thought about time, the end of time, and timelessness.[9]

There has been much debate in the history of Christianity about eternity, almost all focused on whether the term *eternity* denotes timelessness or temporal duration without beginning or end. From Augustine and Boethius up to contemporary arguments made by Eleonore Stump, Norman Kretzmann, D. L. Craig, and others, arguments about eternity have struggled to explain time and timelessness in relation to God, salvation, and transcendence. The *New Englander* tried to make a case in 1875 that in spite of the opinions of "metaphysicians" who argued that eternity referred to timelessness, there was a popular understanding of time as unending duration. The author might have had Friedrich Schleiermacher in mind as a representative of the former group, given the doctrine emphasized in *The Christian Faith*: "By the Eternity of God we understand absolutely timeless causality of God, which conditions not only all that is temporal, but time itself as well." Or the magazine might have been glimpsing the moment in the near future when Ludwig Wittgenstein would make the same point that eternity was timelessness, not everlasting temporal duration. The *New Englander*'s claim that Christians in the pews had a sense of eternity that did not always correspond with the claims of some professional philosophers should not be dismissed as wrongheaded, however. Americans thought in different ways about eternity, depending on the setting and situation. In church services, where prayer and worship often were inspired by considerations of endless reward or endless punishment, a notion of timelessness might have been a reach for some. On other occasions—at the seashore, or facing death, or watching a sunset, or just letting go of the everyday—timelessness made sense. John Ellis McTaggart advised at the beginning of the twentieth century, "Eternity is a more ambiguous word" than "time." Americans juggled both understandings of the term within that ambiguity, always aware of eternity as timelessness but at the same time attempting to imagine eternal duration when theological images such as hell were pressed upon them. The play between those two understandings point to the broader dialectics in the thinking of Americans about eternity. Affective perceptions of time and timelessness, emptiness and fullness, linear duration and circularity, and immortal soul and earthly body were interwoven in Americans' feelings about eternity.[10]

In magazines, journals, books, and diaries, Christians across the spectrum of American denominations, when they imagined eternity as timeless, experimented with language about what that meant. Though they sometimes accommodated other ideas in situations that required them to stretch their thinking, Americans for the most part retained the message of the *Mercersburg Quarterly*, which counseled, in reviewing a book about "the future state," that "eternity's the negation of time," even though it admitted that it was "hard to comprehend a timeless and spaceless state of being." The Catholic position generally was more precisely and consistently articulated by church periodicals and manuals. The *American Catholic Quarterly Review* pithily recommended that Catholics "prepare ourselves for timeless eternity." Ralph Tyler Flewelling, a University of Southern California Christian philosopher, offered a more academic phrasing in pointing out that human "consciousness of immortality attends a timeless order of living" in eternity. Timelessness was difficult to think about, as plenty of theologians, magazines, and correspondents claimed. American Christians nevertheless have continuously reported being able to tell the difference between timeless eternity and history. Their profession of that knowledge rests upon their claims to be able to feel both eternity and history, or, to borrow words from American literature scholar Dana Luciano, Americans relied on "the feeling body as the index of a temporality" whether of linear time or a timeless forever.[11]

Empty Time

In order to understand something of the Christian feeling of the emptiness of time, we have to consider that alongside the Christian sense of eternity. For Christians, timeless eternity was not empty of time; it was full of time, or, in the Christian argot, eternity was, specifically, "the fullness of time." History, on the other hand, could be empty. For some, as the early-twentieth-century literary critic and philosopher Walter Benjamin remarked, the experience of the succession of moments in time could be like the handling of a string of rosary beads, each bead leading monotonously to the next, within a modern experience of "homogenized, empty time." Benjamin's argument, which subsequently was taken up by Benedict Anderson and yoked to an argument about national community, was that with the advent of modern technology for measuring time, lived experience of time became a matter of passing through neutral interchangeable units (seconds, minutes, hours, etc.) that made up an ongoing uniform present, or, as Benjamin proposed, "hell." Benjamin, whose purpose was to clarify the practice of historicism, had much to say about the relevance of empty time to the rise of capitalism, and his influence as a theorist has been felt largely in that regard. But also of importance was his view of the susceptibility of empty time to be interrupted by "chips of Messianic time," in transformative moments that intervened in the succession of temporal units and undermined homogenous, empty time. That insight applies to the practice of Christians in America, whose devotional activities can be characterized as interruptions of empty time, setting the stage for the suffusion of empty time with "chips" of eternity, as represented by prayer, sacraments, worship, meditation, and so forth. As historian of Christianity Carlos M. N. Eire has written about Christian devotion, "time and space were linked directly to eternity through innumerable points of contact," through a material and emotional Christian culture in which "eternity could not only be seen and touched, but also smelled," heard, and tasted. "Any point of contact with the divine realm," observes Eire, "was a link with eternity."[12]

Christians spoke often about the emptiness of time but also about their intentions to fill it. The Christian effort to make empty time full was commonly referred to as "redeeming the time." Robert Louis Stevenson's picturing of "empty time, lolling, strolling, yarns, and disputations," was not what devout Christians in any period in American history would have recommended as a pathway to heaven. Empty time or, as became more common as spatial metaphors of time gained precedence, "vacant time," was to be spent engaging in activities that advanced progress toward salvation. From British colonial America up through the twentieth century, Christians carefully considered the value of time well spent, as in the case of Mrs. Mary Lloyd, of whom colonial Massachusetts minister Ebenezer Pemberton wrote: "She thought it no Burden, but Privilege, to fill up every vacant Space, with something that might be improving to herself." Another well-known strain of the impulse to fill the empty time with profitable activity has been associated with Benjamin Franklin, whose discouragement of "lost time" had to do with another kind of "Way to Wealth." To some extent, as historians have amply demonstrated, the sensibilities of Benjamin Franklin were joined over the years with more specifically religious endeavors to "redeem the time," with consequences both for capitalism in America and for cultural developments such as the late-twentieth-century valorization of work "flow," as we have seen. But the emphasis remained on activities involving prayer and worship and self-discipline—so that filling up the empty time could, paradoxically, be done even by emptying oneself of food, blood, words, and sweat as well as by "filling" one's schedule with prayer, good deeds, Bible study, and Christian fellowship. As Winton U. Solberg and Charles Hambricke-Stowe demonstrated, early New Englanders created a highly articulated schedule of activities designed to fill the hours and days, redeeming the lives of Puritans as they redeemed the time. Sometimes that schedule was set with an eye to starkly stated understandings of time itself, as in Cotton Mather's *Catechism*, which urged "Redeeming the Time, because the Days are Evil." Anglicans, Lutherans, Catholics, Presbyterians, and others brought their own schemes of redeeming the time, and all together promoted the core occasions of the Christian calendar, from Sabbath-keeping to fast days. Such a way of filling empty time has endured in American history, although it is not as forceful or coherent a program as it was in colonial New England, and not as visible in some denominations as previously.[13]

Filling empty time was not as simple as it might seem, however. It was not as clearly articulated a process as the observable patterns of Christian lives over several American centuries might seem at first to suggest. By way of example, take the revivalist Charles Grandison Finney, who preached often about filling time with prayer and with repentance. He argued that experience of conversion was an important stage on the journey to salvation not only for its regeneration of the soul itself, but because of its role in ordering the daily lives of persons around the devotional work of being Christian. Finney, typically economical in his words, informed his audiences that "the moment you grasp the things of Christ, your mind will see, as in the light of eternity, the emptiness of the world." Finney's primary interest was in professing the glories of God in eternity, as revealed by scripture, and juxtaposing that truth to the experiences of people in history, in the "empty time" of the everyday. His rhetorical performance, like that of other Christian preachers, was the refined product of centuries of evangelizing. Its near-flawless execution in the American nineteenth century ostensibly set eternity as a backdrop against which the emptiness of time could be seen in relief. But we should ask if that was a standard nineteenth-century American understanding of what happened in Christian conversion. Did the feeling of eternity lead to a sense of the emptiness of the world? Or was it the case that a sense of the emptiness of the world eventually brought on a vision of "the light of eternity?" Or did both somehow happen simultaneously?[14]

Finney stood in a line of Protestant conversionist preachers descending from English Puritans such as William Perkins, who embraced the view that conversion took place in stages, which included conviction of one's sinfulness and a sense of the emptiness and unholiness of the world. The deeper rhetoric of conversion was always about moving from sinfulness to regeneration and from an experience of the emptiness of the world to the fullness of eternity. Indeed, the core framework of ideas about earthly time and eternity that guided Protestant Americans' thinking about individual regeneration and redeeming the time rested on trust that the transition from "emptiness to fullness" was a core truth of Christianity. Pastors and preachers counseled their congregations to aspire to and anticipate that passage. Writers and teachers likewise informed of the need to appreciate that on the larger canvas of history there was a story equally illustrative, namely, the passage from pagan superstition and false religion to Christianity. The Cornish Methodist Mark Guy Pearse, whose *Daniel Quorm and His Religious Notions* (1875) was popular in America, commented on that narrative by pointing out how "the fullness of time came in the emptiness of time. The world had proved the need of the Gospel by proving the failure of its own gospels." The author of *Glimpses of Jesus* (1858)—devotional reading that slipped some of the harsher theology about human corruption and hell—offered its own encouragement of spiritual striving, wishing for its readers that Jesus would "drive [them] to his fullness through the emptiness of time."[15]

Finney's picturing of the moment of conversion as a vision of "the light of eternity," prompting understanding of the emptiness of the world, would seem to have gotten backward the progression from emptiness to fullness. It might, however, be read more subtly. It is in fact instructive about how emptiness and fullness, time and eternity, were fluid concepts. Finney's reference to the "moment" when the striving Christian felt both eternity and the emptiness of the world probably was not accidental. It was in keeping with much Christian devotional writing to imagine a visionary moment as both in time and out of time, conceived in Christian terms along the lines of Kierkegaard's *öjeblikket*, or "blink of the eye," when "time and eternity come into contact." In fact, Christian writers in America, both Catholic and Protestant, tended to representations of time and eternity that offered the possibility of simultaneity in human experience, where the feeling of the fullness of eternity and the feeling of empty time corresponded in a fleeting moment. As New York pastor John Angell James pointed out, fullness and emptiness, after all, overlapped in time: "To feel your own poverty, emptiness, nothingness, and yet at the same time to feel in all the confidence of faith, our fullness in Christ and our title to an inheritance . . . is one of the most felicitous states of mind we can attain to in this world."[16]

The upshot for American Christianity was that the reporting and discussion of feelings of eternity, of its timelessness and fullness felt in the soul, were always contextualized within a religious culture that valorized the feeling of emptiness. One of the central projects of American Christianity, then, has been to promote the feeling of emptiness as an aspect of the awareness of time and timelessness. When frontier mother Gro Svendsen confided in a letter to her father in 1868, "It seems that the days are filled with emptiness," she was articulating her recognition of something very important about her measurement of time. Within a Christian temporality, her feeling denoted the location of emptiness on the pathway to what the Methodist itinerant John Summerfield called "the fullness of eternity." Summerfield's statement, however, also should remind us that in addition to attending to emptiness, American Christians have sought ways to nurture their feelings of eternity, of timelessness alongside time, fullness alongside emptiness. In many instances that has involved experimenting with paradoxical ideas similar to *öjeblikket*. Such instances can be observed in the apocalyptic eschatology lived by American religious groups.[17]

Apocalypse

Apocalyptic eschatology is a means to managing feelings about time. It does so with narrative that purports to clarify and interrelate those feelings. Apocalyptic contextualizes feelings of eternity and the emptiness of time within a scenario of their intersection or, as Rev. John Angell James might say, their "overlapping." The literary critic Frank Kermode suggested that the central component of apocalyptic literature was "the sense of an ending," an invitation to imagine closure. In order for that sense of an ending to occur, however, the plot has to advance with a view to both the emptiness of time and the fullness of eternity, and so for that reason apocalyptic presents both with a weighty urgency.[18] Apocalyptic has been a central part of Christianity since its first-century beginnings. In *A Very Brief History of Eternity*, Carlos M. N. Eire noted that "it is difficult to find any Christian teaching, symbol, or ritual that is not in some way dependent on the assumption that the end of time is always potentially imminent." In America, apocalyptic has been especially visible. From colonial times up to the twenty-first century, apocalyptic Christian movements—premillennialist and postmillennialist—have formed in the broadest range of settings, from urban centers to rural townships, in every region of the country, among different ethnic groups and all ages of persons. The ubiquity of millennial groups has led one scholar to conclude that "few cultures have embraced millennialism as such a basic component of its DNA, as it were, as Americans have." Historian Paul Boyer concluded that fundamentalist Christian apocalypticism was "a major strand of American religious life," and other scholars have shown its prevalence in Protestant religious life of the nineteenth and twentieth centuries. The publishing successes of Christian writers such as Hal Lindsey (*The Late Great Planet Earth*, 1970) and Tim LaHaye and Jerry B. Jenkins (whose *Left Behind* book series references the end-times rapture of the holy remnant), and the popularity after 1990 of Christian-inflected zombie movies, stories, and games all reflect the important role of Christian apocalyptic in American culture at the beginning of the twenty-first century. Among the many scholarly investigations of American apocalypticism are studies of the role of apocalyptic Marian visions among Roman Catholics, the determinative role of apocalyptic in new religious movements, its hand in shaping music, cinema, and politics, and the centrality of the idiom to American literature, including its place in African American fiction.[19]

With apocalypticism so widespread in American culture, we should be cognizant of its difference from setting to setting. Bernard McGinn has argued with regard to medieval visions of the end that apocalyptic eschatologies form "a pattern of beliefs about time and eternity that are too complex to be reduced to any single essential notion," and the same is true of American versions. There has been such a "bewildering diversity" of apocalyptic groups in America, notes Stephen Stein, that it is difficult to categorize them all, let alone reduce them to a common formula. Nevertheless, some basic defining is possible. Groups are apocalyptic because they expect the imminent end of the world, because notions of time and eternity are central to their beliefs, and because they imagine a passage from the former to the latter. As McGinn suggests, we can see them as "a genus that includes a number of species."[20]

Christian apocalyptic first coalesced in America as Catholic Marian devotion, an emergence traceable to the Spanish Catholic cultures of New World Franciscans and Jesuits. The end-times imagery fashioned by the twelfth-century Italian mystic Joachim of Fiore helped to shape Franciscanism, and a strong cohort of other apocalyptic writers and visionaries over several centuries cultivated and condensed that view of time and eternity so that it was efficiently transmissible to New Spain in the sixteenth century. In works such as *New Apocalypse* (c. 1460), by Joannes Menesius da Silva (aka Blessed Amadeus of Portugal), Mary was incorporated into that eschatological scheme. The Latin American historian David Brading has noted how da Silva's ideas deeply influenced Franciscans and Jesuits in Mexico, fostering belief that the Virgin Mary would be bodily present at the end of the world and that she inhabited her shrines and sanctuaries as a real presence in a manner similar to the presence of Christ in the transubstantiated eucharistic bread. The vision of Juan Diego at Guadalupe in 1531 was the pivotal point for the translation of Spanish apocalyptic thinking into an American idiom that foregrounded the precious relation between Mary and Christians in time and eternity. When Ita y Parra preached *The Image of Guadalupe, Lady of the Ages* in 1731, affirming that the colorful image imprinted on the cloak of Juan Diego was an impeccably true portrait of Mary that had come through eternity to Guadalupe, he brought together themes of the end, the sinful world, the presence of an eternal Mary in time, and the figure of the Lady disclosed in the Revelation to John, the urtext of American Christian apocalypticism. Devotion to what Brading calls "The

Woman of the Apocalypse" became widespread among Catholics in Mexico and the borderlands, taking a variety of forms and eventually serving as a crucial component in the imagination of a national community there. In the United States, the image of the Virgin of the apocalypse underwent an ongoing series of reimaginings, as the Catholicism of Hispanos and Mexican Americans flowed together with traditions of Marian visions that came to America from Europe and with Protestant evangelical ideas about the end.[21]

The complexity of Marian apocalypse embedded in American Catholicism is apparent in the writing of scholars working in several disciplines, including in the ethnographic study of a family living in Phoenix, Arizona, at the close of the twentieth century. In *The Virgin of El Barrio*, Kristy Nabhan-Warren has reported on the manner in which the Virgin's messages to Americans, conveyed through the visions granted Estela Ruiz, delivered an admixture of premillennial and postmillennial ideas with "a sense of apocalyptic urgency." Ruiz, who reported that just prior to the visions, she experienced an "emptiness" that "reached into the depths of my soul," received messages that described the evil of the world in many ways, such as this message in 1994: "Satan has unleashed all the demons in hell, and I have come to help you, each and every one of you, resist this evil which is so powerful throughout the world. You, my children, are not blind and you can see this evil that is so evident all over. You can feel him trying to destroy you and thus overtake all whom he can." Such a view of the world in time was made more pointed by the regular warnings given Ruiz: "I came a while back with messages of warning of imminent destruction of the world and to call you to conversion that this destruction might be avoided." For Ruiz and her community, Mary was a source of hope and a figure of support that the world could be changed, but that vision was poised at the edge of a more dramatic scenario, also given, that time was rushing toward eternity, and as the world became more sinful and empty of faith, that end came nearer.[22]

Marian apocalyptic eschatology in America in some instances has leaned toward a postmillennial view of the Christian future. In other words, it is more inclined to envision a gradual moral improvement of the world leading to a period of millennial glory than a premillennial scenario in which the return of Christ on the Day of Judgment clearly marks the end of time and the commission of souls to eternity in heaven or hell. The reports of Marian visionaries nevertheless are replete with warnings about the end of the world, and even in the more soothing depictions of the future in postmillennialist versions, there is urgency, the bemoaning of the mounting sinfulness of humanity, and a sense of the difference between an evil world in time and the bliss of eternity. Such features characterize instances of Marian visions among Americans in the twentieth century, in Cold Spring, Kentucky; Cleveland, Ohio; Worcester, Massachusetts; Mesquite, Texas; Hillside, Illinois; Batavia, Ohio; San Bruno, California; Lubbock, Texas; Conyers, Georgia; Scottsdale, Arizona; and elsewhere. Such instances variously illustrate a pattern in Marian visions that Sandra L. Zimdars-Schwartz, William A. Christian Jr., Amy Leubbers, and others have characterized as warnings about the approaching judgment of a vengeful God intertwined with assurances that a merciful Mary will save those who are devoted to her. For Michael W. Cuneo, her role in North American Catholic apocalyptic makes her the "vengeful virgin."[23]

Investigating a community in Queens, New York, the folklorist Daniel Wojcik detailed the complexity of a late-twentieth-century American instance of "Marian apocalypse," noting how the "Baysiders," as they called themselves, believed the messages they received were framed specifically for an American audience, an aspect of devotion forthrightly expressed in their literature: "In the United States, Our Blessed Mother knows the American people" and adapts her messages and their delivery for "a nation of television addicts."[24] From the early 1970s to the early 1990s, the Catholic visionary Veronica Lueken reported her encounters with many saints and angels, Jesus, and Mary, whose core message was the emptiness of Americans' souls, the American culture of sin, and the imminent end of the world. Messages saying, "Your children, their hearts, their souls, are empty," were delivered alongside such warnings as "The hourglass is emptying. The prayers of the devout have gained in the past many reprieves, but I say to you my children, the great reprieve will now be denied." The "Great Chastisement" of nuclear holocaust and the destruction of three-fourths of humanity by the crash of a meteor from heaven were imminent: "Oh, and it looks like it only has about—oh, an inch and a half of, of like sand, it looks like, coming through. It's almost empty." The sands were emptying out on a world all but empty of God.[25]

Lueken stressed hundreds of times the difference between time and eternity, affirming how the two were separated by a "veil," but she also emphasized that it was possible to "pass over" from one to the other. Messages informed, "Time is endless when you come over the veil," and although "science will never compensate or penetrate this veil," those who purified themselves with faithful devotion to God would succeed in doing so. Jesus explained (in one of her visions): "You will not understand life beyond the veil until you pass over. . . . Those who purify themselves on earth will come to Us as a shining star." Lueken revealed that in her visions she personally passed over the veil, bringing back with her from eternity into time the urgent warnings of heavenly personages. Her example, moreover, indicated to her followers the truth that one could pass from the emptiness of this world into the fullness of eternity, to be with Jesus, Mary, and the saints and angels, and that in the coming apocalypse, others would do the same. Such passing took place in a moment poised between the emptiness of time and eternity, so that "the moment when the soul will be balanced" and "that moment when they pass beyond the veil" were metaphysically aligned with "the moment of chastisement," "the moment . . . here in the final battle for the spirits" and "the exact moment of infiltration or conception . . . the moment of conception," the last being a frequently recurring phrase in messages to Lueken about human reproduction. Such language illustrates what Douglas Robinson detailed in his sweeping study of apocalyptic eschatology in American literature, in which he explored the centrality of the widespread image of "the veil" for its mediatory position between "*time* and *judgment*," where it represented "a standing between extremes that (these writers hope) will permit vision without loss of self."[26]

On some occasions more than ten thousand persons gathered to witness Lueken's reports of her visions, and a lively community of followers who maintain a website and radio presence has continued to spread the details of her Marian visions since her death in 1995. In this case as in others of Marian apocalyptic, the notion of the emptiness of the sinful world and the possibility of passing through the veil to momentarily experience eternity while still alive in time, to feel time and eternity at once, resonated deeply with an American Catholic view of the emotional search for God, along the lines of what the *Catholic World* explained in 1892: "Man is essentially a longing being. The human soul is a void, aching to be filled with God." That longing, and the apocalyptic vision, characterized popular Catholicism in numerous American settings and informed the lives of commune-minded Catholics such as those who formed the Saint Nazianz Colony in Manitowoc County, Wisconsin in 1854, which grounded its design for communal Christian living in its reading of the Revelation to John. But here, as in other cases, we must bear in mind that the belief that the emptiness of the world is the result of sinfulness and corruption is paradoxically intertwined with ideas about the emptiness of the soul that longs for God. The world is empty because it affords and fosters the selfish pursuit of money, power, and sex, and because of increasing secularity and hedonism. The soul is empty partly because it must live within an environment imbued with such immorality, but at the same time, and in a seemingly contradictory way, the soul is empty in a good way because of self-denial practiced by persons. The feeling of emptiness experienced by the devout is occasioned by a sense of the immorality of the world together with a perception of diminished self that comes with living in that wicked world. But it also is a feeling that arises in the course of a Christian's striving to deny self (a discipline that Christians believe is prompted by a God who wishes to save them), which often is imbued with deep longing for God. The various kinds of emptiness are joined in much American Christian thinking, and especially in apocalyptic: Christians feel empty as they comprehend their participation in a corrupted world, as their practice of self-denial strips away the familiar, and as longing increases. Depending on the moment and the setting, one or the other of those kinds of emptiness might be in the foreground of awareness, while still intertwined with the others.[27]

The trajectory of Marian apocalypticism in America is a long one, its New World manifestation predating the better-known millennialism of English Puritans who settled the Atlantic coast in the seventeenth century. Puritan apocalyptic and its legacies, however, have played a more determinative role in expressing American ideas about emptiness, time, and eternity, and American Protestantism in general has been more visibly marked by apocalyptic than Roman Catholicism in America. But underlying each were common concerns about time and eternity, emptiness and fullness, corruption and the moment of judgment. The feeling of emptiness informed each. John Winthrop, best known for his stirring speech about the "city on the hill" to the English men and women who settled Massachusetts Bay in 1630, cultivated a deeply emotional piety that included recognition of how God "showed mee the emptiness of all my gifts and parts; . . . I knew I was worthy of nothing." Winthrop, along with John Cotton, Thomas Hooker, and others among the first generation of Puritans who came to New England constructed, says Avihu Zakai, an "apocalyptic dramatic vision of the removal to America." Winthrop, in his "eschatological zeal," was instrumental in shaping the "*Exodus*, or judgmental, type of religious migration" and became "wholly preoccupied with the great task of defining the ideological, apocalyptic premises" of the Puritan removal to the New World. Zakai's broader interpretation, which revolves around his attempt to account for the origins of an American exceptionalism, is not our interest here, and in any event appears less persuasive against the work of Theodore Dwight Bozeman and others. But Zakai's point about the place of apocalyptic in Puritan thinking in the seventeenth century is taken. As

Baird Tipson wrote, seventeenth-century New England literature "reeks with apocalyptic." Zakai's close readings of apocalyptic themes reinforces and extends what others have written: in the midst of the "errand into the wilderness" that Roxbury minister Samuel Danforth described in 1671 and that Perry Miller ordained as a key trope of Puritan (and post-Puritan) self-understanding, many New Englanders contemplated their seeming drift from the covenantal promises that suffused the early Massachusetts Bay communities. Ministers such as Danforth increasingly drew upon the Old Testament book of Jeremiah in their warnings to their congregations, Danforth himself cautioning, "The Times are difficult and perilous; the Wind is stormy and the Sea tempestuous; The vessel heaves and fits, and tumbles up and down in the rough and boisterous waters, and is in danger to be swallowed up." New Englanders over the next century remained aware of the various threats to their religious experiment, in part because clergy such as Cotton Mather, who preached on eschatology in more than forty image-rich sermons published after 1691, would not let them forget about the craftiness of Satan the Great Deceiver. By the middle of the eighteenth century, some New Englanders had begun to think in more specific terms about time and eternity, puzzling over the prospects for the future of America as the future of Christianity and wondering about chronologies. Jonathan Edwards, who wrote at length about time, kept a journal in which he made detailed notes about the timetable for the dawning of the millennium, the predictive signs revealed in the Revelation to John, and, especially, the behaviors of popes, the Antichrists whose machinations would become more apparent as the end approached.[28]

One measure of the importance of apocalyptic thinking to Americans is the record of their willingness to form communities around their expectation of the imminent end of the world. Such communities were predicated on anxiety over a sinful world, and they anticipated a moment when time would end and they would pass from the emptiness of the world into the fullness of eternity. Feeling the end of time approaching in various ways, they projected different schedules for that event and wove together ideas about millennial glory that sometimes slipped through the definitions of premillennial and postmillennial that Christian theologians employed in their more systematic writings. The breadth of their thinking about time and eternity was matched by the range of social structuring that communities developed. In some cases persons all but abandoned their lives to prayerful anticipation of an end of time that was expected in a matter of months, or predicted for a specific year in the near future, bearing in mind all the while that prayer itself was "but bringing a man out of time and standing him upon the threshold of the eternal world." Alternatively, they organized their community activities around less definite timetables and less focused agendas. In all cases, however, they devoted much effort to describing and decrying the state of the world, the vanity of humanity, and the resolution of that problem in the coming apocalypse. Their "sense of ending" was closely interwoven with their feelings of emptiness and longing, with their feeling of time, which they actively cultivated in the present.[29]

In apocalyptic communities, from colonial times to the twenty-first century, Americans have experimented with different ways of living out their belief in the imminent end of a sinful world. The Quaker Jemima Wilkinson (1752–1819), calling herself the "Universal Public Friend," began an evangelizing career in the 1770s that gained her three hundred converts who followed her to Genesee County, New York, which at that time was Seneca Indian Territory. They lived communally there from 1790, many of them celibate, expecting the end of the world and the judgment of God upon a corrupt society. Wilkinson urged them, "Feel it daily to kill and mortify that which remains in any of you, which is of the world," because imminently "a midnight is come" upon the "fleshly wisdom of man, which is his utter enemy." She addressed her followers as "ye dear plants of the right hand of eternity," explaining to them that time was rushing toward the moment when God would "take the dark veils from off all faces, that they may come to see [him] who art invisible."[30]

Wilkinson's emphasis on celibacy and her focus on the end of the world was similar to that of Mother Ann Lee (1736–1784), who led the United Society of Believers in Christ's Second Appearing, otherwise known as the Shakers, in New York City from 1774 and then at Watervliet, New York, from the time of their arrival there in 1779. Numbering nineteen settlements at its peak in the mid-nineteenth century, and surviving in diminished numbers during the twentieth century, the Society cultivated a simple agrarian and crafts-oriented lifestyle and became known for its religious dancing and its furniture, among other things. It was profoundly apocalyptic in its early stages, but, as the leading Shaker historian notes, the group softened its expectation of the end into a millennial view less reliant upon an imminent scenario of violent transition from time to eternity. Criticism of the sinful world, which reached its highest note in the robust criticism of "the flesh," constantly reiterated, remained fundamental to the Shakers, but the sense of urgency lessened. The great attention paid to time and eternity remained as well, with members deeply immersed in notions of millennial time and spiritual travel, which together formed a religious practice of a kind of spiritual time travel. As Shaker Frederic McKechnie wrote in the Shaker *Manifesto* (1899), those who "take up the cross of self-denial" and "lay down their lives for Christ's sake" will discover their true self "with some strange element of eternity so worked into it." Put another way, Shakers came to imagine themselves, as Suzanne Youngerman has written, as inhabiting a moment between time and eternity, a notion illustrated in Shaker art and especially, for Youngerman, in the drawing of a flying angel carrying a pocket watch. "Shaker time was transitional time," an elongated moment between synchrony and diachrony, according to Youngerman; or, as art historian Sally Promey subsequently pointed out, Shakers imagined a "new and intimate relationship between past and present, between time and eternity." Shaker writings and art prominently feature the theme of travel, often representing it in relation to time and illustrating the Shaker belief that persons could travel through time, could visit eternity and return to time, in a play across borders that was crucial to the eschatology of the group and to its conceptualization of the spiritual life. Shaker testimonies spoke of members counting upon the "blessing and protection of God in their spiritual travel," but they warned also that separation from the world and its fleshly sinfulness was necessary to "travel to such a degree of purity" as to "be more bright and glorious than the angels." What Shakers called "travel of soul" could include many sorts of journeys, including "to the second and third heavens" and "deeply into the regeneration," and for Mother Ann Lee, it included visits to those suffering in the afterlife in order to redeem them, a process apparent to her followers who heard her screamings and groanings at night as she endured agony for them. Shakers believed that the Second Coming had occurred, as a "spiritual experience," and that Mother Lee, as the female side of the Godhead, now complemented and advanced the work begun by Jesus. Mother Lee, who also was known to Shakers as "the woman of the Apocalypse," was thought by some followers to have "actually risen with Christ, and did travel with him in the resurrection." She also was recognized by her followers for her travel to Eden to see what had gone wrong there. For all, as Promey remarks, "spiritual travel described the state and condition of the Believer's life both in time and eternity."[31]

Shaker spiritual travel in the moment between time and eternity was framed by the notion of "spiritual labor," the work of suffering and repentance that persons pursued as they separated from the world. Mother Lee

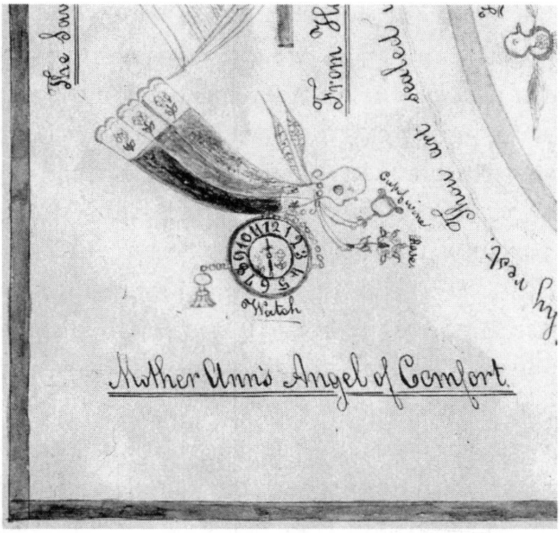

Figure 4.1 Miranda Barber, "Mother Ann's Angel of Comfort" (detail). A moment between time and eternity. The Shaker depiction of an angel, a creature living in eternity, carries a watch measuring time. From *From Holy Mother Wisdom . . . to Eldress Dana or Mother* (Mount Lebanon, NY, 1848). Ink and watercolor on paper, $9^{23}/_{32} \times 7^{23}/_{32}$ in. Andrews Collection, Hancock Shaker Village, Pittsfield, MA.

castigated the elders of the church at Ashfield in 1782, warning them, "The devil deceives you just as he has done heretofore, and just as he does all the rest of the professors in this world. They think they have enough, and so do you; and at the same time no victory over the nature of sin. You are a lazy, idle people." Shakers frequently discussed the emptiness of the world, the corruption of material life, and the intense feelings that were involved in traveling from emptiness to fullness, from time into eternity. They cultivated these ideas together, giving them voice within a long moment of the apocalyptic reality through which they spiritually traveled.[32]

The example of the Shakers illustrates what the Italian philosopher Giacomo Marramao spoke of in an interpretation of Walter Benjamin's idea of Messianic time and its intrusion into empty time. Marramao pointed out that "the Messiah . . . appears in a moment of danger, when a small opening seems to reveal itself: the entryway for the messianic is also the entrance point of contingency, of transience. The entrance point is a contingency that is 'kairological' and that coincides with a sort of interlude between being and nothingness, 'fullness' and 'emptiness,' desperation and hope."

The Shaker belief that the Second Coming had occurred placed believers in such an interlude, within a framework that was millennialist and that remained critical of the world and qualifiedly hopeful for the future.[33]

Another religious group that developed a complex understanding of the interlude between time and eternity was the Jehovah's Witnesses, which began as an association of Bible study groups, Zion's Watchtower Tract Society, in the 1870s. In 1931 the society formally adopted the name by which it commonly is known. The group's founder, Charles Taze Russell, taught that Jesus had returned to earth in 1874 as an "invisible spirit" and that the divine harvest of souls had begun in earnest in anticipation of the end of the world in 1914. Members of the group, who identify the creator God of the Bible as Jehovah, subsequently came to believe that the world had actually entered its "last days" in 1914 and that a battle of Armageddon would take place in the very near future. Russell believed that a degenerated and apostate Christendom was beyond repair and that God would dramatically destroy the wicked, not gradually reform the world. Like the Shakers, the Jehovah's Witnesses opened for themselves a broad moment during which they felt themselves in a transition between time and eternity, between a world that was sinful and destined for annihilation and the millennium that would bring the kingdom of Jehovah fully into existence on earth, where a "great crowd" of believers would live prior to their translation to an eternal home in heaven. In 1879 Russell, who warned against "the emptiness of churchianity," announced to readers of the inaugural issue of *Zion's Watchtower and Herald of Christ's Presence*: "That we are living 'in the last days'—'the day of the Lord'—'the end' of the Gospel age, and consequently, in the dawn of the 'new' age, are facts." The failure of the church in several attempts to predict the date of the end of the world and the cascading problem of theological tenets grounded in predictive analysis of the Bible have made it necessary for leaders to alter some of the claims made by Russell and his successors.[34]

The Jehovah's Witnesses have addressed the problem of failing to predict Armageddon by redoubling their efforts to picture the world as evil. Over the course of the twentieth century, they focused on new and emerging kinds of evil and fostered the emotional cultivation of hopelessness about the overwhelming power of that evil in the world at the same time that they upheld feelings of hopefulness that the millennium is dawning and the pure will be saved. Like the Shakers, they have understood themselves to be in a transitional moment—and one that keeps elongating—and like the Shakers, they continue to condemn the world (and even more forcefully), all the while planning for life in it. Their condemnations have been effective because, as Zoe Knox and David L. Weddle have shown, they have adapted their message and retrained their sights on perceived threats such as Communism, the Soviet Union, and the United Nations, although church teachings stress that the divine plan already has resolved the futures of such threats. More importantly, the church constantly characterizes life as "emptiness and the chasing of wind," as a "'brief span of empty existence through which' we pass 'like a shadow.'" In the early twenty-first century, people are "plagued with feelings of emptiness" and experience "inner emptiness and a lack of meaning and purpose in life," so much so that "the emptiness can be haunting. Having no purpose in life even disturbs some to the point that they no longer wish to live." But humans "possess a keen sense of time and a perception of eternity" that allows them to understand how the transition from one to the other is taking place even as world events reinforce a feeling of emptiness and intensify the desire for a resolving judgment by God: "In themselves, recent world happenings are bad, but what they signify is good, namely, Christ's presence. The conditions mentioned above [wars, lawlessness, persecution] started to be evident in that widely heralded year 1914! It marked the end of the Gentile Times and the beginning of the transitional period from human rule to the Thousand Year (Millennial) Reign of Christ."[35]

The conceptualization of life as activity undertaken in a temporal framework between time and eternity is also manifest in the Latter-day Saints. The Mormon, and especially early Mormon, view of time and eternal destiny has been in flux, partly because of ongoing revelations received by a large cohort of Mormon leaders and partly because of changing circumstances in the life of the core community as it migrated to Ohio, Missouri, Illinois, and Utah. Scholars have debated for years whether nineteenth-century Mormonism, for example, took a premillennialist or a postmillennialist theological perspective. The Mormon historian Grant Underwood writes about the "uniquely Mormon twist on premillennialism" that was grounded in the Mormon belief in a gathering of the Mormon elect before the apocalypse, and historian Richard Bushman has pictured a premillennial Mormonism "tinged with postmillennialism." Most historians nevertheless agree that the Latter-day Saints (the name discloses the group's leanings regarding their feeling about time) organized themselves around a trust that the world was corrupt and that God's imminent judgment would cut off the wicked from the good. In his earliest vision in 1820, Joseph Smith, the founder of the group, received the revelation that the "world lieth in sin at this time and none doeth good no not one they have turned asside from the gospel and keep not my commandments they draw near to me with their lips while their hearts are far from me and mine anger is kindling against the inhabitants of the earth to visit them according to th[e]ir ungodliness and to bring to pass that which hath been spoken." Smith restated that report of the end frequently, as in 1829, when he advised that "the great and dreadful day of the Lord is near, even at the doors." Other leaders of the early LDS community reinforced that vision, depicting, as did Orson Pratt in 1840, "the great events that wait this generation; the terrible judgments to be poured forth upon the wicked, and the blessings and glories to be given to the righteous," who "will be filled with all the fullness of God." At the end of the century, the same view was common, Franklin Dewey Richards exhorting in *A Compendium of the Doctrines of the Gospel* (1882), that a correct reading of Isaiah and the early church "testimonies [which] are becoming historical facts" disclosed that "the earth is made empty because both priests and people have gone astray." That emptiness was a sign of the imminent "destruction of the wicked" in a "commotion" of fearful earthquakes, lightnings, and tempests. Mormon church leaders in the twentieth century deployed such language less often, but as Susan Petersen and Massimo Introvigne have shown, there remains a strong vein of premillennialism in what the former calls the "unofficial literature" of the LDS and the latter describes as a widely practiced "folk premillennialism." Petersen makes the additional, and crucial, point that the circulation and telling of stories about the imminent end in which only the elect Mormons will be saved is a way in which an emotional intensity is cultivated among the membership, a kind of boost to their "spiritual sensitivity" to the present moment between time and eternity.[36]

Writing about the highly dualistic apocalyptic view of early Mormons, Grant Underwood has remarked on how Mormons imagined "an end-time showdown between good and evil," and he underscores the "rhetoric of polarization" redolent in such Mormon messages.[37] Apocalyptic always divides humanity between winners and losers, and those aspiring to salvation typically demonize their opponents. That same polarizing rhetoric can be found in twentieth-century Protestant fundamentalism, which has a highly developed apocalyptic mythology that is dramatically represented in the preaching of jeremiads. As it developed in northern and western American urban settings, Christian fundamentalism elaborated upon the premillennialist view of English evangelist John Nelson Darby, arriving by the time of the Great Depression to a fully articulated doctrine of God's "plan for the ages," which would culminate in the victory of Jesus and the angels over the Antichrist and his evil forces at Armageddon. Fundamentalists believed that the plan, the details of which—including the exact moment of its occurrence—were hidden from humanity, could be glimpsed in properly decoded symbolism of the Bible and especially the violent imagery of the Revelation to John. Fundamentalists such as Dwight L. Moody experimented with narrating the course of future events that would lead to Armageddon, but it was not until the twentieth century that fundamentalist apocalyptic acquired its distinctive cast. In the preaching of Billy Sunday, Aimee Semple McPherson, Billy Graham, Jerry Falwell, Pat Robertson, and dozens of other fundamentalist leaders, apocalyptic and jeremiad developed hand-in-hand as commentary about what such persons believed was wrong with America and how time was rushing toward a moment in which God would put things right.[38]

The emptiness of the world, the difficulties Christians faced living in that world, the identification of specific ideas, persons, and communities as agents of corruption, and the imminent end of time define fundamentalist jeremiad. Baptist pastor Jerry Falwell's lament in *Listen America!* (1980) that Americans "are empty inside" was a platform for the condemnation of those things that brought only emptiness: unmarried sex, abortion, homosexuality, pornography, the dysfunctional family, the "Satanic effects of humanism and naturalism," and "the official campaign to discredit the Bible." As Susan Friend Harding has observed, Falwell took on the persona of an Old Testament prophet to preach a return to "family values" as founder of the Moral Majority. In that role Falwell endeavored to "viscerally define and exclude" not only homosexuals and humanists, but government agencies, welfare, entire nations such as China, the Soviet Union, and Cuba, and rock music, which was "part of the satanic design to destroy our little children." His apocalyptic eschatology foresaw a rapture in which the born-again would be spared the tribulation inflicted on the rest of humanity, and he stated that his mission was to bring in a robust "harvest of souls" before that time. He made much of the cold war, and especially the prospect of nuclear war, in setting his Christian message in the context of "the coming war with Russia," as he did in *Nuclear War and the Second Coming of Jesus Christ* (1983). After the fall of the Soviet Union, Falwell trained his sights on the evils of secularity in stating that the likely scenario for the end of the world would come on January 1, 2000, as part of the Y2K crisis. In so doing, he was following in the footsteps of *700 Club* personality Pat Robertson, whose prediction that the world would end in 1982 spotlighted the Soviet

Union, but who later reshaped his end-time message around homosexuality, abortion, and other issues.[39]

Billy Graham, like almost all American fundamentalists, designated Communism a powerful threat to Christianity, telling his 1949 Los Angeles revival audience, "Communism is a religion that is inspired, directed, and motivated by the devil himself who has declared war against Almighty God." At the end of the twentieth century, after the cold war, Graham leaned more toward the condemnation of "the false gods of materialism and hedonism," which he condemned using a familiar trope: "I find people involved in irresponsible, destructive, and debasing practices, trying to fill the empty space with other things, even trying to fill the spiritual emptiness with sexual excitement." But Graham remained consistent throughout his public life in picturing the dynamics of personal regeneration as analogous to the process by which Christians at the end of time would pass from the emptiness of the world into eternity with God. In a sermon preached at the crusade in Charlotte, North Carolina, in 1958, Graham repeatedly pressed his audiences to be born again—his sermon that evening was in a cycle of dozens that exhorted his audiences to convert—by linking the urgency of conversion to the approaching end of the world: "Ladies and gentlemen, on the dark horizon of the present moment I see no other hope. There is really no other possibility I see at the moment for solving the problems of the world than the coming again of Jesus Christ." Graham blended scenarios of the end, and alarm about its imminence, with calls for persons to give up their attachment to the things of the world and accept Jesus as their personal savior. He depicted the battle between God and Satan as one played out both in the soul of a person and in time, each setting distinctive in certain ways in the telling, but each implicated in the other. Such an approach to evangelizing had been common in America since at least the early nineteenth century and might even be traced to Jonathan Edwards's "Sinners in the Hands of an Angry God" (1741) and other American colonial preaching. What all such preaching presumed was the emotive link between the experience of time and the experience of emptiness, a sensibility that had been in evidence for a long time even before the *New York Evangelist* in 1845 affirmed that "nothing can be more adapted to impress us with the instability and emptiness of earthly things than the constant flight of time."[40]

The historian of American Christian millennialism James H. Moorhead has pointed out that "the struggle between good and evil within the believer's breast mirrored a cosmic struggle between God and Satan; indeed, the two were part of one process." For Moorhead, the coincidence of the two struggles reinforced the pattern of polarization and demonization redolent in each, so that "the internal struggle for faith was projected into the historical process. There it had the latent power to generate radical views, for millennialism interpreted history in extreme terms: Christ and Antichrist faced one another at Armageddon, and there could be no neutral parties." In taking as an example the nineteenth-century Oberlin Seminary professor Rev. Henry Cowles, Moorhead makes a crucial observation on the manner in which the language of such preaching was "a rhetoric of polarization which expected opposition and helped to create it." For Moorhead, "polarizing rhetoric could push persons into extreme positions, thus inviting resistance, and this opposition could in turn become evidence to the believer that the millennium was indeed approaching and that his zeal should be redoubled." Christian preaching about the end, joined as it was with preaching for conversion, leveraged the feeling of emptiness experienced by individuals in depicting a world divided between good and evil. In addressing time and eternity, such preaching continuously aligned the struggle of the soul with the struggle of history, each with its own kinds of emptiness but depicted in their overlapping within an epistemology that set the good against the wicked, the spiritual against the material, the literal Bible against humanism, Americans against Communists, and family values against a corrupt hedonism. Fundamentalist preachers cultivated in their audiences feelings about time and about emptiness. They wove those feelings together in offering a view of the end and in exhorting their audiences to convert. In the process, they demonized their religious and social opponents.[41]

Racial Time

Preacherly warnings, and messages from Mary, to redeem the time, to fill it with prayers, abstinence, rosaries, Bible-reading, family bonding, fasting, and even suffering were directed to those who were understood to have availability in their daily schedules to perform such redemptive exercises. In that context, time was considered empty in the sense that the minutes and hours had not all been dedicated to activities such as a working at a job, eating, and sleeping. There was "free time" to fill. African Americans, while enslaved and then in the long Jim Crow era, had little or no free time. As political scientist Mark Hanchard has argued, we should be cognizant of the reality of "racial time" that differs from the everyday temporality of the dominant white majority in the experience of Afro-diasporic peoples. For

Hanchard, the "inequality of temporality" that is embedded in racial rule meant that persons of color, and particularly African Americans, experienced, among other problems, unequal temporal access to goods, services, and institutions. They had to wait extended periods of time for access in some cases and were obliged to act within rapidly closing windows in other cases. Especially following the Haitian Revolution (1791–1804), Hanchard points out, "the control of slave time (both work and leisure) became a primary concern of slave owners throughout the New World."[42] The remarks of one southern slave owner exemplified that concern: "I have ever maintained the doctrine that my negroes have no time whatever; that they are always liable to my call without questioning for a moment the propriety of it; and I adhere to this on the grounds of expediency and right."[43] The agricultural and industrial exploitation of black labor after Reconstruction and the massive incarceration of black males in U.S. prisons in the decades after the civil rights movement extended the racial time of the plantation. Writing from prison in 1993, a black man expressed cogently the reality of racial time and the manner in which it frustrated his pursuit of filling time with religious exercises of any sort: "Have you ever wondered what it would be like to have no free time, no entertainment, and no place where you could sincerely relax or share peaceful time with God?" Complicating the impossibility of free time for antebellum slaves and their descendants was the erasure of African genealogies, what Henry Louis Gates Jr. identified as the "brilliant substructure of the system of slavery!" Gates observed that "it was the deprivation of time in the life of the slave that first signaled his or her status as a piece of property" so that "a 'slave' was he or she who, most literally, stood outside of time." There are several ways in which to apply Gates's argument, but for our purposes it is useful in prompting reflection on the ways in which lack of "free" time, alongside a life lived "outside of history"—lived as property that could neither be "filled" nor recognized as "empty"—identify a social experience that does not fit within the Christian category of "empty/full" as it has been elaborated in white American Christianity.[44]

The predicament of African Americans who had no "free" time—when all time is labor time—and whose standing in time itself was ambiguous shaped the development of black apocalyptic. Lloyd Pressley Pratt has argued that African American literature links revolution against racial injustices with the intrusion of "messianic time." Timothy E. Fulop has shown how black millennialism in the Nadir could imagine a millennial future that was not in America, was not Anglo-Saxon, and recovered a Golden Age of

African culture rather than extending a white American one. Maxine Lavon Montgomery has argued that descriptions of apocalypse in African American fiction disclose that "to be black in America is to experience calamity as an ever-present reality, to live on the brink of apocalypse." There have been a diversity of African American Christian ideas about apocalypse, but in most of those cases, rhetoric about the end does not warn about the emptiness of the world. At its center, instead, is injustice in the world, a world filled up with injustice and inequality, experienced by a social group who are clearly defined by that inequality. Where white Christian fundamentalism, with control of resources and dominance over blacks, figured the world as empty and so looked forward to the fullness of eternity in the approaching apocalypse, black Christians, whose lives were full of work and, more importantly, made plainly identifiable "substance" by the imposition of chattel slavery and racial rule, looked forward to a world emptied of oppression. Black millennialism accordingly was more concrete, less focused on a transition from empty time to the fullness of eternity, and attuned more to "calamity as an ever-present reality" than to the rhetoric of an imminent end and the timetables predicting it.[45]

> All events fear their words.
> —Elias Canetti

5 Believers

Empty Words

When the Elizabethan Puritan Richard Rogers confessed to his diary in 1587 his anxiety about "myne heart being deceived," he expressed a fear common to Puritans. Puritans explored and monitored their feelings constantly and were especially diligent in seeking out evidence of pride or other "conceits" that they believed could find harbor in their souls even as they labored to live as regenerate Christians. Puritans, for all of the trust they placed in God, the Bible, preaching, and their ministers, had difficulty trusting themselves. They knew that Satan sought always to deceive them, to puff them up with confidence in their spiritual status while leading them down the slippery slope to hell. Puritans questioned their righteousness before God, believing that no one but God knew who was elected to heaven and who was damned. They nervously probed their feelings, an exercise that frequently led them not only to wonder if their feelings were genuine, appropriate, or justified, but to doubt the adequacy and even propriety of the language they used in reporting their feelings and in analyzing them. Puritan men and women deeply devoted to the "Word," the revelation of God in scripture, at the same time suspected that words could mislead. As literary historian Paula Blank has written, "The idea that 'truth' must be distinguished from mere words" was embraced by many Puritans, and especially so as nascent science added an additional troubling component to the investigation of language. The same dilemma was present among other Christian groups in England and Europe, in most cases shaped by a background of centuries-old debates about nominalism—the philosophical position that general ideas were *nomina*, or "empty words"—within the Catholic church.[1]

Puritans in New England preached often about the dangers of empty words. Their audiences, like those of later preachers Alexander Campbell (one of the nineteenth-century founders of the Churches of Christ) and revivalist Billy Graham, were familiar with the scriptural source of that cautioning in Ephesians 5:6: "Let no man deceive you with empty words. For because of these things, the wrath of God comes on the children of disobedience." Those audiences also were aware of the concern of their pastors for the fates of their souls, and especially for the fatal error of deceiving oneself, which, as New England minister Joseph Alleine (d. 1668) had warned, was a process anchored deep in the soul: "But now many conclude, because the work is done, that therefore they are in Christ, when as they do not look into the bottom of their duties, whether they be done in sincerity or hypocrisy, and so do but deceive their own souls by trusting to them." Fellow New Englander Samuel Mather specifically addressed the "duty" of prayer, remarking about the deceived that "they indeed *Pray* for many things, but not from a sight and sense of their wants: they are only *empty words*, which they speak and the Lord abhors their best prayers." Roger Williams of Rhode Island, in a classic of colonial theological polemic, *George Fox Digg'd Out of His Burrowes*, enlarged the arena of deception to include evil provocateurs. He pressed his readers to appreciate how "wolves covered only with sheepskins" could deceive the faithful, warning that "they prate of Scripture, and speak brave swelling empty words as Jude speaketh."[2]

The term *empty words* was often used in theological writings, and in addition it was employed to refer to a wide range of topics about which there could be discussion regarding insincerity, deception, or distrust. John Caldwell preached a sermon in Connecticut in 1741 that was critical (like many other sermons) of the emotional "extravagances" performed during the Great Awakening. Those who promoted such displays were likely "not the Children of our Father which is in Heaven." In his view, "'Tis therefore no more than a Pretence that such things are among them, great boasting empty Words of superior Sense and Knowledge." The depiction of one's theological adversaries in such fashion remained a key part of religious debate in America. The Reformed minister J. Williamson Nevin, displeased with criticism of the doctrines of the Trinity and Incarnation in the nineteenth century, reflected in his remarks something of the debate over nominalism that was important in America at the time, asking his readers a question about doctrines: "What must we think of our Christianity, then, if we see in them no practical relation to either, but imagine we have to do with them only as abstractions, which cannot enter our intelligence or will in any way, but resolve themselves at last into empty words simply and nothing more." The Unitarian Edgar Buckingham took a similar approach in condemning the "error of sectarian convictions," writing that it "not only in past ages led to indescribable confusion, crimes, and miseries, but still corrupts individual minds and the Church at large. It satisfies the conscience with empty words, the mind with strange imaginations." Roman Catholics identified adversaries using the same language. The *American Catholic Quarterly Review*, remembering in 1915 the "wonderful thirteenth century," scolded that Dante's Catholic paeans to Mary were "infinitely beyond the empty words of praise that have at times been wrung from protestant poet pens." The Masons, for their part, asked the leading question "[Are] the duties of a Mason nothing but naked ceremonies?" and wondered, "Is this a semblance of a reality—a shadow without the substance—empty words?"[3]

Like many other Christian publications, the *Christian Advocate* asserted that "Christian faith is not built on empty words or vain assumptions." But Christian writers, and others, extended the use of the phrase to discussion of related issues. The *Independent*'s "An Argument on Slavery" (1851) asked whether America would "ever . . . introduce a real liberty or constantly deceive the world with empty words." The *American Catholic Quarterly Review*, reviewing Thomas H. Huxley's *Three Lectures on Evolution* (1876), suggested that the "theory must be rejected as but a tissue of empty words." Madame Helena Blavatsky, whose ideas inspired the founding of the Theosophical Society in New York in 1875, wrote in *The Secret Doctrine* that, since the universe was a passing illusion, "it stands to reason that life and death, good and evil, past and future, are all empty words." Lucy Maud Montgomery, author of *Anne of Green Gables* (1908), expressed little interest in the veiled universe but did judge badly of "idle words—words that desecrate the sacredness of language meant to convey heart and soul's deepest meaning to heart and soul, debased coin of speech that discredits the image and superscription of the godhead inscribed on it; weak words, silly words, *empty* words." Montgomery's fears about the degradation of words, a worry that informed much Christian writing, remained a part of Christian reflection on the reporting of emotional experience, and particularly with regard to conversion. Just as Joseph Caldwell had expressed doubts about the words of Great Awakening converts, the authors of *11 Innovations in the Local Church: How Today's Leaders Can Learn, Discern, and Move into the Future* (2007) warned that "when people are forced to make a salvation prayer too soon, they only repeat empty words and are therefore not truly born again."[4]

The challenges posed by empty words were clear in cases of individual lives: words could mislead and damage the soul. Doctrines that were empty words could mislead individuals as well, but more importantly, they formed a threat to the collective, to the body of believers. Empty doctrines threatened like-minded believers as a group. Just as the English *Lancet* was "opposed to all 'empty doctrines'" because of their threat to the practice of medicine as whole, and the defenders of the tailoring craft opposed "false and empty doctrines of cutting," Christian writers were opposed to what Pope Leo XII in 1826 called "false and empty doctrines" about God because they endangered the community of believers. The practice of a religious faith, as scholars have stressed and restressed, is a complex of beliefs, prayers, rituals, feelings, visions, art, ethical behaviors, community gatherings, fastings, dress styles, food, and many other things. Christians in America always have thought doctrine to be important, in keeping with the meaning of orthodoxy, or "right words," and have always insisted—unlike some academics who study them—that community was defined largely by belief in Christian doctrines (even though many members of the community were unaware of some or most of those doctrines that comprised the official theology). The claim of the influential German Lutheran historian Adolf von Harnack in "The Idea of the Church," a part of his influential *History of Dogma* (1890s), that membership in a religious community was first and foremost an assent to doctrine articulated the view held by of American Christians both before and after he wrote. Harnack described how, for the (admired) early Christian writer Origen, "all who call themselves Christians and yet do not adhere to the traditional apostolic creed, but give themselves up to vain and empty doctrines, are regarded as heretics," their false doctrines "as a rule traced to the devil." Harnack's contemporary Charles von Gerock, the court preacher at Stuttgart, was more direct in stating the relation between doctrine and community: "Yes, Christ is risen; it is not a dead Saviour to whom we pray, but a living one; it is not an empty doctrine that binds believers together." That idea of individuals in a group bound together by doctrine, which was not new to Americans when Harnack and Gerock were published in America in the late nineteenth century, framed estimations about the nature of Christian community and made the seriousness of empty doctrines all the more grave for the life of the religious body, the church.[5]

Warnings about empty doctrine took a variety of forms, including references to the ideas of Jews in antiquity and wayward leaders from medieval and early modern Christianity. The *Methodist Review* pointed out how Jesus "had cast out the Pharisees' magic and their empty doctrine," while the Lutheran writer George Fritschel condemned "the empty doctrine of Zwingli." The bishop of the Protestant Episcopal Church in the diocese of Ohio, Charles Pettit M'Ilvaine, proposed that "empty doctrine" was "a fiction of ages of Papal darkness," in the sense that if one were to look beneath the surface of such doctrine, one would "find nothing left but a name." The Roman Catholic position, explained in detail in the papal bull for the universal jubilee of 1826 (published in Baltimore that year), was straightforward in its estimation of the threat: "You are surrounded by false christs and false prophets." Those impostors come to the faithful "in the clothing of sheep, but inwardly they are ravening wolves," presenting such cause for alarm that Catholics should follow the example of primitive Christians who "collected the books that contained the false and empty doctrines, and burnt them publickly." All such remarks were calculated to preserve the viability of the group as a collective of individual believers bonded together through each person's embrace of approved doctrine. That did not mean, however, that the emotional experiences of individuals were underrated in various writers' references to the threats posed by empty doctrines. American Christians remained aware of the relation between the feeling of emptiness, the longing for God, and the promise of fullness, so that discussions of empty doctrine often were framed in language signifying personal and collective spiritual disaster but equally in images of hope for the rewards of cleaving to right doctrine. Such discussions also navigated the very complicated and at times paradoxical understandings of a personal feeling of emptiness as both a blessing and a curse. For example, Adam Clark's Bible and commentary published in Philadelphia in 1838 juxtaposed for its readers the fullness of Christ with empty doctrines of non-Christians. Explaining the letter of Paul to the Colossians (Col. 2:9), Clarke noted: "*For in him dwelleth all the fulness*. This is opposed to the vain or empty doctrines of the Gentile and Jewish philosophers: there is a fulness in Christ suited to the empty, *destitute* state of the human soul." For Clark, the "groundless traditions of Jewish and Gentile teachers" deprived persons of the experience of being filled by God. That interpretation recognized the undesirability of a personal experience of emptiness and at the same time reminded readers that feeling empty was a stage in the process of the longing for God that ended in being "*filled* with Him." "Empty philosophy" was evil and the experience of emptiness was trying, but for the individual, the gospel would lead to "*completeness in Christ.*"[6]

For those who were seduced by the empty words of empty doctrines, there was "empty belief," and as in the case of the phrase *empty doctrines*, the term was deployed in writing about more than Christianity. From livestock reports in Pennsylvania ("knowledge is what is needed, not empty belief") to U.S. Senate Committee meetings on commerce ("the empty belief that security can be found"), to disapproval of Buddhism ("an empty belief that the constant saying over of his name . . . will cause a man to be saved"), the phrase recurs. Christian use of the term, like other applications, was intended to mark some belief as groundless, adulterated, or in some cases irrational. The accent given it in Christian literature is that the emptiness of belief is linked to the behavior of the believer. Empty belief (as it arose from empty doctrine) itself placed the soul in jeopardy. All were agreed about that. But to pay lip service to sound doctrine, to appear to believe without exhibiting the fruits of orthodox belief, also imperiled the soul. The redoubtable Lutheran pastor Henry Onderdonk (1789–1858) preached that "faith and works separated from each other are counterfeits" and that "empty belief" in time would become misery. James E. Talmage, of the Mormon Council of the Twelve, offered the same counsel, "that actions, not words alone, works, not empty belief, doing, not merely knowing what to do, are conditions indispensable to the salvation of the soul." The Unitarian Joseph Allen (1790–1873) advised that "true religion" evidently "means something more than the empty belief in God" and something "more earnest, than a little psalm-singing," namely "the performance of all those high behests" that will suit one for an afterlife, because "the future world will not be a place for sloth and laziness." Allen's compatriot, the rebel Bostonian Theodore Parker, brought to his theological reflections a broader understanding of activity in the world. Professing an eagerness to remind his readers of "the permanent substance of Religion," Parker prefaced one of his most provocative writings with an expression of intent to recall persons "from a worship of Creeds and empty Belief, to a worship in

Spirit and in Life." Criticism of empty belief for Parker, and for most others who spoke of it, included the notion that performing one's faith in acts of devotion was crucial to the spiritual health of the Christian, but there were differences of opinion (and much ambiguity) about which behaviors, precisely, were required.[7]

Although it would overstate the case to suggest that there was a strong preoccupation with the idea of empty belief, it is fair to say that the idea was common and amply diffused through American Christian religious groups across the denominational spectrum. The appeal of the idea of empty belief can be gauged, oddly, even in a denomination such as Christian Science, the religion founded by Mary Baker Eddy in the latter part of the nineteenth century. The Church of Christ, Scientist, built upon a scriptural foundation that included Baker's *Science and Health* (1875) alongside the Bible, stressed healing as the elimination of empty belief, or, as the *Christian Science Journal* put it, "truth-empty belief." Sin, disease, the body, and death likewise were not real, but merely empty belief, so that healing was always spiritual healing that exorcised empty belief from the mind. Empty belief in this case, then, was not understood in the way that most writers supposed, namely, as belief without action. Rather, it was belief in the unreality of action in the unreal world, a radically Platonic view of the harmony of all reality in Mind.[8]

Christians' thinking about empty words, doctrines, and beliefs made them wary of being deceived and contributed toward their distrust of words. The *Christian Observer* of Louisville addressed early-twentieth-century Christians with the caveat "This generation needs to heed the warning of Paul to the Church of Ephesus, 'let no man deceive you with vain words'—not vain in the sense of frivolity of self-conceit, but empty words" that "make a good showing, but when you get to the bottom there is nothing there." The Rev. Ellwood Hall of New Jersey about the same time narrated how the "hypocritical members of the Jewish Church" made such a habit of concocting phony doctrines that in the afterlife they would "try to deceive the great Judge with empty words the same as they have deceived men." During the runup to prohibition, the Boston Wesleyan Association's *Zion's Herald* offered an extended Sunday school lesson that spelled out for children the nature of the linguistic deception. Taking as his text Ephesians 5:6, given as "Let no man deceive you with vain (R.V. 'empty') words," the retired U.S. naval chaplain Rev. W. O. Holway asked, "What are some of the . . . empty words with which men try to deceive others?" He listed a few examples of men covering for their sins: "That they are only 'sowing wild oats';

that to commit them is part of a man's 'personal liberty'; . . . that a strong man can "drink or let it alone." All such explanations essentially ended up in the same place, cautioning Christians about deceivers who would speak empty words in order to work evil. The point was still being made insistently by Billy Graham in the late twentieth century. In a book section titled "The Deceivers," Graham mixed cautions about false prophets derived from the Gospel of Matthew with the "empty words" text from Ephesians to conclude that "sometimes the 'sheep's clothing' is a clergyman's robe." The deceiver might be a liberal or a fundamentalist, said Graham, but it will be "difficult sometimes for a Christian to discern a false teacher, since in some ways he resembles the true teacher," and, in any event, and more momentously, "the person behind the Great Deception is Satan himself." And if it were not frightening enough that deceivers who spoke empty words might be masquerading as clergy, there was the possibility of persons deceiving themselves with their own words. During the War of 1812, a Boston publication discussed the problem of empty words together with the observation that God "knows our blindness and how ready we are to deceive ourselves, even where the deception leads directly to our ruin."[9]

The importance of Christian thinking about emptiness in language and doctrine is more clearly perceptible as part of a broader pattern of American nervousness about words. In *Representative Words: Politics, Literature, and the American Language, 1776–1865*, Thomas Gustafson analyzed a side of the American democracy that often has been underestimated, namely, the deep American distrust of words. Gustafson demonstrated how that distrust evolved through a process that involved Americans "questioning . . . rhetoric or the uses to which it has been put by confidence men, demagogues, Indian haters, slave masters, lawyers, presidents, ministers, and other members of the word-slinging class." American writers such as Charles Brockden Brown and Herman Melville, among many others, "invited their readers to discover for themselves the unreliability of narrators and of representation itself." Such writers helped to build a political culture that prompted voters to distrust government and contributed to a literature that "called upon its readers to distrust language as an instrument of false representation."[10]

The crucial framework for this distrust of words and the platform for challenges to oratory (and writing) was the Baconian view of the unreliability of language to define the world, the ease with which words mediated a false sense of reality. Gustafson relates how the English philosopher and scientist Francis Bacon described words as leading "men into empty controversies," how they "throw all (things) into confusion," "forcibly disturb the judgment," and are "full of trickery and deceit." For Bacon, "the beginning of wisdom is the distrust of words." Bacon's influence in America was especially important in religion, and the aspects of his thinking that were appropriated by religious writers converged with the influence mapped by Gustafson. The historian of American Christianity E. Brooks Holifield, in a sweeping analysis of Christian thought in America up to the Civil War, has stressed the crucial role played by Baconian thought in the development of theology in America. Referring to Bacon (1561–1626) as "the patron saint of evidential Christianity in America," Holifield detailed the ways in which Bacon's *Novum Organum* "furnished an ideal that sustained theologians in America" for half a century. Bacon's modeling of a method of inquiry grounded in induction was braided with his suspicion of words, and American Christian writers, affected by both of those aspects of Baconian thought, crafted theologies that attempted to assure believers of spiritual truths based on empirical evidence at the same time that those writers undermined and made uncertain those very words of assurance. The vaunted mission of many early-nineteenth-century American Christians to fashion a thoroughly Christian republic accordingly proved to be a complex project, fraught with contradictions and ironies. The distrust that churches fostered vibrated alongside the hope they gave for a democratic Christianity in an exceptional geography. As historian Amanda Porterfield has shown in an analysis of the central role of doubt in the early Republic, "the churches manipulated distrust as well as relieved it, feeding the uncertainty and stability they worked to resolve." A central part of that conjoined effort was the characterization of the doctrines of adversaries as spurious and the beliefs of other groups as empty. Distrust of words was a perspective on language that was easily instanced with reference to someone else's words. As Gustafson notes, "American novelists from the beginning have made distrust of words as much a part of their story as politicians in pursuit of office have made distrust of a competitor's campaign rhetoric a part of their speeches." In religious circles—which overlapped with those of both novelists and politicians—persons doubted others and doubted themselves. They distrusted the words of others and questioned the truth of their own words, the doctrines and beliefs of their own denominations. Christians were aware of an emptiness outside their group, wary of the empty doctrines of other groups known to them through the oratory of their ministers and priests. At the same time they wondered about their own religious leaders, their own doctrines, the emptiness inside the group. They sensed the precarious collective self-understanding of their own group, whose power and authority just might prove to be the teeth of a wolf in sheep's clothing, gobbling up the souls of the unwary.[11]

In the view of those who sought to blend Enlightenment emphases on reason and science with Christian theology, words were dangerous. The "Scientific Spirit in Theology" that informed much American Christianity, and especially liberal Protestantism in the latter part of the nineteenth century, Nicholas Gilman opined in the *Unitarian Review* in 1879, rejected dogmatic theology that "patches together a theory of human nature out of ejaculations in the Psalms." For the scientific-minded Christian, if genuine knowledge was acquired through appeal "to facts, to the abiding realities in the natures of all things and beings, then distrust of words alone and independence of personal authority" would be "held to be of prime importance." Even clergy who were anxious about the seeming undermining of ministerial authority and institutional stability were aware, as Rev. Ezra Siles Gannett (d. 1871) preached, that in discussions about theology, it was "not unusual to hear men speak of it with distrust if not with derision." A key philosophical debate for Christians in America for most of the nineteenth century was between nominalism and realism, and the nominalist suspicion of language remained a part of the habits of thought of many Christians even after new empiricisms began to emerge at the turn of the century. In their popular form, those suspicions were manifest in the writings of the nominalist Mark Twain, against a more formal opposition that included the Mercersburg theologian John W. Nevin, who urged realism.[12]

The nineteenth-century Congregational theologian Horace Bushnell took the problem of language and religion more seriously than most other religious writers. Bushnell argued that there were no words that exactly represented particular things. His "Dissertation on Language" (1849), which historian Sydney Ahlstrom considered "a milestone in American thought" that "altered traditional views of creeds," was a philosophically fluid (and sometimes contradictory) argument for the emptiness of words and the tentativeness of doctrines. His central claim in that work was forcefully stated: "There are no words, in the physical department of language, that are exact representatives of particular things. For whether we take the theory of the Nominalists or the Realists, the words are, in fact, and practically, only the names of genera, not of individuals or species. To be even more exact, they represent only certain sensations of sight, touch, taste, smell, hearing—one or all. Hence the opportunity in language for endless mistakes and false reasonings, in reference to matters purely physical." For

Bushnell, "physical language" was grounded in an empirical approach to the world and supplied names for things based upon that orientation. Accordingly, it was more effective in treating concrete realities, the "certain sensations of sight, touch," and the other senses. Alongside that kind of language was "intellectual language," which, in spite of the name, which might sound inappropriate to twenty-first-century ears, relied upon emotion and poetry in communicating religious ideas. All religious language, as Bushnell saw it, was poetic language, with its symbols and metaphors and, especially, its prompts to feeling. As William Baird has pointed out, Bushnell believed that "no language is adequate for the expression of truth," so that "efforts to prove theological doctrine, in Bushnell's opinion, are futile." Bushnell's estimation of words, and especially, as he wrote, the distinguishing of "separate truths from their forms" represented much about Christianity as it was practiced in America in the nineteenth century and in the centuries since. Bushnell proposed, instead, the romantic notion that the communication of religious ideas, and especially between minister and congregation, was best effected through the utilization of "poetic language" that relied upon analogy and aimed to stimulate emotion.[13]

Arguably, there is no better instance of romantic language than glossolalia. While glossolalia technically is not a language, but a vocal ejaculation of series of phonemes, some American Christians in the early twentieth century and since have believed it to be a holy language given as a gift to the born-again as a sign of their regeneration. The surge of interest in Pentecostal charisms after the Azusa Street gatherings began in 1906 grew into a full-blown movement in the century afterward, and in so doing it came to embody the ongoing Christian distrust of words. Pentecostalists who embrace glossolalia as prophetic speech that can be interpreted by others—that is, "translated" into English—place their trust in the revelational character of glossolalia as it is manifest, above all, in its emotional delivery to a group of other Christians. Pentecostalism typically is practiced as a highly emotional form of Christianity and in its more striking forms includes weeping, shouting, clapping, jumping, rolling on the floor, and even, in rare instances, snake-handling. It places a premium on emotional performance and takes such performance as one indication, among others, of the experience of God. For such persons, as historian of Pentecostalism Grant Wacker has shown, the seemingly less emotional worship of mainline Protestant denominations was a sign of its hollowness and poverty of spirit. Pentecostals had a name for that kind of barren Christianity, writes Wacker: "In pentecostals' view, nominalism—Christianity in name only—bedeviled all the mainline churches." Pentecostals were keenly aware of what they believed was a disjuncture in the mainline churches between professions of embracing Christian doctrine and heartfelt Christian emotion that came with a real experience of Jesus Christ. The doctrines preached in mainline churches, in other words, were empty words, and the members of those churches accordingly were nominalists. The degree to which Pentecostals distrusted language is impressively displayed in their choice, alternatively, to trust in the phonemes of glossolalia. What non-Pentecostals might judge as the most empty of words, emptier even than the inadequate English language deployed in the service of communicating religious truth, Pentecostals espoused as the richest of language, the fullest linguistic representation of the truths of Christianity. This is not say that Pentecostals distrusted the Bible or that they had no doctrines of their own. Rather, they found glossolalia as religious speech to be the key marker of Christian religious experience. Pentecostal rejection of nominalism was a judgment upon other kinds of Christianity and a judgment upon language. Because it was known to come from God, glossolalia was to be trusted. That trust was a bold commentary on the untrustworthiness of other languages.[14]

Biblical literalism, like glossolalia, is an approach to language that incorporates a distrust of words, and specifically the ambiguity of words. Its excessive preoccupation with literal meaning masks an anxiety about words, their slipperiness, ambiguity, contradictoriness. Literalism is the insistence that words correspond to "things" (e.g., the word *table* corresponds to a wooden platform). For Christians, a robust biblical literalism is a style of reading scripture that aims to leave no room for recognizing ambiguity and thus endeavors to permit no opening for deception. Meanings are thought to be plain and language fully representative of revealed truth. Fundamentalists in faith traditions the world over, in the words of Malise Ruthven, "avoid addressing ambiguities of language by arguing that the plain meanings of scriptures are a part of their moralizing." In America, literalism is particularly noticeable among fundamentalists. Its practice within that community is characterized, writes the philosopher Walter A. Davis, by "an absolute certitude that can be established at the level of facts that admit no ambiguity or interpretation." It is a claim to certitude that "puts an end to all doubt, even to the possibility of doubt"—presumably the doubt, as T. L. Luhrman recently has argued, that suffuses Protestant evangelicalism. According to Davis, it is, moreover, the product of a compelling need to do so. As Peter Harrison and others, including Davis, have observed, that kind of confidence in language—however it has been acquired—has made fundamentalists collaborators with the development of science (and with constitutional originalism). The central issue, however, concerns the trustworthiness of words. That trustworthiness was expressed unwaveringly by the Princeton school of Reformed Christianity in the mid-nineteenth century, and no better than Charles Hodge, who declared that "the inspiration of the scriptures extends to the words" (a pronouncement reiterated by many ever since). Historian Mark A. Noll has written persuasively about how the hermeneutic of the Princeton theology permeated much of American Christianity, noting that by 1860 it compounded "Reformed theological instincts and commonsense literalism" that had been developing in America for over two centuries. Indeed, for Noll, the Reformed preference for a literal interpretation became the "prevailing American hermeneutic" two full generations before the Civil War. That approach included a tendency to think about verbal ambiguity together with the prospect of being deceived, as we can glimpse in "How to Interpret Scripture" (1823), which proposed that choosing the correct meaning of a word when several are possible (e.g., whether *will* is an auxiliary verb or a noun) was as uncomplicated as understanding the meanings of words in everyday conversation: "The use of them in common discourse, in these different senses, occasions no ambiguity unless it is designed by the speaker for the purpose of deception." A century and a half later, at the time when Hal Lindsey's drama of deceived Christians *The Late Great Planet Earth* became a bestseller, sociologist Jeffrey K. Hadden set out to survey American Christianity in transition (as fundamentalists and some other evangelicals became more visible and vocal in American public life). He found that there was a strong noncorrelation between Christians who embraced biblical literalism and tolerance for doubt and ambiguity. The degree to which Christians who embraced a biblical literalism insisted upon the plain meaning of words has been their radical means by which to deny the possibility of the emptiness of words. Literalists' professed trust in words was a loudly voiced denial of their deep distrust of them. The dogmatic insistence upon the inspired authenticity of each word in the Bible reflects an orientation to language that recognizes the deep structural deficiencies of language, its potential emptiness, and its profound capability to deceive in matters of doctrine and belief. That suspicion of language has been noted by scholars reading literatures of many languages. It has, as well, been at the heart of some research in the field of religious studies itself, where it has manifested as a claim for the inadequacy of words to characterize embodied religion, which nevertheless is ontologically taken as primal, plain, and inspired in its performances.[15]

Believing Communities

Fundamentalism is a specific kind of Christianity but also a brand that encompasses several subspecies. Its biblical literalism, which often is accompanied by a millennialist view of time, makes it easily recognizable among other groups in the American religious landscape. The predilection of fundamentalist Christians to display an overweening confidence in their brand also marks them. If, as one scholar has written, "fundamentalist certainty always becomes rectitude," we should expect that fundamentalists will engage other religious groups in a way that draws sharp distinctions between themselves and their competitors. The literary theorist Wayne C. Booth, writing about fundamentalist rhetoric, remarked that "every fundamentalist I've looked at provides jumbo jets loaded with enemies." The suspicion that words might be empty and the related demand for diligent avoidance of empty doctrines played a central role in American Christian fundamentalist groups' efforts to differentiate themselves from other groups. That is, they viewed other religious groups as proponents of dangerous empty doctrines. Fundamentalists have not been alone in that enterprise, however. To some extent all Christian groups in America have differentiated themselves from competitors by developing a wariness of empty words and empty doctrines noticed in other groups. In varying degrees, Christian groups have played out the relational dramas summarized by Kenneth Burke in his aside "I know you're a Christian, but what are you a Christian against?"[16]

The crucial context for understanding competition among Christian groups in America is the disestablishment of religion and the restructuring of institutional life that followed in its wake. The relationship between church and state in America is a complex one, marked by patterns of strong resistance to any kind of collaboration between the two entities as well as by urges to enact coordinated cross-denominational programs of social reform and other causes. The historical investigation of this aspect of American religious history has been particularly lively in recent years, with the publication of groundbreaking works by Philip Hamburger, David Sehat, Winnifred Sullivan, and other legal scholars and religious historians. The debates that have emerged from this growing literature have left intact at least one central interpretation of the historical development of denominations in America, namely, that the withdrawal of state money for the support of religion triggered an energetic competition among denominations for members. States such as Massachusetts and Connecticut dragged their feet in bringing state policy into line with disestablishment as enacted in the First Amendment, but several decades after the Bill of Rights, the effects of disestablishment were visible. A crucial aspect of that transition was the response of local and regional organizations to the loss of funding for clerical salaries, the maintenance of buildings, outreach, and education. Churches began to compete very actively for members, not just out of a desire to attract persons to doctrines thought to be superior, but because without significant support from church members, the congregation would be limited in its activities and possibly forced to disband. Churches did close and persons subsequently did join neighboring churches. At the same time, religious groups at every level—local, regional, and national—engaged in vigorous debate that would differentiate them from each other. That process of differentiation was undertaken partly as a matter of survival, out of the need to stake out theological and social ground that would ensure membership and fiscal health. Religion became a more competitive market, and with that development engagements between groups became more adversarial. That is not to say that collaboration disappeared. Antebellum America was a time of proliferation of voluntary societies and shared projects of publishing and missionizing. The process of differentiation itself, however, coalesced as a matter of defining targeted out-groups as what the in-group was not. It became a matter of pushing off against other groups in an effort to reinforce difference and in so doing set recognizable group boundaries.[17]

Christian groups pushed off from other groups by criticizing the doctrines of those groups. Christian history is replete with such frictions. In America after disestablishment, however, in a social environment where, as Candy Gunther Brown, David Nord, and Barton Price have observed, the publication and dissemination of Christian doctrinal literature and the formation of Christian reading communities greatly increased, some things were different. As local congregations were born, failed, relocated, realigned, began anew, or tentatively carried tradition forward, they sharpened their criticisms of others. The competitive environment and the transitory nature of congregational life in some locales (and the fear of that in others) raised the stakes for building a sense of unity and belonging in a congregation, and that factor was reflected in the tone and frequency of rhetoric that was deployed to characterize out-groups. In some places, such as the Burned-Over District of New York, an additional feature of the process was the simultaneous call for a stop to "sectarianism" that was thought to divide churches. Such calls, which came equally from persons such as revivalist Charles Finney and Mormon founder Joseph Smith, underscore just how keenly aware Americans were of the breadth of religious possibilities open to them and how earnestly many persons desired to belong to a single, somehow authenticated Christian social body. At various times in the two centuries following disestablishment, Christian churches have evidenced that they could view themselves as collaborators, whether in social causes such as prohibition and civil rights, or in organizations such as the National Council of Churches. Mainline Protestant churches such as the Episcopalian, United Church of Christ, United Methodist, and several others became notably more inclined to collaboration after the mid-twentieth century. Such denominations at the same time began losing members, however, and that pattern of loss remained constant for the rest of the century. The more vocal evangelical churches, on the other hand, and especially those with fundamental and Pentecostal leanings and a greater willingness to define boundaries, gained members.[18]

In the nineteenth and twentieth centuries, Christian groups criticized their competitors, and differentiated from those groups, by accusing them of preaching false doctrines. Again, it is important to note that strongly adversarial positions were more common in some religious bodies than in others. But even in denominations where there was vocal support for unity among churches and statements by leadership playing down differences, in some cases such statements provided cover for heated debate among factions within a denomination, or they came in the wake of highly public airing of differences between denominations. Henry Sloane Coffin, the president of Union Theological Seminary, presented his view of Christianity in one of the essays commissioned for the 1926 *Forum* series on reasons for membership in various denominations. His "Why I Am a Presbyterian" made the case that "the perpetuation of our meaningless divisions means inefficiency, waste, and the continued impoverishment of Christians by their separation from their rightful colleagues in thought and worship and labor." For Coffin, the "time [was] ripe" for "inclusive organic union among the churches of the United States." Coffin, however, wrote against the backdrop of the highly visible heresy trials of the previous several decades, the divisive theological arguments within Presbyterianism that resulted in the Auburn Affirmation of 1924, and the momentous fundamentalist-modernist controversy as it was manifested in the Scopes trial of 1925. His conciliatory words conveyed the seriousness of the divisions among Christian groups as much as they offered a vision of unity. Other Christians were less optimistic about unity, and they made that plain in broadcasting their disapproval of the doctrines of their opponents. Walter M. Langtry in 1909 criticized nonmainstream groups in a common fashion, as cults: "Mormonism was the first great cult of modern times based on a pretended revelation. Then followed Christian Science with a similar basis which denies the material altogether; and spiritualism, which is a thinly veiled materialism." Such errors were transparent when one clung to "the authority of the Bible as a guide which is the test of all false doctrines." Mormonism was an especially useful Other for Christian churches. Beginning with condemnations such as E. D. Howe's *Mormonism Unvailed* (1834), some part of the national population identifying as Christian since then has answered the question, "Are Mormons Christians?" in the negative, understanding equally that to be a Christian was to be not a Mormon. A twenty-first-century critic of Mormonism explicitly articulated that corollary: "Rather than asking 'Are Mormons Christians?,' a better question would be 'Are Christians Mormon?'" The answer to the latter was in the negative "because Christians do not believe what Mormons believe. They are not Mormons."[19]

Toleration of false doctrines, as the *Lutheran Church Review* explained, was the initial tragic step down a pathway to perdition. In "A Picture of an Apostate Christian" (1902), which introduced the discussion as "the apostacy—how brought about," the *Review* sketched a clear series of progressions that began with "accepting false doctrines," progressed into more dangerous territory as persons "drift[ed] away into every possible form of heresy," and finally, and most importantly for appreciating the American religious scene, arrived at the moment when the deceived became "avowed enemies." The *Review* entertained various sorts of possible sources of false doctrines but was especially concerned with Roman Catholicism, whose "pernicious false doctrines" included the priesthood, works, Mariology, and the mass, among others. A century later, in *Heresies of Catholicism: The Apostate Church*, John Schroeder was still arguing that most Catholic doctrines were "empty words" in order to make sweeping criticisms of the Catholic church in America. Catholics, for their part, used the same language in criticizing their opponents. The *Month and Catholic Review* (1881), describing the "futility" of Anglican ordination, added another layer of meaning to the phrase in telling how "the unordained Anglican clergy are to be pitied when they say their empty words over the bread and wine." Many publications, not content to limit their surveillance to just one or two groups, made lists of offenders. The *Christian Telescope and Universalist Miscellany* identified false doctrines with "the winds" of Matthew 7:25 and condemned all those groups "by whom they were put in motion; whether by Methodists, Freewillers, Christian Baptists, Free Thinkers, or whatever name people may assume." The *American Catholic Quarterly Review* had its own lists of "false doctrines" that deceived, and in one issue it focused on "Spiritism" groups, reaching deep into the American hinterland to identify the threat posed by groups such as "The Mountain Cove, the Kiantone Movement, The New Motive Power, the Sacred Order of Unionists, the Order of the Patriarchs, and worst of all, the Arkansas Angelites." It is unlikely that such rhetorical attacks were undertaken thoughtlessly, and religious writers, while evidencing awareness of the complicated dynamics of warning in-group members of false doctrine, clearly set an adversarial tone. The Episcopal *Church Weekly* in 1863 owned up, "We have detailed the underlying principles of the recent attacks on the Bible and shown their fallacies. Our argument has been negative; for our object has been simply to fortify you." *Brownson's Quarterly Review*, a Catholic voice, was similarly aware that much discussion of out-groups was negative and made that point strongly but somewhat inadvertently in observing: "We repeat here what we have often said in our Review, that we do not refute false doctrines simply by pointing out their falsehood; we must do it by distinguishing between the true and the false, and showing that we accept the true." The standard for most religious polemic in eighteenth- and nineteenth-century America, and among many groups in the twentieth, was the practice of defense of the group through pushing off from opponents' doctrines. The Episcopal diocese of South Carolina in 1850, for example, formally charged its leaders to "'defend' this congregation 'from the sins of heresy and schism' . . . 'from all false doctrine, heresy, and schism.'" Making a similar point, Hosea Ballou, the Unitarian clergyman and proponent of universalism (the salvation of all souls), in a sermon titled "Criteria of False and True Preaching," sketched what he believed were the life stages, religiously speaking, of the typical Protestant minister. Even before any seminary training, the young man "begins to consider it his duty to defend his faith against heretic opposers." While having, "as yet, no question respecting the propriety of his own creed," he is full of zeal for his creed and wondering "at the stupidity of all who oppose it."[20]

Something of the complexity of the defensive posturing of much American Christianity can be seen in the example of the well-traveled and widely published Methodist minister Hiram Mattison, who made a name for himself by preaching and writing against all manner of false doctrines and the groups that embraced them. He explicitly cast many of his efforts as "defenses" of true doctrine, as in *A Scriptural Defense of the Doctrine of the Trinity or a Check to Modern Arianism, as Taught by Campbellites, Hicksites, New Lights,*

Universalists, and Mormons; and Especially by a Sect calling Themselves "Christians" (1846). The raft of a dozen endorsements for the book rang with delight over Mattison's having "exposed the false doctrines" of various opponent groups and how "the author [had] done a good service in attacking that grand feature of almost all modern heresies." His *Popular Amusements: An Appeal to Methodists in regard to the Evils of Card-Playing, Billiards, Dancing, Theatre-Going, Etc.* (1868) similarly gave him occasions to censure Episcopalians, Unitarians, Swedenborgians, Spiritualists, Mormons, and "dead level Unitarians," among others. His nineteenth-century biographer made a point of explaining just how deeply committed Mattison was to defensive preaching by relating the background to some of Mattison's writing, including his book on the Trinity. With regard to that book, Mattison was said to be at a gathering in which false doctrines were being proposed and "he arose, in his wonted calmness and clearness of utterance" and "exposed the false teachings of the Arian preacher" with such devastating criticism that "his discomfited opponents lingered in the congregation only to see their boasted theology completely dissected." Such an account allows us to glimpse something of the competitive environment of American Christianity in the mid-nineteenth century and something as well of the urge to defend it. But to understand Mattison's response more fully, we must consider that Methodism at the time was in turmoil. It was growing rapidly, but as membership increased, it experienced growing pains that included disagreement among persons about doctrine as well as about forms of association. Indeed, those two elements of Methodism were closely related. A. Gregory Schneider has shown how Mattison was active at a time when Methodism was buffeted by disagreements between holiness advocates and their in-house opponents. "There were at stake here," writes Schneider, "the issues of what it meant to be a Christian and belong to a Christian community." Rhetoric was pitched to define the boundaries of the group, and the tone of that rhetoric often was defensive, whether it was aimed at in-group factions or out-group (non-Methodist) bodies.[21]

It is important to note, however, that Mattison also attempted defenses of what he believed were true doctrines by explaining the reasons why those doctrines were to be embraced, and he drew on a broad range of historically significant discussions of doctrine, some theological argumentation grounded in his own grasp of the Bible, and "the testimony of reason and nature" in order to do so. His *The Immortality of the Soul* (1864) and *The Resurrection of the Dead* (1866), while illustrating his sense of the centrality of doctrine to in-group solidarity, equally demonstrate that not all polemic was purely negative and not all assertions of identity were blatant caricatures of religious opponents. In the competitive religious economy of the nineteenth century—and in the twentieth century as well—setting one's own group against others was a crucial part of coalescing in-group identity and enhancing it, but it was not the only kind of argumentation that mattered.[22]

The formation of in-group identity among American Christians has required that groups involve themselves in a process of differentiating from other groups. Such a process increasingly is recognized by scholars investigating the broad field of Western religious history as a crucial component of group solidarity and stability. One step in understanding the nature of that process is to appreciate how Alister McGrath, synthesizing the work of other scholars, has conceptualized "that it is impossible to offer an account of the 'essence' of heresy" from a "supposed position of objective historical truth," that is, by taking "a view from nowhere." Heresy "is not an observable or empirical reality, but a socially constructed entity." Consequently, "what makes a heresy is not so much its ideas as the way it is characterized and categorized by others." When an American Unitarian writer in 1822 complained that "neither the word *heretic* nor *heresy* is ever used in that sacred book with the least reference to true or false doctrines," he was attempting to steer discussion into a similar channel, but without the benefit of postmodern theory and a deep critical historiography. A reference to heresy is an effective way for one group to distinguish itself from another, and although each side might have reasons for its approval or disapproval of a certain doctrine, the process of contestation is one in which the central dynamic is much less one of proof of "objective historical truth" than it is a means of rhetorically differentiating one group from another.[23]

Differentiation among religious groups as a matter of conflict in which each group develops and sustains identity by pushing off from others has been the topic of a growing body of scholarly work. With a nod to Hegel, and building on the theories of George Simmel and his interpreter Lewis Coser (whose thinking informs parts of chapter 3), as well as identity theorists such as Henri Tajfel, Bruce Fireman, and William A. Gamson, historians of religion have analyzed the social development of communities across a broad chronological spectrum ranging from ancient Judaism and early Christianity to recent North American Christianity. Susan Haber, in a study of purity in early Judaism, has argued that the social predicament of a community represented by the Epistle to the Hebrews can be understood as "the struggle to establish a distinct self-definition" through "social conflict," which is "a catalyst for establishing and strengthening group identity." John G. Gager made a similar point with regard to relations between Christianity and Judaism in the ancient world, Evert-Jan Vledder has described the "clarifying effect" of conflict on group identity in the Gospel of Mark, and Mikael Telbe, in a study of Christian believers in Ephesus, illustrated with regard to that community how conflict served "as a boundary-maintaining and group-binding function. This means that conflict with other groups contributes to the establishment and reaffirmation of the identity of the groups and to the maintenance of their boundaries against the surrounding world." We have seen previously how sociologist Christian Smith has analyzed American evangelicalism by drawing deeply on such thinking, his research echoing the view of Kai Erikson, who observed in *Wayward Puritans* (1966): "One of the surest ways to confirm an identity, for communities as well as for individuals, is to find some way of measuring what one is *not*." Recent work by Jolle Demmers makes the same point more broadly in summarizing this aspect of social theory: "Social identities are relational in the sense that they are limited: we are what we are *not*: Catholic not Protestant, female not male; Serb not Albanian." All of this research is especially important for understanding American Christianity in the wake of disestablishment, as competition for members, the rapid proliferation of religious groups, and the migration of persons from group to group over the course of their lives has marked American Christianity in a distinctive way. All of this was noted a hundred years ago by the English author D. H. Lawrence, who, in his groundbreaking *Studies in Classic American Literature* (1923), argued that the Puritans "came largely to get away—that most simple of motives. To get away. Away from what? In the long run, away from themselves. . . . And people in America have always been shouting about the things they are *not*."[24]

Debate among Christian groups in America has been lively and continuous throughout the nation's history. At its worst, it has resulted in violence.[25] The American Christian valorization of the feeling of emptiness has informed that debate. To feel empty as a Christian in America is understood to be a preliminary to feeling full of God. To feel empty is to feel as if one is not this, that, or something else. It is understood to be an emptying of the self before God and a deep longing for God. It is an feeling that fosters a hollowness with regard to social identity and translates especially to a weak collective self-understanding (except as what the group is "not"), as that collective is conceptualized in space and time, two categories that in many cases also are complicated by their construction as empty. As Kai

Erikson argued with regard to New England Puritans, the individual's sense of what one is *not* overlaps with the social sense of what one is not. To feel empty personally as part of a social body that values that experience is to belong to a social body that is itself experienced to some extent as empty. The way in which such a social body defines itself is through saying what it is not. American Christian groups that are engaged in debate with each other about doctrine, in a postestablishment environment where constant competition is required for survival, act out their emptiness, marking their boundaries by "defending against enemies" and saying, constantly, what they, the in-group, are not.

The process of making collective identity out of emptiness is complicated. Christian groups do have beliefs, and they deploy a rhetoric about the importance, the centrality, of those beliefs to membership in the group. Some members have an understanding of the group's doctrines and can take a lead role in the performance of defending them. Many persons, however, do not have a strong grasp of more than just a few doctrinal points. Taking recent history as an example, the sociologist Alan Wolfe has observed that "the leaders of a major denomination in the United States may know what differentiates a Baptist from a Methodist or John Calvin from Martin Luther, but those who join their churches, even when they are comparison shopping, are not usually comparing denominational histories and theologies. ('I haven't the slightest idea,' says one Presbyterian to the question of whether he believes what others of his denomination believe.)" If we look closer at the recent scene, we see, according to surveys by the Pew Forum on Religion and Public Life, that members of American Protestant groups scored an average of 45% on a multiple-choice test designed to measure overall religious knowledge and that contained sections on the Bible and Christianity. Catholics scored 40% correct, while atheists/agnostics scored 80%. In terms of specific doctrinal beliefs, 16% of all Christians surveyed answered correctly that the doctrine that salvation comes by faith alone is traditionally Protestant. Such figures suggest that it has been Christians' trust that doctrine must be defended, rather than learned, that underlies differentiation. Sermons about the importance of defending doctrine have served more as a call for group solidarity than as a charge to master the language of doctrine and to communicate it to others. The "empty words" and "empty doctrines" of out-groups make vulnerable targets during periods of active in-group self-definition because the members of the in-group—who, like the Puritans, are aware at some level of the danger of self-deception—to some extent experience their own doctrines as empty words. That experience is not an isolated aspect of their Christian faith or an accident. It is a part of a web of commitments they have made to emptiness that includes their feeling of an emotion, their practice of bodily disciplines, their feeling space, and their feeling time.[26]

In a section of his history of Baptists in America entitled "Baptists and the Twentieth Century," historian Bill J. Leonard described how "in many regions of the country, Baptist identity seemed 'up for grabs.'" Baptist groups, while agreeing on a few common points of doctrine, such as those regarding election and biblical inspiration, debated "what constitutes a true Baptist with frequency," sometimes denouncing each other as heretical. Leonard stresses, however, "Yet not all Baptists believe that confessions are useful"; and, drawing on the work of William L. Lumpkin, he cautions that "Baptists have 'traditionally been non-creedal' and have 'not erected authoritative confessions of faith as official bases or organization and tests of orthodoxy.'" In Lumpkin's words, "the desire to achieve uniformity has never been strong enough to secure adoption of a fixed creed." The character of debates about doctrine among members of different branches of a religious group that is indisposed to creedal statements suggests that something more than the debate of doctrine is occurring in confrontations between rivals. While it is likely that some measure of doctrinal articulation and rearticulation is important to the groups involved, more central to the process is the fact of enactment of performative scripts of defense and attack, as Baptists, in Leonard's words, are "compelled to revisit who they are and how they relate to changing times." That kind of theater is visible as well in the public performances of Louisiana Pentecostal minister Jimmy Swaggart. In analyzing Swaggart's anti-Catholicism in sermons and books such as *Catholicism and Christianity* (1986), David A. Harvey drew on the organizational research of Fireman and Gamson to describe how Swaggart's preaching and writing were keyed to evoke "'a sense of common identity, shared fate, and a general commitment to defend the group.'" That defense took place as part of a process in which adversarial groups were part of a terrain where encounter is "polarized, metaphoric language employed to raise and focus anger, and everyday events distorted, exaggerated, or placed in a new context all to make plain the vision and reveal the imminent danger." Swaggart's criticism of Catholics (like his criticisms of other out-groups) was in essence "an appeal to solidarity."[27]

What to make, however, of *False Doctrines* (1970), the manual of errors compiled by the popular Baptist evangelist John R. Rice (1895–1980)? Rice attended graduate school at the University of Chicago and Southwestern

Baptist Theological Seminary before founding *Sword of the Lord*, a fundamentalist newspaper, in Dallas in 1934. When he relocated to Wheaton, Illinois, in the 1940s, he took the paper with him, and it grew into an enormously successful enterprise, publishing many millions of copies of the newspaper as well as pamphlets and books. Rice nevertheless left Wheaton and began a decade-long process of distancing himself from evangelicals, whom he believed had compromised their fundamentalist faith; finally he broke with even Billy Graham in the late 1950s. Much of the prime of his career accordingly was spent debating his opponents and urging Baptists to reject false doctrines. His book on that subject was as comprehensive as anything else published in the twentieth century, a guide to doctrinal error even more detailed than volume 4 of *The Fundamentals*. Rice's thoughtfulness about false doctrine was represented by the thorough listing of errors on the book's cover: "I. Errors of Romanism; II. Baptismal Regeneration; II. Unchristian 'Christian Science'; IV. Errors of Seventh-Day Adventists; V. The Tongues Heresy; VI. Hyper-Calvinism—A False Doctrine; VII. Jehovah's Witness Errors; VIII. Ultra-Dispensational Heresy; IX. Spiritualists and Fortune-Tellers; X. Anglo-Saxon People are Not Israel; XI. Mormonism; XII. Communism and Socialism; XIII. Modernism–Religious Liberalism." Rice's concern in fact extended beyond such a list, his introduction explaining, "In this book we discuss some false doctrines, not all." He opined that theologians would not be fooled by such heresies, but that "common Christians . . . would most likely be misled by these false doctrines," an implicit question about how much "common Christians" actually knew about doctrine but also a statement of concern for the potential gullibility of Christians. What Rice emphasized was the particular danger posed by active agents of evil, who foisted such false doctrines upon the faithful. Referencing Matthew 7:15, where "Jesus warned of false prophets who are not sheep but wolves," he pointed out how such agents "are pretending to be sheep, but they are wolves. They are pretending to be preachers of the Gospel, but they are Infidels." In an elaboration of that warning, he called out his own enemies: "Some born-again Christians compromise until it is hard to tell the scabby, dirty sheep from the wolf in sheep's clothing." What complicated Rice's take on false doctrine was his view, stated elsewhere, that in beseeching God for the gift of service—that is, an endowment from the Holy Spirit to enable righteous preaching—it was necessary for a person to come to God as "an empty vessel." That message about the importance of emptiness, which drew upon a sermon of Dwight L. Moody, was one of the lessons of *The Power of Pentecost: A Classic Bestseller on the Fullness of the Spirit* (1949).[28]

But, again, why *False Doctrines*? Was it a book that drew the family to the dining room table on Sunday afternoons or became the focus of Wednesday evening study sessions? Did members of the congregation discuss it with their fellows and neighbors, and their ministers? Or was it, like the Bible in many homes, something for the coffee table or fireplace mantle, something placed near the Bible, where, as an icon representing purity or as a talisman redolent with defensive powers, it warded off wolves in sheep's clothing? If the latter, its role likely was understood within the context of a larger environment of deception and distrust and, in many cases, conspiracy.

Historians and literary scholars have written extensively about conspiracy fears in America in recent decades, taking up the threads of interpretations by David Brion Davis and Richard Hofstadter, among others. Hofstadter, who coined the term "paranoid style," described how American political life was replete with pronouncements that secret, subversive, conspiratorial organizations are pursuing and preying upon righteous Americans. According to Hofstadter, nativists and right-wingers believed that a "'vast' or 'gigantic' conspiracy" was "the motive force in historical events," and that "history [was] a conspiracy, set in motion by demonic forces." That view of political life had much in common with the feeling of apocalyptic time and the belief that wolves dressed as sheep were spreading false doctrines among Christians. Belief in conspiracies has extended well beyond the groups discussed by Hofstadter and has been, in the words of historian of conspiracy Robert Goldberg, "part of a long and central tradition in our nation's history"; it "is part of the national birthright and offers community to believers." A recent encyclopedia of conspiracy theories in American history numbered more than five hundred items. David H. Bennett has written about how the identification of enemies in conspiracy theories has served at times to "unite a disparate people in a lonely land," and Robert S. Levine has shown how the coalescence of a "counter-conspiratorial discourse" that is visible as early as Washington's Farewell Address of 1796 prompted social cohesion through its depiction of lurking conspiratorial enemies. I have noted in another study how in the area of religion, such fears of conspiracy have been a standard part of the landscape since colonial times and have evolved to include a broadening array of potential opponents as the number of religious groups has grown and the translation of religious tropes into a more generic language of conspiracy and secrecy has taken place.[29]

Classicist Eli Sagan and historian Timothy Tackett, writing about democracy in ancient Athens and the revolutionary Terror in France, respectively, have noted how paranoia in individuals often presents as a profound mistrust not only of others, but of oneself. They have suggested that just as a "frail sense of identity" in a person often correlates with paranoia, so collective paranoia, arising from weak collective identity, correlates with broader social fears of secrecy and conspiracy. Their analyses prompt consideration of the possibility that individual Christians who were concerned about deceiving themselves and about being deceived—by their own empty words, by preachers of empty doctrines—organized themselves into groups that took on those characteristics in the process of coalescing a collective self-understanding. A group that cultivates personal emptiness, that promotes a systematic denial of self, always runs the risk of creating a social environment that constructs a "frail sense of identity." In so doing, it not only can foment responses to perceived opponents and conspiracies that will serve the purpose of reinforcing group solidarity; it also raises the likelihood of demonizing those opponents. Just as apocalyptic that is framed by a sense of the emptiness of time leads, as James H. Moorhead has stated, to "demonizing opponents," so also does the distrust of words, one's own and, especially, those of others, open a pathway to building lists of enemies and painting them as demons.[30]

In the end, when viewed over several centuries, it appears that Christian groups in America have committed to surveilling themselves just as they have focused on investigating other groups. Various branches of American Christianity at times have taken the form of "strong group/low grid" that anthropologist Mary Douglas proposed as the social framework for witchcraft cosmologies in which persons are highly wary of demons and witches who have infiltrated the group, bent on destroying it from within. The wolf in sheep's clothing, while often depicted as a fraud attempting entry to the group, equally has been the cause for wariness within the group. When the *Christian Observer* in 1902 presented its readers with an exposition of "False Teaching within the Church," it intended to focus their attention on the wolves within. Celebrating the dismissal of a professor from Northwestern University "on account of unsoundness of doctrine," the *Observer* condemned the toleration of "false teachings, such as the horrid one that the Pentateuch is a collection of myths" and affirmed that "when they are heard from the lips of an enemy, the hearer is on his guard, he knows that the enemy is plotting his ruin." The reporting of such cases among Christians in American religious history has been constant and has always been grounded in biblical warnings about impostors. The Presbyterian minister Albert Barnes (1798–1870) provided a template for scriptural prooftexting in his analysis of a key Matthean pericope in *Notes on the Gospels: Designed for Sunday School Teacher and Bible Classes*. But Barnes's analysis, meant to fortify believers against deception, might have had more the character of a poisonous gift. Anyone who read it learned that "Satan sows false doctrine" and does so "in the very place where the truth is preached." Most importantly, "while the hearts of people are open to receive it, by false but plausible teachers, he takes care to inculcate false sentiments." Satan, the "enemy who deceives," working through his witting or unwitting human agents, "knows that in the human heart it will take deep and rapid root." Such language urged wariness of false doctrine, but it also cast suspicion upon feeling itself, and in so doing left persons with little confidence in their ability to defend against anything. It left them, in such a predicament, hoping to be empty.[31]

Notes

Introduction

Epigraphs: Teofilo F. Ruiz, *The Terror of History: On the Uncertainties of Life in Western Civilization* (Princeton, NJ: Princeton University Press, 2011), 47; Phillips Brooks quoted in *New York Observer*, April 20, 1911, 508.

1. E. V. G., "Religion and Christianity: Second Article," *Mercersburg Review* (April 1860), 251.

2. Orestes Brownson, *The Works of Orestes Brownson*, collated and arranged by Henry F. Brownson (Detroit: Thorndike Nourse, 1884), 14:36; J. W. Mendenhall, *Plato and Paul; or, Philosophy and Christianity* (Cincinnati: Cranston and Stowe, 1886), 750; Joseph Krauskopf, "A Sunday Lecture before the Reform Congregation Keneseth Israel, January 4, 1891," in *Jewish Converts and Perverts. I. True and False Converts* (Philadelphia: W. Goodman, 1891), 11; Lyman Abbott, "Summer Vesper Sermons: What Is a Christian?," *Outlook*, Aug. 15, 1908, 850; Charles M. Sheldon, "What Does It Mean to Be a Christian: I. What Is a Christian," *Congregationalist and Christian World*, Oct. 3, 1903, 457.

3. Douglas John Hall, *What Christianity Is Not: An Exercise in Negative Theology* (Eugene, OR: Wipf and Stock, 2013).

Chapter 1

Epigraph: Charles Simic, *Jackstraws* (New York: Harcourt, 1999), 32.

1. Laurel Fulkerson, *No Regrets: Remorse in Classical Antiquity* (New

York: Oxford University Press, 2012); William R. Reddy, *The Navigation of Feeling: A Framework for the History of Emotions* (New York: Cambridge University Press, 2001); Susan Karant-Nunn, *The Reformation of Feeling: Shaping the Religious Emotions in Early Modern Germany* (New York: Oxford University Press, 2010); Lila Aba-Lughod, *Veiled Sentiments: Honor and Poetry in a Bedouin Society* (Berkeley: University of California Press, 2000); Barbara Rosenwein, *Emotional Communities in the Early Middle Ages* (Ithaca, NY: Cornell University Press, 2006); Mick Smith, Joyce Davidson, Laura Cameron, and Liz Bondi, eds., *Emotion, Place, and Culture* (Farnham, Surrey, UK: Ashgate, 2009); Martha C. Nussbaum, *Upheavals of Thought: The Intelligence of Emotions* (Cambridge: Cambridge University Press, 2001); Catherine A. Lutz, *Unnatural Emotions: Everyday Sentiments on a Micronesian Atoll and Their Challenge to Western Theory* (Chicago: University of Chicago Press, 1988); Peter N. Stearns and Jan Lewis, *An Emotional History of the United States* (New York: New York University Press, 1998).

2. John Corrigan, Eric Crump, and John M. Kloos, *Emotion and Religion: A Critical Assessment and Annotated Bibliography* (Westport, CT: Greenwood Press, 2000).

3. John Corrigan, ed., *The Oxford Handbook of Religion and Emotion* (New York: Oxford University Press, 2008); Corrigan, *Religion and Emotion: Approaches and Interpretations* (New York: Oxford University Press, 2006); Corrigan, "Religion and Emotions," in *Doing Emotions History*, ed. Susan Matt and Peter N. Stearns (Urbana: University of Illinois Press, 2014), 140–59; Corrigan, "Appendix I: History, Religion, and Emotion: An Historiographical Survey," in *Business of the Heart: Religion and Emotion in the Nineteenth Century*, by Corrigan (Berkeley: University of California Press, 2002), 269–80.

4. Clive G. Hazell, "A Scale for Measuring Experienced Levels of Emptiness and Existential Concern," *Journal of Psychology* 117 (1984), 177–82; "Experienced Levels of Emptiness and Existential Concern with Different Levels of Emotional Development and Profile of Values," *Psychological Reports* 55 (1984), 967–76; "Levels of Emotional Development with Experienced Levels of Emptiness and Emotional Concern," *Psychological Reports* 64 (1989), 835–38; E. David Klonsky, "What Is Emptiness? Clarifying the 7th Criterion for Borderline Personality Disorder," *Journal of Personality Disorders* 22 (2008), 418–26; Ivri M. Kumin, "Emptiness and Its Relation to Schizoid Ego Structures," *International Review of Psycho-Analysis* 5 (1978), 207–16; Carlos Farate, "O vazio psiquico contra a depressão: Agir, fultidade e 'falha' na representação de si/Psychic emptiness versus depression: To act, futility, and to fail in the representation of self," *Revista Portuguesa de Psicanálise* 28 (2008), 133–55; John R. Peteet, "Approaching Emptiness: Subjective, Objective and Existential Dimensions," *Journal of Religion and Health* 50 (2011), 558–63; Michael Washburn, *Transpersonal Psychology in Psychoanalytic Perspective* (Albany: SUNY Press, 1994), 214–16; Jean-Paul Sartre, "The Flies (Les Mouches)," in *No Exit and Three Other Plays* (New York: Knopf Doubleday, 1976), 57; David R. Law, *Kierkegaard's Kenoptic Christianity* (Oxford: Oxford University Press, 2012); Richard A. Shweder, "Menstrual Pollution, Soul Loss, and the Comparative Study of Emotions," in *Culture and Depression: Studies in the Anthropology and Cross-Cultural Psychology of Affect and Disorder*, ed. Arthur Kleinman and Byron Good (Berkeley: University of California Press, 1985), 182–205; Philip Cushman, "Why the Self Is Empty: Toward a Historical Situated Psychology," *American Psychologist* 45 (1990), 599–611; James H. Leuba, "The Contents of Religious Consciousness," *Monist* 11 (1901), 536–72.

5. Urs App, *The Cult of Emptiness: The Western Discovery of Buddhist Thought and the Invention of Oriental Philosophy* (Kyoto, Japan: UniversityMedia, 2012); Roger-Pol Droit, *The Cult of Nothingness: The Philosophers and the Buddha*, trans. David Streight and Pamela Vohnson (Chapel Hill: University of North Carolina Press, 2003); Newman Robert Glass,

Working Emptiness: Toward a Third Reading of Emptiness in Buddhism and Postmodern Thought (Atlanta, GA: Scholars Press, 1995); Robert J. J. Wargo, *The Logic of Nothingness: A Study of Nishida Kitarō* (Honolulu: University of Hawaii Press, 2005); Robert E. Carter, *The Logic of Nothingness: An Introduction to the Philosophy of Nishida Kitarō*, 2nd ed. (St. Paul, MN: Paragon, 1997); Keiji Nishitani, *Religion and Nothingness*, trans. with an introduction by Jan Van Bragt (Berkeley: University of California Press, 1982).

6. Masao Abe, "Kenosis and Emptiness," in *Buddhist Emptiness and the Christian Trinity* (Mahwah, NJ: Paulist Press, 1990); Bettina Baumer and John R. Dupuche, eds., *Void and Fullness in the Buddhist, Hindu, and Christian Traditions: Śūnya—Pūrna—Plerôma* (New Delhi: DK Printworld, 2005); Robert E. Carter, "God and Nothingness," *Philosophy East and West* 59 (2009), 1–21; John Raymaker, *A Buddhist-Christian Logic of the Heart: Nishida's Kyoto School and Lonergan's "Spiritual Genome" as World Bridge* (Lanham, MD: University Press of America, 2002); Gordon D. Kaufman, "God and Emptiness: An Experimental Essay," *Buddhist-Christian Studies* 9 (1989), 175–87; Frederick J. Streng, *Emptiness: A Study in Religious Meaning* (New York: Abingdon, 1967); Randall Nadeau, "Frederick Streng, Madhyamika, and the Comparative Study of Religion," *Buddhist-Christian Studies* 16 (1996), 65–76; John P. Keenan, "Emptiness as a Paradigm for Understanding World Religions," *Buddhist-Christian Studies* 16 (1996), 57–64.

7. Louise Sundararajan, "*Kong* (Emptiness): A Chinese Buddhist Emotion," in *Religious Emotions: Some Philosophical Explorations*, ed. Willem Lemmens and Walter Van Herck (Newcastle: Cambridge Scholars Press, 2008), 192.

8. I am indebted to Peter Thuesen for pointing out a salient passage in book 9 of Augustine's *Confessions*: "For those who try to find joys in things outside themselves easily vanish away into emptiness. They waste themselves on the temporal pleasures of the visible world. Their minds are starved and they nibble at empty shadows." Augustine, *Confessions*, trans. R. S. Pine-Coffin (New York: Penguin, 1961), book 9, n.p.

9. Rudolf Otto, *The Idea of the Holy*, trans. John W. Harvey (New York: Oxford University Press, 1958); and *Mysticism East and West: A Comparative Analysis of the Nature of Mysticism*, trans. Bertha L. Bracey and Richenda C. Payne (New York: Macmillan, 1932). Robert Roberts discusses in "The Feeling of Absolute Dependence," *Journal of Religion* 57 (1977), 252–66, how Schleiermacher's *feeling* of absolute dependence can be separated from *belief* in the attributes of God. Christine Helmer comments on Schleiermacher's differences with mysticism in "Mysticism and Metaphysics: Schleiermacher and a Historical-Theological Trajectory," *Journal of Religion* 83 (2003) 517–38.

10. Saint John of the Cross, *The Dark Night of the Soul*, trans. and ed. Kurt F. Reinhardt (New York: Ungar, 1957), 195; Laura L. Garcia, "St. John of the Cross and the Necessity of Divine Hiddenness," in *Divine Hiddenness: New Essays*, ed. Daniel Howard-Snyder and Paul Moser (New York: Cambridge University Press, 2002), 89; Thomas Cogswell Upham, *The Life of Madame Catharine Adorna: Including Some Leading Facts and Traits in Her Religious Experience*, 3rd ed. (New York: Harper, 1858), 164.

11. Saint Augustine, *The Confessions of St. Augustine*, trans. and ed. Albert Cook Outler (Mineola, NY: Dover, 2002), 10.43–44; Algar L. Thorold, *An Essay in Aid of the Better Appreciation of Catholic Mysticism Illustrated from the Writings of Blessed Angela of Foligno* (London: Paternoster, 1900), 155. On Upham's interest in Saint Catharine, see *Purgation and Purgatory: The Spiritual Dialogues*, by Catherine of Genoa (Mahwah, NJ: Paulist Press, 1979), 39–43.

12. Jorge Luis Borges, *Everything and Nothing* (New York: New Directions, 1999), 76; Catherine Gimelli Martin, *Milton among the Puritans: The Case for Historical Revisionism* (Farnham, Surrey: Ashgate, 2010), 113; Jerald C. Brauer, "Types of Puritan Piety," *Church*

History 56 (1987), 53, 49; Thomas Hooker, *The Soules Humiliation* (London, 1640; reprint, New York: AMS Press, 1981), 145.

13. Thomas Shepard, *The Autobiography of Thomas Shepard* (Boston: Doctrinal Tract and Book Society, 1853), 1:72; Andrea Knutson, *American Spaces of Conversion: The Conducive Imaginaries of Edwards, Emerson, and James* (New York: Oxford University Press, 2011), 45. See the confession of "Mitchell," in "Thomas Shepard's Record of Relations of Religious Experience, 1648–1649," *William and Mary Quarterly*, third series, 48 (1991), 457.

14. John Cotton, *Spiritual Milk for Boston Babes* (Boston, 1684), 2; John Calvin, *Institutes of the Christian Religion*, ed. John T. McNeill, trans. Ford Lewis Battles (Philadelphia: Westminster Press, 1960), 1:37; Anne Bradstreet, *The Works of Anne Bradstreet*, ed. Jeannine Hensley (Cambridge, MA: Harvard University Press, 1967), 60; Anne Bradstreet, "Meditations Divine and Morall," in *The Works of Anne Bradstreet in Prose and Verse*, ed. John Harvard Ellis (Charlestown, MA: A. E. Cutter, 1867), 61.

15. Evan Carton, "Getting a Life: History, Identity, and Desire in American Writing," *Texas Studies in Literature and Language* 35 (1993), 146; Rosemary Fithian, "'Words of My Mouth, Meditations of My Heart': Edward Taylor's Preparatory Meditations," *Early American Literature* 20 (1985), 93; Edward Taylor, "Meditation I.27," in *The Poems of Edward Taylor*, ed. Donald E. Stanford (New Haven, CT: Yale University Press, 1960), 39; Karl Keller, "The Example of Edward Taylor," *Early American Literature* 4 (1969–70), 19; Belden C. Lane, "Two Schools of Desire: Nature and Marriage in Seventeenth-Century Puritanism," *Church History* 69 (2000), 396; Michael Wigglesworth, "A Song of Emptiness to Fill Up the Empty Pages Following: Vanity of Vanities," in *The Day of Doom* (Boston: John Allen, 1715), 69–72. The poem originally was published in 1657.

16. Jonathan Edwards, *Personal Narrative*, in *Jonathan Edwards: Representative Selections*, ed. Clarence H. Faust and Thomas H. Johnson (New York: American Book Company, 1935), para. 27, 22; Jonathan Edwards to Thomas Gillespie, July 1, 1751, in *The Works of Jonathan Edwards*, vol. 16 of 22, general editors Perry Miller, John E. Smith, Harry S. Stout (New Haven, CT: Yale University Press, 1957), 383.

17. Jonathan Edwards, *Personal Narrative*, in *Jonathan Edwards: Representative Selections*, ed. Clarence H. Faust and Thomas H. Johnson (New York: American Book Company, 1935), para. 22, 12.

18. Jonathan Edwards, *A Treatise concerning Religious Affections* (Worcester, MA: Isaiah Thomas, 1808), 410, 328.

19. Jonathan Edwards, *Personal Narrative*, para. 33, 12.

20. William J. Scheick, *Design in Puritan American Literature* (Lexington: University Press of Kentucky, 1992), 118, 119.

21. See John Corrigan, *The Hidden Balance: Religion and the Social Theories of Charles Chauncy and Jonathan Mayhew* (New York: Cambridge University Press, 1987).

22. John Corrigan, "Meaninglessness," in freq.uenci.es: *a collaborative genealogy of spirituality*, Nov. 14, 2011, http://freq.uenci.es/2011/11/14/meaninglessness/, accessed April 22, 2013.

23. William Carlos Williams, *In the American Grain* (Norfolk, CT: New Directions, 1925), 65; D. H. Lawrence, *Studies in Classic American Literature* (New York: Viking, 1923), 3.

24. John Greenleaf Whittier, "To Oliver Wendell Holmes" (1892), in The Project Gutenberg EBook of *The Works of Whittier*, vol. 4 of 7, www.gutenberg.org/files/9586/9586-h/9586-h.htm, accessed Aug. 8, 2012.

25. *The Emptiness and Vanity of a Life Spent in the Pursuit of Worldly Profit, Ease, or Pleasure* (Philadelphia: Henry Miller, 1767). A copy of the tract has "Jonathan Kolb" written

by hand below the title. *The Interesting Narrative of the Life of Olaudah Equiano* (London, 1794), 263; "The Emptiness of Human Glory," *New York Evangelist* 22 (1851), 92; "Emptiness of Worldly Fame," *Friends' Review* 5 (1852), 767; Lorenzo Dow and Peggy Dow, *History of Cosmopolite: Or the Writings of Rev. Lorenzo Dow* (Cincinnati: Applegate, 1864), 684.

26. Robert Richardson, *Memoirs of Alexander Campbell* (Cincinnati: Standard, 1980), 1:379; Charles Hodge, *Conference Papers; or, Analyses of Discourses, Doctrinal and Practical* (New York: Scribner's, 1879), 190; Francis Asbury, *The Journal of the Rev. Francis Asbury*, 3 vols. (New York: N. Bangs and T. Mason, 1821), 1:101. The term *kenosis* is derived from κενός.

27. "The New Unitarian Church," *New York Evangelist* 27 (1856), 2; Sylvester Bliss, *Memoirs of William Miller* (Boston: Joshua V. Himes, 1853), 284.

28. Sister Saint Francis Xavier, "Letter from Sister St. Francis Xavier, December 4, 1843," in *The Life and Letters of Sister St. Francis Xavier (Irma LeFer de la Motte) of the Sisters of Providence of St. Mary-in-the-Woods, Indiana* (St. Louis: Herder Books, 1917), 197–98; Sarah Morey Underwood Hunt, "The Diary of Sarah Morey Underwood Hunt, January, 1849," in *Journal of the Life and Religious Labors of Sarah Hunt* (Philadelphia: Friend's Book Association, 1892), 45–46; Elizabeth Emma Sullivan Stuart, "Letter from Elizabeth Emma Sullivan Stuart to William Chapman Baker April 4, 1853," in *Stuart Letters of Robert and Elizabeth Sullivan Stuart and Their Children, 1819–1864* (New York: Privately published, 1861), 505–6; Rev. J. S. Buckminster, *Sermons* (Boston: John Eliot, 1814), 189.

29. "Henry James on Creation," *Christian Examiner* 75 (1863), 217; Henry Alline, *Henry Alline: Selected Writings*, ed. George A. Rawlyk (Mahwah, NJ: Paulist Press, 1987), 78. Alline was a preacher whose influence was strong in Nova Scotia and New England. "The Orthodox Doctrine of Everlasting Punishment," *Christian Inquirer*, April 6, 1861, 1; Eliza Paul Gurney Kirkbride, "Diary of Eliza Paul Gurney, January, 1850," in *Memoir and Correspondence of Eliza P. Gurney*, ed. Richard F. Mott (Philadelphia: J. P. Lippincott, 1884), 191.

30. Lyman Beecher, *Autobiography, Correspondence, etc., of Lyman Beecher, D. D.*, ed. Charles Beecher, 2 vols. (New York: Harper, 1865), 1:300. See also 2:60. Mary Maclane, *The Story of Mary Maclane* (Chicago: H. S. Stone, 1902), 25, 222. Maclane fantasized a union with the Devil. Anne Charlotte Lynch Botta, "Letter Anne Lynch Botta to Andrew Dickson White," Dec. 26, 1888, in *Memoirs of Anne C. L. Botta Written by Her Friends*, ed. Vincenzo Botta (New York: Selwin Tate, 1893), 293–94; Lucy Larcom, *Lucy Larcom: Life, Letters, and Diary* (Boston: Houghton Mifflin, 1894), 116–17; Abigail Abott Bailey, *Memoirs of Mrs. Abigail Bailey* (Boston: Samuel T. Armstrong, 1815), 11–12; Elizabeth Sullivan Stuart, "Letter from Elizabeth Emma Stuart to Kate Stuart Baker," in *Stuart Letters of Robert and Elizabeth Sullivan Stuart and Their Children, 1819–1864* (New York: Privately published, 1964), 1:267.

31. Ellen G. White, *God's Amazing Grace* (N.p.: Review and Herald, 1973), 230; Roy F. Baumeister, *Escaping the Self: Alcoholism, Spirituality, Masochism, and Other Flights from the Burden of Selfhood* (New York: Basic Books, 1991); Sacvan Bercovitch, *The Puritan Origins of the American Self* (New Haven, CT: Yale University Press, 1975), 19, 22–23. On the "paradox of the self" in early American Protestantism, see Rodger M. Payne, *The Self and the Sacred: Conversion and Autobiography in Early American Protestantism* (Knoxville: University of Tennessee Press, 1997).

32. Isabella Marshall Graham, "Letter from Isabella Marshall Graham, July, 1797," in *The Unpublished Letters and Correspondence of Mrs. Isabella Graham* (New York: John S. Taylor, 1838), 217; Hannah Hobbie, "Diary of Hannah Hobbie, 1830," in *Memoir of Hannah Hobbie, or Christian Activity, and Triumph in Suffering*, by Rev. Robert G. Armstrong (New

York: American Tract Society, 1837), 221; Mary Coombs Greenleaf, "Letter from Mary Coombs Greenleaf, 1834," in *Life and Letters of Miss Mary C. Greenleaf, Missionary to the Chickasaw Indians* (Boston: Massachusetts Sabbath School Society, 1838), 107; Catharine Beecher, "Letter to Dr. Beecher, New Year, 1823," in Beecher, *Autobiography*, 1:502.

33. "Self-Emptiness," *Friends' Review* 17 (1864), 452; Joseph Lathrop, *Sermons on Various Subjects* (Worcester, MA: Isaiah Thomas, 1809), 384; E. Brooks Holifield, *Theology in America: Christian Thought from the Age of the Puritans to the Civil War* (New Haven, CT: Yale University Press, 2003), 452–66; "Thoughts for the Thoughtful," *Zion's Herald*, May 10, 1893, 150.

34. "A Complaint Not to Be Complained Of," *New York Evangelist*, March 3, 1881, 4; "A Baptism of Love," *Christian Advocate and Journal*, July 6, 1845, 193; Philip Schaff, *History of the Apostolic Church*, trans. Edward D. Yeomans (New York: C. Scribner, 1859), 183; Deborah H. Cushing Porter, "Diary of Deborah H. Porter, April, 1838," in *Memoir of Mrs. Deborah H. Porter*, by Anne T. Drinkwater (Portland, ME; Sanborn and Carter, 1848), 78; "Mrs. Sarah Pierpont Edwards: Narrative of Personal Experience," *Circular*, July 4, 1870, 126. Her account was included in Sereno Dwight, *The Works of President Edwards: With a Memoir of His Life* (New York: G. & C. & H. Carvill, 1830), 1:171–86.

35. Beecher, *Autobiography*, 2:60; Thomas Smith, "Letter Boston, Jan 30 1726–7," in *Journals of the Rev. Thomas Smith, and the Rev. Samuel Deane: Pastors of the Church in Portland* (Portland, ME: Joseph Bailey, 1849), 9; Mother Theodore Guerin, "Letter from Mother Theodore Guerin to Augustine Martin, October 19, 1841," in *Journals and Letters of Mother Theodore Guerin*, ed. Sister Mary Theodosia Mug (Saint-Mary-of-the-Woods, IN: Providence Press, 1937), 77; "Extracts from the Memoirs of Stanley Pumphrey," *Friends' Review*, Feb. 2, 1888, 423; Angelina Emily Grimke Weld, "Letter from Angelina Emily Grimke Weld to Sarah Moore Grimke, August 1, 1836," in *The Grimke Sisters: Sarah and Angelina Grimke, the First American Women Advocates of Abolition and Women's Rights*, ed. Catherine H. Birney (Boston: Lee and Shepard, 1885), 147.

36. Charles G. Finney, *Lectures on Revivals of Religion* (New York: Fleming H. Revell, 1868), 115; Timothy Dwight, *Sermons* (Boston: Hezekiah Howe and Durrie and Peck, 1828), 2:233; Augustus Hopkins Strong, *American Poets and Their Theology* (Philadelphia: Griffith and Rowland, 1916), 223; "A Real Religion," *Independent . . . Devoted to the Consideration of Politics, Social and Economic Tendencies*, July 15, 1893, 11. The "depth of need" being "beyond words" is typically articulated in "Selections from the Writings of John Barclay," *Friends' Intelligencer*, Feb. 23, 1867, 801; "This Sunday School. Second Quarter. Lesson VI," *Christian Advocate*, April 27, 1899, 674.

37. Leigh Eric Schmidt, "The Making of Modern 'Mysticism,'" *Journal of the American Academy of Religion* 71 (2003), 294; Catherine L. Albanese, *A Republic of Mind and Spirit: A Cultural History of American Metaphysical Religion* (New Haven, CT: Yale University Press, 2007), 11, 12.

38. Many Protestants converted to Catholicism in the nineteenth century. Annual conversions to Catholicism peaked in 1960 at 146,000. See Jay P. Dolan, *The American Catholic Experience* (Garden City, NY: Doubleday, 1985), 391.

39. Jenny Franchot, *Roads to Rome: The Antebellum Protestant Encounter with Catholicism* (Berkeley: University of California Press, 1994), 281; Robert A. Orsi, *Thank You, St. Jude: Women's Devotion to the Patron Saint of Hopeless Causes* (New Haven, CT: Yale University Press, 1996), 151 ("pain purged" and "nurses were encouraged"); Robert A. Orsi, *Between Heaven and Earth: The Religious Worlds People Make and the Scholars Who Study Them* (Princeton, NJ: Princeton University Press, 2005), 44 ("thus emptied").

40. *Isaac T. Hecker: The Diary: Romantic Religion in Ante-Bellum America*, ed. John

Farina (Mahwah, NJ: Paulist Press, 1988), 305, 304, 308, 161; Orestes Augustus Brownson, *The Convert: or, Leaves from My Experience* (New York: D and J Sadlier, 1889), 78.

41. Amanda Porterfield, *The Transformation of American Religion: The Story of a Late-Twentieth-Century Awakening* (New York: Oxford University Press, 2001), 64; Upham, *Life of Catherine Adorna*; Dougan Clark, *The Offices of the Holy Spirit*, 1st American ed. (Philadelphia: Henry Longstreth, 1880), 45.

42. Dorothy Day, *The Long Loneliness: The Autobiography of a Legendary Catholic Social Activist* (New York: Harper and Row, 1952), 20; Daniel Berrigan, *The Dark Night of Resistance* (Garden City, NY: Doubleday, 1971); Richard Gray, *A History of American Literature*, 2nd ed. (New York: Wiley Blackwell, 2012), 594; Sylvia Plath, "Tulips," in *Ariel: The Restored Edition* (New York: Harper Perennial, 2004), 18, 19; Luis Montoya and Ricardo Archuleta, "La Despedida de la Virgen (Farewell to the Virgin)," in "Music and Culture of the Northern Rio Grande: The Juan B. Rael Collection," Library of Congress, *American Memory*, http://memory.loc.gov/cgi-bin/query/r?ammem/raelbib:@1(La+Despedida+de+la+Virgen++Farewell+to+the+Virgin++[textual+transcription]), accessed May 11, 2014.

43. CBN TV, www.cbn.com/media/player/index.aspx?s=/vod/BIO_062509_WS, accessed May 11, 2014.

44. Quoted in David Edwin Harrell Jr., *Pat Robertson* (San Francisco: Harper and Row, 1987), 30.

Chapter 2

Epigraph: Paul Zweig, "Against Emptiness," in *Against Emptiness* (New York: Harper and Row, 1971), 35.

1. Jonathan H. Turner, *Face to Face: Toward a Sociological Theory of Interpersonal Behavior* (Palo Alto: Stanford University Press, 2002), 42–48; and "Dramaturgical and Cultural Theorizing on Emotions," chap. 2 in *The Sociology of Emotions*, by Turner and Jan E. Stets (Cambridge: Cambridge University Press, 2005), 26–68.

2. Birgitt Röttger-Rössler, "Gravestones for Butterflies: Social Feeling Rules and Individual Experiences of Loss," in *Emotions as Bio-cultural Processes*, ed. Birgitt Röttger-Rössler and Hans Jürgen Markowitsch (New York: Springer, 2009), 176; John Leavitt, "Meaning and Feeling in the Anthropology of Emotions," *American Ethnologist* 23 (1996), 526, 527. "This would involve identifying components of emotionally marked action, locating situations in which these recur, and identifying feeling-tones typically associated with these situations" (527). See also Leavitt, "Structure et émotion dans un rite kumaoni, Himalaya central," *Culture* 4 (1984), 9–31; Roy A. Rappaport, "The Sacred in Human Evolution," *Annual Review of Ecology and Systematics* 2 (1971), 23–44; William R. Reddy, *The Navigation of Feeling: A Framework for the History of Emotions* (New York: Cambridge University Press, 2001). The strand of scholarly investigation of the body from Merleau-Ponty through George Lakoff and Mark Johnson, the authors of *The Embodied Mind*, and recent research in Arthur Glenberg's Laboratory for Embodied Cognition at the University of Wisconsin has developed a framework for appreciating how "language understanding is directly grounded in bodily states, that is, that language understanding requires the appropriate bodily states to derive meaning from the words." Arthur M. Glenberg, David Havas, Raymond Becker, and Mike Rinck, "Grounding Language in Bodily States: The Case for Emotion," in *The Grounding of Cognition: The Role of Perception and Action in Memory, Language, and Thinking*, ed. R. Zwaan and D. Pecher (New York: Cambridge University Press, 2005), 126. Elsewhere Glenberg and co-workers note that "emotional systems contribute to language comprehension much as they do in social interaction. . . . Emotion simulation affects comprehension processes beyond initial

lexical access." "Emotion Simulation during Language Comprehension," *Psychonomic Bulletin and Review* 14 (2007), 4360. Maurice Merleau-Ponty, *Phenomenology of Perception*, trans. Donald A. Landes (New York: Routledge, 2012), originally published as *Phénoménologie de la perception* (Paris: Gallimard, 1945); George Lakoff and Mark Johnson, *Philosophy in the Flesh: The Embodied Mind and Its Challenge to Western Thought* (New York: Basic, 1999); Franceso J. Varela, Evan T. Thompson, and Eleanor Rosch, *The Embodied Mind: Cognitive Science and Human Experience* (Cambridge, MA: MIT Press, 1992).

3. Heather Wood, "Space and Gender in the *Antigone*," *Critical Sense* (2001), 87–120; Sydney Whiting, *Memoirs of a Stomach* (London: W. E. Painter, 1850); Bernard Moncriff, *The Philosophy of the Stomach* (London: Longman, Brown, Green, and Longmans, 1855); Constantine Hering, *New Provings of the Following Remedies: Cistus Canadensis* (Philadelphia: Tafel, 1866), 50; Bernhard Baehr, *The Science of Therapeutics, According to the Principles of Homeopathy*, trans Charles J. Hempel (New York: Boericke and Tafel, 1872), 606; Joseph Laurie, *Elements of Homeopathic Practice of Physic* (Philadelphia; Rademacher and Sheek, 1853), 596; Samuel Hahnemann, *Treatise on the Effects of Coffee* (Louisville: Bradley and Gilbert, 1875), 19.

4. "Soul Starvation," *Christian Observer*, Feb. 27, 1907, 5.

5. Theodore L. Cuyler, "The Next Revival," *Christian Advocate*, Jan. 21, 1904, 96; "The Seed-Time and Harvest," *Littel's Living Age*, Jan. 28, 1871, 275.

6. Henry Ward Beecher, "Plymouth Pulpit: The Realm of Faith," *Christian Union*, Nov. 5, 1879, 368.

7. William James, "What Is an Emotion?," *Mind* 9 (1884), 188–205; Jonathan Edwards, "Miscellany 854," in *The Miscellanies: Entry Nos. 833–1152*, ed. Amy Pantinga Pauw (New Haven, CT: Yale University Press, 2002), 81. Pauw cited Thomas Case's *The Morning Exercise Methodized* (London, 1660), 360, on 82n6. Edwards, *Treatise concerning the Religious Affections* (Boston: S. Kneeland and T. Green, 1745), 175. It is doubtful that Beecher meant to argue for emotion in the same way as James, and he did not in his writings, whatever his intention. But his attraction to James's ideas was noticed by his biographer Lyman Abbott, who observed: "His experience accorded with and interprets practically the philosophy of Professor William James." *Henry Ward Beecher* (New York: Houghton Mifflin, 1904), 395–96.

8. Orestes Brownson, quoted in "Mr. Brownson's Notion of Fourierist Doctrine," *Phalanx: Organ of the Doctrine of Association*, July 13, 1844, 1–2.

9. John Calvin, *Institutes of the Christian Religion*, 2 vols., ed. John T. McNeill, trans. Ford Lewis Battles (Philadelphia: Westminster, 1960), 2:1242, 1241; Theodore Dwight Bozeman, *The Precisionist Strain: Disciplinary Religion and Antinomian Backlash in Puritanism to 1638* (Chapel Hill: University of North Carolina Press, 2004), 118; Raymond A. Mentzer, "Fasting, Piety, and Political Anxiety among French Reformed Protestants," *Church History* 76 (2007), 330–62. See also Patrick Collinson, *The Religion of Protestants: The Church in English Society, 1559–1625* (Oxford: Oxford University Press, 1982), 260; Horton Davies, *Worship and Theology in England*, 3 vols. (Grand Rapids, MI: Eerdmans, 1996), vol. 1, pt. 1:260, 268, 288–89, 441; pt. 2:126–27, 238, 247–49. Approximately one in five Protestants reported fasting regularly in 2011, and over 50 percent of Catholics reported doing so. "Asian Americans: A Mosaic of Faiths," *Pew Forum on Religion*, www.pewforum.org/Asian-Americans-A-Mosaic-of-Faiths-religious-practices.aspx, accessed Oct. 10, 2012. The popularity of the "Daniel fast" among Protestants in the early twenty-first century is reflected in the bestselling *The Daniel Fast: Feed Your Soul, Strengthen Your Spirit, and Renew Your Body*, a manual for a twenty-one-day fast by "Christian life coach"

Susan Gregory (Carol Stream, IL: Tyndale Momentum, 2010); and John Piper, *A Hunger for God: Desiring God through Fasting and Prayer* (Wheaton, IL: Crossway Books, 1997).

10. Josiah Gilbert Holland, *Lessons in Life* (New York: C. Scribner, 1861), 19; Julius H. Rubin, *Religious Melancholy and Protestant Experience in America* (New York: Oxford University Press, 1994), 109, 102–8; Jesse Lee, *A Short History of the Methodists* (Baltimore: Magill and Clime, 1810), 33, 187; "African American Layman John Stewart Begins Mission to Wyandott Indians in Ohio," in *The Methodist Experience in America*, ed. Russell Richey, Kenneth E. Rowe, and Jean Miller Schmidt (Nashville: Abingdon, 2000), 2:172–73; Candy Gunther Brown, "The Spiritual Pilgrimage of Rachel Stearns, 1834–1837: Reinterpreting Women's Religious and Social Experiences in the Methodist Revivals of Nineteenth-Century America," *Church History* 65 (1996), 584; Stephen J. Stein, *The Shaker Experience in America: A History of the United Society of Believers* (New Haven, CT: Yale University Press, 1992), 174–75; *The Book of Common Prayer . . . of the Protestant Episcopal Church* (New York: Protestant Episcopal Press, 1831), 32; *A Companion for the Festivals and Fasts of the Protestant Episcopal Church* (New York: Swords, Stanford, 1840), 148; Anthea D. Butler, "Observing the Lives of the Saints: Sanctification as Practice in the Church of God in Christ," in *Practicing Protestants: Histories of Christian Life in America, 1630–1965*, ed. Laurie F. Maffly-Kipp, Leigh E. Schmidt, and Mark Valeri (Baltimore: Johns Hopkins University Press, 2006), 162; Bill McCartney, *From Ashes to Glory* (Nashville: Thomas Nelson, 1995), 124, 2; Wilford Woodruff, *Wilford Woodruff's Journal*, vol. 1, *1833–1840* (Salt Lake City: Signature, 1991), 129–31; Joseph Smith, *History of the Church of Jesus Christ of Latter Day Saints*, with an introduction and notes by B. H. Roberts (Salt Lake City: Deseret News, 1902), 1:200; Elder Spencer Condie (Mormon General Authority), *General Conference Address*, 2002, Church of Jesus Christ of Latter-day Saints, www.lds.org/general-conference/2002/04/becoming-a-great-benefit-to-our-fellow-beings, accessed May 11, 2014. Protestant reformers in America such as John Harvey Kellogg, Bronson Alcott, Sylvester Graham, and Ellen Gould White recommended abstinence from certain foods and drinks and occasionally fasting, and their writings evidence their involvement in a broader pattern of American thinking about emptiness. Their proposals for fasts rarely had an explicitly religious tenor, however. I thank Christopher Blythe for his help in interpreting the practice of fasting among Mormons.

11. *The Golden Manual: Being a Guide to Catholic Devotion Public and Private* (New York: P. J. Kenedy, 1902), 30, 994. An earlier British version (London: Burns and Lambert, 1850) added a few more days (p. 3).Vernon Staley, *The Catholic Religion: A Manual of Instruction for Members of the Anglican Church*, 4th ed. (London: Mowbray, 1894), 231; "Life of Penance and Mortification: Excerpt from the Regula Sancti Michaelis (Constitution), Order of the Legion of St. Michael," sections 19, 30, 31, St. Michael's Call, www.saint-mike.org/library/rule/excerpts/penance_and_mortification.html, accessed May 11, 2014; Rev. William Dodd, *The Nature and Necessity of Fasting* (London: E. Dilly, 1756), 48.

12. Adalbert de Vogüé, "To Love Fasting: An Observance That Is Possible and Necessary Today," *American Benedictine Review* 35 (1984), 312; United States Conference of Catholic Bishops, "Penitential Practices for Today's Catholics," http://old.usccb.org/doctrine/penitential.shtml, accessed Oct. 21, 2013; and Our Lady of Divine Providence Catholic Church, www.oldpmiami.org/ip.asp?op=Catholictalk_Ash_Wednesday&lg=E&m=, accessed May 11, 2014; Caroline Walker Bynum, *Fragmentation and Redemption: Essays on Gender and the Human Body in Medieval Religion* (Cambridge, MA: MIT Press, 1991), 133; and Bynum, *Holy Feast and Holy Fast: The Religious Significance of Food to Medieval Women* (Berkeley: University of California Press, 1987). An Orthodox view is Alex-

ander Schmemann, *Great Lent: Journey to Pascha* (1969; Crestwood, NY: St. Vladimir's Seminary Press, 2001), 93–98. Kathleen M. Dugan, "Fasting for Life: The Place of Fasting in the Christian Tradition," *Journal of the American Academy of Religion* 63 (1995), 539–48; R. Marie Griffith, "Apostles of Abstinence: Fasting and Masculinity during the Progressive Era," *American Quarterly* 52 (2000), 614; Teresa Shaw, *The Burden of the Flesh: Fasting and Sexuality in Early Christianity* (Minneapolis: Fortress, 1998); "Sermon XCIX: The Proper Method of Religious Fasting," *American National Preacher* 5 (March 1831), 153; Piper, *Hunger for God*.

13. Edward Taylor, "The Reflexion," Fire and Ice: Puritan and Reformed Sermons, www.puritansermons.com/poetry/taylor15.htm, accessed May 11, 2014. The sexual imagery in the poem and the issue of gender are explored by John Clendenning in "Piety and Imagery in Edward Taylor's 'The Reflexion,'" *American Quarterly* 16 (1964), 203–10; Francis Asbury, *The Journals and Letters of Francis Asbury*, ed. Elmer C. Clark, J. Manning Potts, and Jacob S. Payton, 3 vols. (Nashville: Abingdon, 1958), 3:433, 324, 415, 341–45; Jacques Derrida, *Memoirs of the Blind*, trans. Pascale-Anne Brault and Michael Naas (Chicago: University of Chicago Press, 1993), 126, 127.

14. *The Pious Guide to Prayer and Devotion* (New York: Bernard Dornin, 1808), 232; "Female Habitual Self-Mutilators," *Acta Psychiatrica Scandinavica* 79 (1989), 283; J. R. Parkin and J. M. Eagles, "Bloodletting in Bulimia Nervosa," *British Journal of Psychiatry* 162 (1993), 246–48; E. David Klonsky, "What Is Emptiness? Clarifying the 7th Criterion for Borderline Personality Disorder," *Journal of Personality Disorders* 22 (2008), 418–26; Greta Olson, "The Monster Within: Demonic Images of Food, Bodies, and the Desire to Eat in Recent American Literature on Eating Disorders," in *The EmBodyment of American Culture*, ed. Heinz Tschachler, Maureen Devine, and Michael Draxlbauer (Münster: Lit Verlag, 2003), 115.

15. Jimmy Yu, *Sanctity and Self-Inflicted Violence in Chinese Religions, 1500–1700* (New York: Oxford University Press, 2012); See also an early scholarly notice of Chinese "blood-letting as a religious rite" in *Medicine, Magic, and Religion: The Fitzpatrick Lectures Delivered before the Royal College of Physicians of London, 1915–1916*, ed. W. H. R. Rivers and G. Elliot Smith (New York: Harcourt, Brace, 1927), 98.

16. Angela Montford, *Health, Sickness, Medicine, and the Friars in the Thirteenth and Fourteenth Centuries* (Aldershot, England: Ashgate, 2004), 234; J. Codell Carter, *The Decline of Traditional Bloodletting and the Collapse of Traditional Medicine* (New Brunswick, NJ: Transaction, 2012), 43–44; M. K. K. Yearl, "Medieval Monastic Customaries on Minuti and Infirmi," in *The Medieval Hospital and Medical Practice*, ed. Barbara S. Bowers (Aldershot, England: Ashgate, 2007), 178, 176.

17. Richard Kieckhefer, *Unquiet Souls: Fourteenth-Century Religious Saints and Their Religious Milieu* (Chicago: University of Chicago Press, 1984), 89–121; Caroline Walker Bynum has finely detailed the blood piety associated with the Passion of Jesus and the Eucharist in early modern Germany, but does not address the bleeding of Christians, in *Wonderful Blood: Theology and Practice in Late Medieval Northern Germany and Beyond* (Philadelphia: University of Pennsylvania Press, 2007); and she offers additional insights in *Fragmentation and Redemption: Essays on Gender and the Human Body in Medieval Religion* (New York: Zone Books, 1992), 79–239. Elspeth von Oye and Ita von Hohenfels quoted in David F. Tinsley, "The Spirituality of Suffering in the Revelations of Elspeth von Oye," *Mystics Quarterly* 21 (1995), 133–34, 132; see also Tinsley's translation: http://webspace.pugetsound.edu/facultypages/tinsley/Courses/Eval2010/ItaEngl.pdf, accessed May, 11, 2014.

The religious studies scholar Robert Orsi, like Kieckhefer, Bynum, and historians who have studied medieval piety, has stressed the centrality of pain to Catholic thinking about holiness. Orsi, commenting on twentieth-century American Catholicism, notes that for Catholics, "pain purged and disciplined the ego, stripping it of pride and self-love; it disclosed the emptiness of the world." That understanding resonates with my own, although I would stress that personal emptiness for Catholics, beyond the absented pride and self-love, is a felt emotional state, and one that is highly prized even as it is lamented. Pain, as it annihilates language and "obliterates all psychological content," according to Elaine Scarry, *The Body in Pain: The Making and Unmaking of the World* (New York: Oxford University Press, 1985), 34, 4–5, erases self, but at the same time it condenses the self into a "self in pain." Robert Prince, "The Self in Pain: The Paradox of Memory. The Paradox of Testimony," *American Journal of Psychoanalysis* 69 (2009), 279–90. Pain as such is conceptualized as a means of cultivation of a feeling of emptiness. From that perspective, the "wounded" about whom Orsi writes, such as the cripples who are "emptied of all but their holiness and innocence," are emblematic, for observers, of a kind of holy emptiness; whether the wounded themselves always feel holy emptiness is another question. Robert A. Orsi, *Between Heaven and Earth: The Religious Worlds People Make and the Scholars Who Study Them* (Princeton, NJ: Princeton University Press, 2005), 44; and Orsi, *Thank You, St. Jude: Women's Devotion to the Patron Saint of Hopeless Causes* (New Haven, CT: Yale University Press, 1996), 151.

18. Henry Suso, *The Life of Blessed Henry Suso by Himself* (London: Burns, Lambert, and Oates, 1865), 21, 58, 78. One branch of Christianity in which emptiness has been highly visible is Orthodoxy. With a comparatively greater emphasis on *apophasis* (denial) than *kataphasis* (affirmation) Orthodoxy has stressed the necessity of emptying the self. More precisely, and in keeping with the richer meaning of the term, Orthodox practice more commonly defines the self by saying what it is not. Rather than filling the mind with words and images, apophatic practice empties it, defining self through differentiation. Because of scholarship that previously has analyzed this aspect of Orthodoxy, there is less mention of Orthodoxy in what follows. Orthodoxy's stressing of the importance of emptiness resonates with what I have described with regard to other kinds of Christianity in America.

19. Paula Kane, "'She offered herself up': The Victim Soul and Victim Spirituality in Catholicism," *Church History* 71 (2002), 80–119.

20. Paula Fredriksen, ed., *On the Passion of the Christ: Exploring the Issues Raised by the Controversial Movie* (Berkeley: University of California Press, 2006), xix; Martha Sawyer Allen, "'Passion of the Christ' Rouses Faithful, Worries Others," *Minneapolis–St. Paul Star Tribune*, Feb. 14, 2004.

21. David Carrasco characterizes the letting of one's own blood among Aztecs as part of a "sacred exchange with the gods." "Identity and Archaeology: David Carrasco," in *Conversations with Ian Stavans*, by Ian Stavans (Tucson: University of Arizona Press, 2005), 42. Rivers and Smith, *Medicine, Magic, and Religion*, 99; John M. Kloos Jr., A Sense of Deity: The Republican Spirituality of Dr. Benjamin Rush, Chicago Studies in the History of American Religion 10 (Brooklyn, NY: Carlson, 1991); Heinrich Stern, *Theory and Practice of Bloodletting* (New York: Rebman, 1915), 96; Susan E. Lederer, *Flesh and Blood: Organ Transplantation and Blood Transfusion in Twentieth-Century America* (New York: Oxford, 2008), 34.

22. Harry S. Stout, *Upon the Altar of the Nation: A Moral History of the Civil War* (New York: Viking, 2006), quotes on 405, 72, 454, 82–83, xxi; see also 249–50; Drew Gilpin Faust, *This Republic of Suffering: Death and the American Civil War* (New York: Random House, 2009), 189–91; Henry B. Smith, "Report to the Evangelical Alliance," *American Presbyterian and Theological Review* 5 (Oct. 1867), 560.

23. Donald G. Mathews, "The Southern Rite of Human Sacrifice," *Journal of Southern Religion* 3 (2000), n.p., http://jsr.fsu.edu/mathews.htm, accessed May 5, 2013; Kenneth Burke, *A Grammar of Motives* (Berkeley: University of California Press, 1945), 405–7; Rene Girard, *The Scapegoat* (Baltimore: Johns Hopkins University Press, 1989); Orlando Patterson, *Rituals of Blood: Consequences of Slavery in Two American Centuries* (New York: Basic Civitas, 1998), 197. Mathews does not believe that identification with the victim played a role in the lynching of blacks but that it eventually made its way into southern thinking about the process. Mathews believes that southerners initially "could not see that they were party to a ritual of human sacrifice in which the shedding of blood restores order, resolves violence, and fulfills the requirements of 'justice.' They identified not with the victim of their violence but with the Law that demanded and therefore justified punishment; it was in the very logic of the predominant white Christian understanding of the Universe." Later, as part of the decline of lynching, things began to change:

> That African Americans could see lynching as a sacrificial act in which they identified with the victim meant that existentially at least they understood an alternative view to the orthodox (white) emphasis on penal sacrifice. A few whites could begin to see that Christ, too, had been lynched and to challenge both theology (implicitly) and white conceptions of justice (explicitly). . . . Because the myth of God's just vengeance permitted whites' obsession with punishment to rule their relations with blacks there was no restriction within the myth to the racism that clouded their vision. E. T. Wellford, however, had sensed that atonement demanded empathy with sacrificial victims so that there might be no more "victims"; but his insight remained hidden from most Southern whites. They could not see, as black Christians did, that in a sacrifice celebrated in such dramatic and public fashion, the Christ had become black. Mathews, "Southern Rite of Human Sacrifice"

24. James P. Morris, "An American First: Blood Transfusion in New Orleans in the 1850s," *Louisiana History* 16 (1975), 341–60. Morris traces the experiment in New Orleans to French influences (333–44).

25. Henry Clay Trumbull, *The Blood Covenant: A Primitive Rite and Its Bearing on Scripture* (Philadelphia: John D. Wattles, 1898), 287, 116; Frederik A. Fernald, "Science and 'Christian Science,'" *Popular Science*, April 1889, 808; *HIS* 30 (1969), 41; Father Divine, *New Day*, June 2, 1938, 43, 57, quoted in R. Marie Griffith, *Born Again Bodies: Flesh and Spirit in American Christianity* (Berkeley: University of California Press, 2004), 150.

26. Philip Yancey and Paul Brand, *In His Image* (Grand Rapids: Zondervan, 2008), chap. 8, "Transfusion," n.p.; Billy Graham, *Hope for a Troubled Heart* (Nashville: Thomas Nelson, 1991), 52; Walter Farquhar Hook, *The Cross of Christ; or, Meditations on the Death and Passion of our Blessed Lord and Savior* (New York: D. Appleton, 1845), 109 (quote), 96; "Notes," *New York Observer*, July 11, 1895, 43.

27. Bishop E. R. Hendrix, The Chief Asset of Christianity," *Herald of Gospel Liberty*, Aug. 27, 1903, 559; "Outlines of the Doctrine of the Mystical Life," *American Catholic Quarterly Review*, Oct. 1914, 562; "The HOLY GHOST—the Lifeblood of the Mystical Body of Christ" is in Alfred G. Mortimer, *Catholic Faith and Practice: A Manual of Theology* (New

York: Longmans, 1898), lii, 376; Derick Mack Virgil, *The Holy Ghost: He Is the Blood of Jesus* (Bloomington, IN: AuthorHouse, 2011), 24; M. R. DeHaan, *The Chemistry of the Blood* (Grand Rapids: Zondervan, 1943), 39–40.

28. Michael P. Carroll, *The Penitente Brotherhood: Patriarchy and Hispano-Catholicism in New Mexico* (Baltimore: Johns Hopkins University Press, 2002), 82, 83; Jane T. Merritt, "Dreaming of the Savior's Blood: Moravians and the Indian Great Awakening in Pennsylvania," *William and Mary Quarterly* 54 (1997), 742, 744. On the side hole, see also Rachel Wheeler, *To Live upon Hope: Mohicans and Missionaries in the Eighteenth-Century Northeast* (Ithaca, NY: Cornell University Press, 2013). As Emile Durkheim argued and Gilbert Lewis restated in a study of ritual bloodletting in New Guinea, "ritual is not exactly like language; it is not exactly like communication by means of a code nor can it be decoded like one. The complexity and uncertainty about a ritual's meaning . . . may sometimes sustain and preserve ritual performance." Emile Durkheim, *The Elementary Forms of the Religious Life*, trans. Karen E. Fields (New York: Free Press, 1995), 389–91; Gilbert Lewis, *Day of Shining Red: An Essay on Understanding Ritual* (New York: Cambridge University Press, 1980), 8–9. We should bear in mind that the power of bloodletting, in the Moravian context and in others, has historical depth (much prior to Benjamin Rush), and not only with reference to a deep Catholic tradition of blood devotions. The mingling of bloodletting as a medical procedure with Moravian blood mysticism grounded in a devotion to the wounds of Jesus coalesced against a background of medical perspectives on phlebotomy itself. Bloodletting for centuries had been understood precisely as a practice of emptying the body. Bernard de Gordon's *De flebotomia* (1308) and late-thirteenth-century writings by Arnau de Vilanova had set the frame for such thinking, asserting that "the first and principal reason why phlebotomy is performed is that of evacuation" and that "it purges the whole body." That understanding remained strong into the late nineteenth century, with bloodletting typically allied therapeutically with purging brought on by emetics. Vomiting and bloodletting both evacuated the body. As purgation, bloodletting joined religious thinking to medical practice, resulting in rituals that both reenacted the Passion of Christ and emptied the body. That process served equally to cognize and cultivate the emotion of emptiness. Bernard de Gordon quoted in Pedro Gil-Sotres, "Derivation and Revulsion: The Theory and Practice of Medieval Phlebotomy," in *Practical Medicine from Salerno to the Black Death*, ed. Luis García-Ballester, Roger French, John Arrizabalaga, and Andrew Cunningham (New York: Cambridge University Press, 1994), 119. Examples of nineteenth-century medical lectures that associated purges leading to vomiting with bloodletting but also indicate the rapid decline of the practice of bloodletting are "Northern Medical Association of Philadelphia. Subject for Discussion: Bloodletting," *Medical and Surgical Reporter*, Dec. 17, 1859, 271–74; and Prof Dujardin-Beaumetz, "Original Lectures: Bloodletting," *Medical News*, Oct. 6, 1883, 365.

29. Saint Gertrude (the Great), *The Herald of Divine Love*, trans. Margaret Winkworth (Mahwah, NJ: Paulist Press, 1993), 126; Ann Willson, "Letter from Ann Willson, April 11, 1827," in *Familiar Letters of Ann Willson* (Philadelphia: William D. Parrish, 1850), 50–51; Julia Kristeva, *Powers of Horror: An Essay on Abjection* (New York: Columbia University Press, 1982), 101.

30. Michael B. Lewis, "Exploring the Positive and Negative Implications of Facial Feedback," *Emotion* 12 (2012), 852–59; "Botulinum Toxin Cosmetic Therapy Correlates with a More Positive Mood," *Journal of Cosmetic Dermatology* 8 (2009), 24–26; Ursula Hess, Arvid Kappas, Gregory J. McHugo, John T. Lanzetta, and Robert E. Kleck, "The Facilitative Effect of Facial Expression on the Self-Generation of Emotion," *International Journal of Psychophysiology* 12 (1992), 251–65; Chris L. Kleinke, Thomas R. Peterson, and

Thomas R. Rutledge, "Effects of Self-Generated Facial Expressions on Mood," *Journal of Personality and Social Psychology* 74 (1998), 272–79; Congregation of the Holy Cross, *The Rules of the Congregation* (Notre Dame, IN: Ave Maria Press, 1871), 30; Charles Darwin, *The Expression of Emotions in Man and Animals*, ed. Francis Darwin (1872; New York: New York University Press, 1989); James, "What Is an Emotion?," 188–205.

31. Schmemann, *Great Lent*, 104; *St. Vincent's Manual . . . and Devotional Exercises* (Baltimore: John Murphy, 1856), 30, 630, 300, 322; *The Ursuline Manual; or, A Collection of Prayers, Spiritual Exercises, etc., Interspersed with the Various Instructions Necessary for Forming Youth to the Practice of Solid Piety, Originally Arranged for the Young Ladies Educated at the Ursuline Convent, Cork*, rev. by John Power and approved by John Hughes (New York; E. Dunigan, 1857), 220, 334; *St. Joseph's Manual Containing Selection of Prayers and Public and Private Devotions with a Brief Exposition of the Catholic Religion* (Boston, Patrick Donahoe: 1853), 470; *Rule of St. Benedict*, chap. 6, "Of Silence," in *Benedict's Rule: A Translation and Commentary*, by Terrence G. Kardong, O.S.B. (Collegeville, MN: Liturgical Press, 1996), 119.

32. Lawrence S. Cunningham, *The Catholic Experience* (New York: Crossroads, 1985), 65, 73; John F. Teahan, "The Place of Silence in Thomas Merton's Life and Thought," *Journal of Religion* 61 (1981), 370.

33. Benjamin Harrison, *Speeches of Benjamin Harrison, Twenty-Third President of the United States: A Complete Collection of His Public Addresses from February, 1888, to February, 1892, Compiled by Charles Hedges* (New York: United States Book, 1892), 510; John A. Hostetler, *Amish Society* (Baltimore: Johns Hopkins University Press, 1993), 306; Bohdan Szuchewycz, "Silence in Ritual Communication," in *Silence: Interdisciplinary Perspectives*, ed. Adam Jaworski (Berlin: Mouton de Gruyter, 1997), 243; T. L. Harris, "The Problem of Worship in American Protestantism," *Journal of Religion* 4 (1924), 640.

34. Kieran Flanagan, "Liturgy, Ambiguity, and Silence: The Ritual Management of Real Absence," *British Journal of Sociology* 36 (1985), 214; Alan Davies, "Talking in Silence: Ministry in Quaker Meetings," in *Styles of Discourse*, ed. Nikolas Coupland (New York: Croom Helm, 1988), 118. Commenting on the Quaker meeting, Davies writes: "Speaking arises out of silence and is the means to the end of an even deeper silence" (118). Roger Lenaers, *Nebuchadnezzar's Dream or an End of the Medieval Catholic Church* (Piscataway, NJ: Gorgias Press, 2007), 232; "Prayer for Revivals," *Christian Advocate*, Sept. 18, 1879, 600; Robert Dilday, "Contemplative Worship Consistent with Baptist Principles," *Texas Standard: The Newsmagazine of Texas Baptists*, Sept. 15, 2012. The Foucauldian statement on the artificiality of a distinction between speech and silence: "There is no binary division to be made between what one says and what one does not say; we must try to determine the different ways of not saying such things, how those who can and those who cannot speak of them are distributed, which type of discourse is authorized, or which form of discretion is required in either case. There is not one but many silences, and they are an integral part of the strategies that underlie and permeate discourses." Michel Foucault, *The History of Sexuality*, trans. Robert Hurley (New York: Vintage, 1990), 1:27.

35. William Leonard, "Labor as Worship," *Shaker*, Aug. 1871, 58; Orestes Brownson, "Mr. Brownson's Notion of Fourierist Doctrine," *Phalanx*, July 13, 1844, 3; Robert Anthony Bruno, *Justified by Work: Identity and the Meaning of Faith in Chicago's Working-Class Churches* (Columbus: Ohio State University Press, 2008).

36. George Ovitt Jr., "The Cultural Context of Western Technology: Early Christian Attitudes Towards Manual Labor," *Technology and Culture* 27 (1986), 486, Saint Basil quoted on 490; Ovitt, *The Restoration of Perfection: Labor and Technology in Medieval Culture* (New Brunswick. NJ: Rutgers University Press, 1986), 106; Evagrius of Pontus

quoted by David E. Linge, "Leading the Life of Angels: Ascetic Practice and Reflection on the Writings of Evagrius of Pontius," *Journal of the American Academy of Religion* 68 (2000), 554; Lynn Townsend White Jr., *Medieval Religion and Technology: Collected Essays* (Berkeley: University of California Press, 1978), 320. White argues that for monks to pray in such manner was a matter of praising God, not asceticism; Jacques LeGoff stresses that monks viewed labor as penitential mortification of the flesh. *Time, Work, and Culture in the Middle Ages* (Chicago: University of Chicago Press, 1980), 280–81.

37. Max Weber, *The Protestant Ethic and the Spirit of Capitalism*, trans. Talcott Parsons (London: Unwin, 1930); Huldreich Zwingli, *Huldreich Zwinglis Werke: Erste vollständige Ausgabe*, ed. Melchior Schuler and Johannes Schulthess (Zurich, 1841), vol. 6, pt. 1, pp. 209, 269. R. H. Tawney, in *Religion and the Rise of Capitalism* (London: Murray, 1926), emphasized this aspect of Zwingli's thinking. I consulted a more recent publication: Tawney, *Religion and the Rise of Capitalism* (New York: Transaction, 1998), 115. Martin Luther, *Luther's Works*, ed. Helmut T. Lehmann and Jaroslav J. Pelikan (New Haven, CT: Yale University Press, 1955–86), 44:189; Stephen Innes, *Creating the Commonwealth: The Economic Culture of Puritan New England* (New York: Norton, 1995), 9; Perry Miller, *The New England Mind: From Colony to Province* (1953; Cambridge, MA: Harvard University Press, 1981), 42.

38. Thomas Carlyle quoted in Keith Thomas, ed., *The Oxford Book of Work* (Oxford: Oxford University Press, 1999), 113; Hamilton Wright Mabie, *Essays on Work and Culture* (New York: Dodd, Mead, 1898), 22; William Graham Sumner, *The Challenge of Facts and Other Essays*, ed. Albert G. Keller (New Haven, CT: Yale University Press, 1914), 352; Jacob Abbott, *Rollo at Work; or, the Way to Be Industrious* (Philadelphia: Hogan & Thompson, 1841), 125; Daniel T. Rogers, *The Work Ethic in Industrial America, 1850–1920* (Chicago: University of Chicago Press, 1978).

39. William M. Willett, "The Spirit of Christ in His Followers," *Methodist Magazine and Quarterly Review* 12 (1830), 382; *Farm and Garden*, May 9, 1895, 30; *The Reformed Presbyterian and Covenanter* (Pittsburgh: Bakewell and Marthens, 1875), 13:334; *The Pilgrim of Our Lady of Martyrs* 12 (1896), 63; Thomas Tiplady, *Social Christianity in the New Era* (New York: Fleming H. Revell, 1919), 56; "A Word of Encouragement," *Christian Observer*, Dec. 10, 1847, 197; "Estimates of Men," *Congregationalist*, April 12, 1894, 538; "The Grace of God in Providence," *Christian Observer*, Jan. 21, 1844, 97; *Eliot Anniversary, 1646–1896: City of Newton, Memorial Exercise* (Newton, MA: City Council, 1896), 76; Len Gaston Broughton, *The Revival of a Dead Church* (New York: Fleming H. Revell, 1900), 54; "Christian Unfaithfulness," *New York Evangelist*, Dec. 29, 1842, 1.

40. "A Modern Knight of Missions," *Congregationalist and Christian World*, Sept. 23, 1905, 411; "Laying Up for Yourselves Treasures upon Earth," *Christian Register and Boston Observer*, Dec. 12, 1839, 1; *Ohio Cultivator*, March 1, 1851, 72; "The Farmer's Index: Grass and Clover in Georgia," *Christian Index*, May 31, 1883, 14; "Do Your Own Fishing," *Peoples Advocate*, Dec. 1, 1883, 4; *Wisconsin Weekly Advocate*, Sept. 9, 1900, 8; "The Common People," *Washington Bee*, July 27, 1918, 4; "Heaviness through Manifold Temptations," *Christian Advocate*, June 18, 1903, 987; Robert Laird Collier, *Every-Day Subjects in Sunday Sermons* (Boston: N.p, 1872), 11; Menno Simons, *The Complete Works of Menno Simon* (Elkhart, IN, 1871), 304; Henry Ward Beecher, *Seven Lectures to Young Men* (Indianapolis: Thomas B. Cutler, 1844), 14.

41. *Christian Work Illustrated Family Newspaper* 66 (Jan. 5, 1899), 867; James B. Gilbert, *Work without Salvation: America's Intellectuals and Industrial Alienation, 1880–1910* (Baltimore: Johns Hopkins University Press, 1977); Martin Delany quoted in Jean Matthews, "Race, Sex, and Dimensions of Liberty in Antebellum America," *Journal of the Early*

Republic 6 (1986), 284; Edward Everett Hale, "XIV. Work and Labor," in *How They Lived in Hampton* (Boston: J. Stillman Smith, 1888), 232–49; "Editor's Table," *Appleton's Journal* 1 (1876), 477; "Views of the Labor Movement," *Catholic World* 10 (1870), 796; Major L. Wilson, "Paradox Lost: Order and Progress in Evangelical Thought of Mid-Nineteenth-Century America," *Church History* 44 (1975), 361–62. On the shift from independence and self-sufficiency in farming to a leading interest in calculation for profit in nineteenth-century America, see Herbert Applebaum, *The American Work Ethic and the Changing Work Force: An Historical Perspective* (Westport, CT: Greenwood Press, 1998), 64–72.

42. Richard J. Callahan Jr., *Work and Faith in the Kentucky Coal Fields: Subject to Dust* (Bloomington: Indiana University Press, 2009).

43. Elizabeth Cady Stanton, *The Woman's Bible*, pt. 2 (New York: European, 1898), 25–26.

44. Peter Simpson, *Vices, Virtues, and Consequences: Essays in Moral and Political Philosophy* (Washington, DC: Catholic University of America, 2001), 256; Mihaly Csikszentmihalyi, *Flow: The Psychology of Optimal Experience* (New York: Harper and Row, 1990); Csikszentmihalyi, *Creativity: Flow and the Psychology of Discovery and Invention* (New York: Harper Perennial, 1996), 1; John Geirland, "Go with the Flow," *Wired* 4 (Sept. 1996), www.wired.com/wired/archive/4.09/czik.html, accessed May, 11, 2014. The encyclical by Pope John Paul II "Of Human Work" (1981), expanding and revising Leo XIII's "Rerum Novarum" (1891), oriented Catholic thinking more clearly toward "uniting work with prayer." The Holy See, www.vatican.va/holy_father/john_paul_ii/encyclicals/documents/hf_jp-ii_enc_14091981_laborem-exercens_en.html, accessed May 11, 2014.

45. "A Poem for Today," *Plumbers, Gas, and Steamfitters Journal* 16 (1911), 38; *Rhode Island Schoolmaster* 5 (1859), 138; John LaBriola, *Christ-Centered Selling: A Scripturally Based Guide to Principled, Profitable Persuasion* (Mustang, OK: Tate, 2007); Danah Zohar and Ian Marshall, *Spiritual Capital: Wealth We Can Live By* (San Francisco: Berrett-Koehler, 2004); Diane Paddison, *Work, Love, Pray: Practical Wisdom for Young Professional Christian Women* (Grand Rapids: Zondervan, 2011); Thomas Moore, *A Life at Work: The Joy of Discovering What You Were Born to Do* (New York: Broadway Books, 2008); John Elster, "Self-Realization in Work and Politics," *Social Philosophy and Policy* 3 (1986), 97–126.

46. Horace Bushnell, "The Hunger of the Soul," *Wellman's Miscellany*, March 1, 1870, 84, 85, 86, 88.

47. Gary Taylor, "Gender, Hunger, Horror: The History and Significance of 'The Bloody Banquet,'" *Journal for Early Modern Cultural Studies* 1 (2001), 15; Sylvester Graham, *A Lecture to Young Men on Chastity* (Boston: Charles H. Peirce, 1848), 187, 46, 122. For a discussion of gender and gluttony, see Nina Corazzo, "The Social Construction of Sexual Difference: The Representation of Woman as the Deadly Sin Gluttony," *Semiotics* (1993), 445–64.

48. Noah Webster, *A Dictionary of the English Language* (New York, 1828); Joseph E. Worcester, *An Elementary Dictionary of the English Language* (Boston: Swan, Brewer, and Tileston, 1860), 77; *Catholic Telegraph*, Oct. 10, 1839, 346; "Lust," in *The Catholic Encyclopedia*, vol. 9, *Laprade-Mass Liturgy* (New York: Encyclopedia Press, 1913). William Whewell, expressing the typical belief about desire, stressed that "bodily desires, are sensual, carnal." *The Elements of Morality, Including Polity* (New York: Harper, 1856), 181. Presbyterian pastor Albert Barnes instructed the readers of his *Notes* on the non-Pauline epistles that when Peter wrote "abstain from fleshly lusts," he meant "such desires and passions as the carnal appetites prompt to." Early in the next century, an article on the New Testament intended for family reading explained simply that "lust is appetite run wild." Albert Barnes, *Notes, Explanatory and Practical, on the General Epistles of James, Peter,*

John and Jude (New York: Harper and Brothers, 1857), 164. Edwin F. Hallenbeck, D.D., "Through the New Testament," *New York Observer and Chronicle*, May 4, 1905, 576.

49. "The Contemplator, No. 5," *Philadelphia Repository and Weekly Register*, May 21, 1803, 164; Edward Meyrick Goulburn, *The Pursuit of Holiness* (New York: D. Appleton, 1870), 251, 255; "The Pericopes, or Selections of Gospels and Epistles," *Mercersburg Review*, April 1870, 291; Rev. George Shepard, "Sermon CCXXVI: The Evils and the Remedy of Covetousness," *American National Preacher*, June 1842, 222; A Lady, *The Young Lady's Mentor: A Guide to the Formation of Character* (Philadelphia: H. C. Peck and Theo Bliss, 1851), 118; "The Morals of Money," *Bankers' Magazine and Statistical Register*, June 1854, 962; J. Heinrich Arnold, *Discipleship: Living for Christ in the Daily Grind* (Farmington, PA: Plough, 1994), 56. On money, see also Rev. James M. Macdonald, "Sermon DCCIV: Christian Moderation," *American National Preacher*, March 1857, 62–63.

50. Jonathan Edwards, *The Works of Jonathan Edwards*, ed. Edward Hickman (Edinburgh: Banner of Truth, 1974), 438, 230; Edmund Morgan, "The Puritans and Sex," *New England Quarterly* 4 (1942), 592–93; John D'Emilio and Estelle B. Freedman, *Intimate Matters: A History of Sexuality in America* (New York: Harper and Row, 1988), 19; Billy Graham, *World Aflame* (New York: Doubleday, 1965), 20.

51. Charles G. Finney, *Lectures on Revivals of Religion*, 2nd ed. (New York: Leavitt, Lord, 1835), 39; Nancy F. Cott, "Passionlessness: An Interpretation of Victorian Sexual Ideology, 1790–1850," in *A Heritage of Her Own*, ed. Nancy F. Cott and Elizabeth H. Pleck (New York, Simon and Schuster, 1979); Barbara Welter, *Dimity Convictions: The American Woman in the Nineteenth Century* (Athens: Ohio University Press, 1976), 115; Michael Ditmore, "A Prophetess in Her Own Country: An Exegesis of Anne Hutchinson's 'Immediate Revelation,'" *William and Mary Quarterly*, third series, 57 (2000), 374.

52. "Religious Intelligence: The Brooklyn Revival," *Independent*, Nov. 18, 1875, 16; "Outlines of the Doctrine of the Mystical Life," *American Catholic Quarterly Review*, Jan. 1916, 83.

53. Jan Shipps, "From Satyr to Saint: American Perceptions of the Mormons, 1860–1960," in *Sojourner in the Promised Land: Forty Years among the Mormons*, by Shipps (Urbana: University of Illinois Press, 2000), 51–97; Sophia Peabody, cited in Larry J. Reynolds, "Hawthorne's Labors in Concord," in *The Cambridge Companion to Nathaniel Hawthorne*, ed. Richard H. Millington (New York: Cambridge University Press, 2004), 25–26; Alice Timmons Toomy, Eleanor C. Donnelly, and Katherine E. Conway, "The Woman Question among Catholics," *Catholic World* 57 (1893), 679; Amy D. Rogatis, "What Would Jesus Do? Sexuality and Salvation in Protestant Evangelical Sex Manuals, 1950s to the Present," *Church History* 74 (2005), 114; and Rogatis, "Born Again Is a Sexual Term": Demons, STDs, and God's Healing Sperm," *Journal of the American Academy of Religion* 77 (2009), 131; Terry Wier and Mark Carruth, *Holy Sex: God's Purpose and Plan for Our Sexuality* (New Kensington, PA: Whittaker House, 1999), 77. Recent historical scholarship has challenged readings of nineteenth-century female sexuality that downplay female desire. See, for example, Peter Laipson, "'Kiss without Shame, for She Desires It': Sexual Foreplay in American Medical Advice Literature, 1900–1925," *Journal of Social History* 29 (1996), 507–25.

54. Daniel K. Williams, "Sex and the Evangelicals: Gender Issues, the Sexual Revolution, and Abortion in the 1960s," in *American Evangelicals and the 1960s: Revisiting the "Backlash,"* ed. Axel Schaefer (Madison: University of Wisconsin Press, 2013); Tim LaHaye, *The Act of Marriage: The Beauty of Sexual Love* (1976; Grand Rapids: Zondervan, 2009), 302; Pastor Frantz Lamour, *Thank God for Sex* (Maitland, FL: Xulon Press, 2010), 42; A. Herbert Gray, *Men, Women, and God: A Discussion of Sex Questions from the*

Christian Point of View (Teddington, Middlesex: Echo Press, 2008), 22 (Gray's book was widely available in American Christian bookstores); Diane Roberts and Dr. Ted Roberts, *Sexy Christians: The Purpose, Power, and Passion of Biblical Intimacy* (Grand Rapids: Baker Books, 2010), 168; Ed Wheat and Gaye Wheat, *Intended for Pleasure: Sex Technique and Sexual Fulfillment in Christian Marriage* (Grand Rapids: Fleming H. Revell, 1977), 20; Adrian Thatcher, *God, Sex, and Gender: An Introduction* (Oxford: Blackwell, 2011), 112; Sheila Wray Gregoire, *The Good Girl's Guide to Great Sex: (And You Thought Bad Girls Had All the Fun)* (Grand Rapids: Zondervan, 2012), 167.

55. Gregoire, *Good Girl's Guide*, 167.

56. Richard H. Pratt, "The Advantages of Mingling Indians with Whites," from an extract of *Official Report of the Nineteenth Annual Conference of Charities and Correction* (1892), 46. The salient parts of the report are reprinted in *Americanizing the American Indians: Writings by the "Friends of the Indian," 1880–1900*, comp. Francis and Paul Prucha (Cambridge, MA: Harvard University Press, 1973), 260–71.

57. Saidiya V. Hartman, *Scenes of Subjection: Slavery and Self-Making in Nineteenth-Century America* (New York: Oxford, 1997), 21; Cortlandt Vann Rensselaer, *A Reply to George D. Armstrong, D.D. of Norfolk on Slaveholding and Colonization* (Philadelphia: Joseph M. Wilson, 1858), 5; Jon Butler, *Awash in a Sea of Faith: Christianizing the American People* (Cambridge, MA: Harvard University Press, 1990), 129–63; Charles L. Perdue, Thomas E. Barden, and Robert K. Phillips, *Weevils in the Wheat: Interviews with Virginia Ex-Slaves* (Charlottesville: University of Virginia Press, 1976), 268; Janet D. Cornelius, *Slave Missions and the Black Church in the Antebellum South* (Columbia: University of South Carolina Press, 1999), 116.

58. Father Placide Tempels quoted by Moya Deacon in "The Status of Father Tempels and Ethno-Philosophy in the Discourse of African Philosophy," in *Philosophy from Africa: A Text with Readings*, 2nd ed., ed. P. H. Coetzee and A. P. J. Roux (Cape Town: Oxford University Press Southern Africa, 2002), 103; Wallace D. Muhammad, "Self-Government in the New World," in *African American Religious History: A Documentary Witness*, 2nd ed., ed. Milton C. Sernett (Durham, NC: Duke University Press, 1999), 503–4.

59. Rev. George H. Hepworth, "Beyond the Horizon," *Rising Son*, June 24, 1904, 2.

60. "Self-Emptiness," *Friend's Review*, March 19, 1864, 452.

61. Jean Kilbourne, *Can't Buy Me Love: How Advertising Changes the Way We Think and Feel* (New York: Free Press, 2000), 258; Rev. Ike, "Curse Not the Rich" (Jan. 1976), in *Speaking with Sacred Fire: An Anthology of African American Sermons, 1750 to the Present*, ed. Martha J. Simmons and Frank A. Thomas (New York: Norton, 2010), 652.

Chapter 3

Epigraph: Robert Frost, "Desert Places," in *A Further Range: Book Six* (New York: Henry Holt, 1936), 44.

1. William James, *The Varieties of Religious Experience* (New York: Modern Library, 1902); James, *The Principles of Psychology* (New York: Henry Holt, 1890), 2:134–282; James, "The Spatial Quale," *Journal of Speculative Philosophy* 13 (1879), 68, 66–67; Brenda Jubin, "'The Spatial Quale': A Corrective to James's Radical Empiricism," *Journal of the History of Philosophy* 15 (1977), 213, 216; Martin J. Farrell, "Space Perception and William James's Metaphysical Presuppositions," *History of Psychology* 14 (2011), 171. Most scholars see James's thinking as a development from an approach that is vaguely intuitionist to one in which experience rather than inner states guides the theorizing. Brenda Jubin places particular emphasis on intuitionism in James's early writing about space, while

Martin J. Farrell emphasizes the development of James's spatial theories as a branch of his radical empiricism.

2. J. Frederic Dutton, "A Priori," *Unitarian Review*, May 1891, 6, 3.

3. Jonathan Edwards, *The Works of Jonathan Edwards*, vol. 6, *Scientific and Philosophical Writings*, ed. Wallace E. Anderson (New Haven, CT: Yale University Press, 1980), 203. For a discussion of how Edwards shifted his thinking about space, see Jasper Reid, "Jonathan Edwards on Space and God," *Journal of the History of Philosophy* 41 (2003), 385–403; James McCosh, *The Intuitions of the Mind Inductively Investigated* (New York: Robert Carter, 1866); Augustus Strong, *Systematic Theology: A Compendium and Commonplace*, 3 vols. (Philadelphia: American Baptist, 1907), 1:279; Charles Beecher, *Spiritual Manifestations* (Boston: Lee and Shepard, 1879), 96–97; E. Victor Bigelow, "Genesis of Spatial Sensation," *New Englander and Yale Review*, Sept. 1891, 244; Stephen Eyre Jarvis, *Rosmini, A Christian Philosopher*, 2nd ed. (Market Weighton, Yorkshire: St. Paul's Press, 1888), 37.

4. Jennie M. Burr, "The 'Sky Farm' Region," *Christian Union*, Oct. 5, 1882, 277; Benjamin Colman, *The Glory of God in the Firmament of His Power* (Boston: S. Kneeland and T. Green, 1743), 16; Mather Byles, *A Discourse on the Present Vileness of the Body* (Boston: S. Kneeland and T. Green, 1732), 2; Jonathan Brace, "Sermon DCXXXIII: This World Not Our Place of Rest," *American National Preacher*, Oct. 1854, 222–23.

5. John Locke, *Two Treatises of Government* (1689; London: Whitmore and Fenn, and C. Brown, 1821), 228–29 (I thank Peter Thuesen for suggesting this citation); Thomas J. J. Altizer, *Genesis and Apocalypse: A Theological Voyage toward Authentic Christianity* (Philadelphia: Westminster/John Knox, 1990), 98–99; Michel de Certeau, "Walking in the City," in *The Practice of Everyday Life*, trans. Stephen Rendall (Berkeley: University of California Press, 1984), chap. 7, 91–110; Rob Wilson, *American Sublime: The Genealogy of a Poetic Genre* (Madison: University of Wisconsin Press, 1991), 68.

6. Perry Miller, *Errand into the Wilderness* (New York: Harper and Row, 1956), preface, i; Douglas McKnight, *Schooling, The Puritan Imperative, and the Molding of an American National Identity: Education's "Errand into the Wilderness"* (Mahwah, NJ: Lawrence Erlbaum, 2003), 31; Thomas Brainerd, *The Life of John Brainerd* (Philadelphia: Presbyterian Publication Committee, 1865), 62.

7. Richard Slotkin, *Regeneration through Violence: The Mythology of the American Frontier, 1600–1860* (Middletown, CT: Wesleyan University Press, 1973), 38; William Bradford, *Of Plymouth Plantation, 1620–1647*, ed. Samuel Eliot Morison (New York: Knopf, 1952), 25.

8. Miller, *Errand into the Wilderness*; Edward Johnson, *The Wonder-Working Providence of Sion's Saviour in New England*, ed. J. Franklin Jameson (New York: Scribner's, 1910), 111, 43, 44, 88, 21; Cotton Mather, "Address of Council and Assembly, July 12, 1704," in *Collections of the Massachusetts Historical Society*, fifth series (Boston: The Society, 1879), 6:92; and Mather, *The Wonders of the Invisible World* (Boston: Benjamin Harris for Samuel Phillips, 1692), n.p.; Solomon Stoddard, *An Answer to Some Cases of Conscience respecting the Country* (Boston: B. Green, 1722), 12; Alexis de Tocqueville, *Democracy in America* (Washington, DC: Regnery, 2002), 20.

9. Scott Simmon, *The Invention of the Western Film: A Cultural History of the Genre's First Half-Century* (Cambridge: Cambridge University Press, 2003), 96; John Wall, *Mediations in Cultural Spaces: Structure, Sign, Body* (Cambridge: Cambridge Scholars, 2008), 125.

10. *An Act for Opening the Land Office* (Savannah, GA: James Johnson, 1783), 23; John Reed, *An Explanation of the Map of the City and Liberties of Philadelphia* (Philadelphia: John Reed, 1774), 22–23, 4–5, 14–15, 16, 20–21; *The Laws of the Province of South Carolina*

(Charlestown, SC: Lewis Timothy, 1736), vol. 2, entry 572; Robert David Sack, *Human Territoriality: Its Theory and History* (New York: Cambridge University Press, 1986), 33–34; John Noyes, *Colonial Space: Spatiality in the Discourse of German South West Africa* (Philadelphia: Harwood Academic, 1992), 195.

11. Thomas Jefferson, "Description of Louisiana, Communicated to Congress, on the 14th of November, 1803," in *American State Papers, Miscellaneous Volume I*, 344, 345, 346, online at American Memory, http://memory.loc.gov/ll/llsp/037/0300/03520344 .tif, accessed May 11, 2014; *The Southwest Journals of Zebulon Pike, 1806–1807*, ed. Stephen Harding Hart and Archer Butler Hulbert (Albuquerque: University of New Mexico Press, 2006), 126; "these vast plains" in *The Journals of Zebulon Montgomery Pike*, ed. Donald Dean Jackson (Norman: University of Oklahoma Press, 1966), 2:27; Richard H. Dillon, "Stephen Long's Great American Desert," *Proceedings of the American Philosophical Society* 111 (1967), 95, 103; Timothy Flint, *History and Geography of the Mississippi Valley* (Cincinnati: E. H. Flint, 1833), 459; Francis Parkman, *The California and Oregon Trail* (New York: Thomas Y. Crowell, 1901), 31; Horace Greeley, *An Overland Journey from New York to San Francisco in the Summer of 1859* (New York: C. M. Saxton, Barker, 1860), 99. Some of the historiography is tracked in in Ralph C. Morris, "The Notion of a Great American Desert East of the Rockies," *Mississippi Valley Historical Review* 13 (1926), 190–200. See also Martyn J. Bowden, "The Great American Desert in the American Mind: The Historiography of a Geographical Notion," in *Geographies of the Mind: Essays in Historical Geosophy*, ed. David Lowenthal and Martyn J. Bowden (New York: Oxford University Press, 1976), 119–48. Walter Prescott Webb thought that Coronado first reported the Great American Desert, but he mentions as well that Coronado's reference might have been to uninhabited land rather than dry wasteland. *The Great Plains* (Boston: Ginn, 1933), 153, 107n2.

12. *Abridgement of the Debates of Congress, from 1789 to 1856* (New York: D. Appleton, 1857–61), 132; W. E. Hamilton, "The Faithful Engineer," *New York Observer and Chronicle*, Jan. 27, 1876, 1; "Birth-Day of California," *Littell's Living Age*, March 15, 1851, 515; J. W. Powell, "Scenery on the Colorado," *American Antiquarian and Oriental Journal*, June 1895, 240; "Review 4," *Knickerbocker*, Feb. 1849, 156; Charles Rhoads, "The Desert State," *Friend*, Oct. 17, 1891, 93; Hamlin Garland, "The Prairie Route to the Golden River," *Independent*, Jan. 26, 1899, 247, 248; Herbert George Wells, *The Future in America: A Search after Realities* (London: Chapman and Hall, 1906), 95.

13. "Seasonable Literature," *Methodist Review*, July 1894, 613; Robert Sproul Carroll, *The Soul in Suffering: A Practical Application of Spiritual Truths* (New York: Macmillan, 1919), 117; "Faith Meeting in Boston," *New York Evangelist*, July 24, 1873, 6; "A Cup of Cold Water," *Friends' Intelligencer*, May 25, 1867, 180; Rev. A. W. Cash, "Soul-Thirst," *Herald of Gospel Liberty*, Aug. 6, 1914, 1006; Ray Stannard Baker, "The Great Southwest: II. The Desert," *Century Illustrated Magazine* 64 (June 1902), 225; Mrs. Joanna Bethune, journal entry for March 26, 1827, in *Memoirs of Mrs. Joanna Bethune, by Her Son, the Rev. George W. Bethune, D.D.* (New York: Harper, 1863), 159; George B. Ide, "Sermon III: Duty, Individual and Imperative," *National Preacher and Village Pulpit*, March 1863, 59, 60.

14. W. Barrows, "'The Great American Desert'—There Is None," *Magazine of Western History*, June 1885, 2; Baker, "Great Southwest," 213–14; Richard Slotkin, *The Fatal Environment; The Myth of the Frontier in the Age of Industrialization, 1800–1890* (New York: Athenaeum, 1985); Henry Nash Smith, *Virgin Land: The American West as Symbol and Myth* (Cambridge, MA: Harvard University Press, 1950); Patricia Limerick, *The Legacy of Conquest: The Unbroken Past of the American West* (New York: Norton, 1987); Mary Lawlor, *Recalling the Wild: Naturalism and the Closing of the American West* (New Brunswick, NJ: Rutgers University Press, 2000); Husan L. Hsu, *Geography and the Production of Space in*

Nineteenth-Century American Literature (New York: Cambridge University Press, 2010), esp. 3–8 on "spatial feeling."

15. "God's Plan in Geography," *Zion's Herald and Wesleyan Journal*, Jan. 28, 1857, 1; Edwin Earle Sparks, "Irrigation and the American Frontier," *Chautauquan*, Sept. 1902, 568; B. O. Flowers and Frank Parsons, "On the Stoa of the Twentieth Century: An Army of Wealth-Creators vs. an Army of Destruction," *Arena* 25, no. 5 (1901), 524; *Maine Farmer*, May 13, 1900, 7; Cy Warman, "Linking the Atlantic with the Pacific," *Independent*, Dec. 29, 1904, 1480–83; "Literature: A Miracle in the Desert," *Congregationalist*, June 14, 1900, 882.

16. Nathaniel Ames cited in "Prophecy Fulfilled," *Western Luminary*, Oct. 19, 1825, 232–33; "The Spectator," *Outlook*, May 27, 1905, 216.

17. There are different ways of understanding collective identity, and the term prompts debate among scholars. I have found useful in my thinking about this issue Marilynn B. Brewer's "The Many Faces of Social Identity: Implications for Political Psychology," *Political Psychology* 22 (2001), 115–25. I also thank Professor Andrew Rojecki of the University of Illinois–Chicago for his assistance in making sense of the broader field of identity studies.

18. David Chidester, *Authentic Fakes: Religion and American Popular Culture* (Berkeley: University of California Press, 2005), 227, 226; A. V. D. Honeyman, ed., *The Danites: And Other Choice Selections from the Writings of Joaquin Miller* (New York: American News, 1878), 193; Jean Baudrillard, *Amérique*, trans. Chris Turner (London: Verso, 1988), 7, 8, 37; Robert Bellah, *The Broken Covenant: American Civil Religion in Time of Trial* (Chicago: University of Chicago Press, 1975), 142, 158.

19. Henri J. M. Nouwen, *The Way of the Heart: The Spirituality of the Desert Fathers and Mothers* (New York: HarperCollins, 1981), 25; Kent Ira Goff, *Honest to God Prayer* (Woodstock, VT: Skylight Paths, 2013), 101; Anne Graham Lotz, *The Magnificent Obsession: Embracing the God-Filled Life* (Grand Rapids, MI: Zondervan, 2009), 122; Tommy Tenney, *God's Eye View: Worshipping Your Way to a Higher Perspective* (Nashville: Thomas Nelson, 2012), n.p., see chap. 2, "The Virtue of Zero"; Alan W. Jones, *Soul Making: The Desert Way of Spirituality* (New York: HarperCollins, 1985), 6; R. Kent Hughes, *Acts: The Church Afire* (Wheaton, IL: Crossway Books, 1996), 35. For an example of the manner in which Christianity is defined against Islam in the Holy Land experience, see Ronald Lukens-Bull and Mark Fafard, "Next Year in Orlando: (Re)Creating Israel in Christian Zionism," *Journal of Religion and Society* 9 (2007), 1–20.

20. Wallace Earle Stegner, *Mormon Country* (Lincoln: University of Nebraska Press, 2003), 44; Revelation, Nov. 3, 1831, in *Doctrines and Covenants*, section 133 in *The Doctrine and Covenants of the Church of Jesus Christ of Latter-day Saints Containing Revelations Given to Joseph Smith, the Prophet, with Some Additions by His Successors in the Presidency of the Church* (Salt Lake City, UT: Intellectual Reserve, 1981), verse 29; Emma Smith, *A Collection of Sacred Hymns for the Church of the Latter Day Saints* (Kirtland, OH: F. G. Williams, 1835), 8.

21. Edward W. Said, *Orientalism* (New York: Vintage, 1979), 49–72; Benedict Anderson, *Imagined Communities* (New York: Verso, 2006); Derek Gregory, "Imaginative Geographies," *Progress in Human Geography* 19 (1995), 448. Gregory notes, however, that the dialectics between "land" and "territory" make mapping more complicated than just a will to power.

22. Frederic Jameson, *Postmodernism; or, The Cultural Logic of Late Capitalism* (Durham, NC: Duke University Press, 1991), 16; Certeau, "Walking in the City," 91–110. I take my leads here from a few who have written about the spatial turn in the humanities and social sciences: Fredric Jameson, Edward Soja, David Harvey, and some others, and espe-

cially Foucault, whose ideas about space have been much discussed and debated of late. Foucault located power in space and theorized the ways in which the spatial and the social were intertwined. Power flowed through spatial fields by way of relays and capillaries and could be concentrated in institutions, such as the clinic or the penitentiary. The *movement of bodies in space* proceeded as part of a process that included the ongoing renegotiation of social orders, the policing of social boundaries, and the surveillance of individuals. Michel Foucault, "Of Other Spaces," *Diacritics* 16 (Spring 1986), 22–27. Nigel Thrift, in "Overcome by Space: Reworking Foucault," in *Space, Knowledge, and Power: Foucault and Geography*, ed. Jeremy Crampton and Stuart Elden (London: Ashgate, 2007), 55, argues that because Foucault focused so much on space in terms of orders, he missed some of the vitality of space. But, according to Foucault: "Power must be analyzed as something which circulates, or rather as something which only functions in the form of a chain. It is never localized here or there, never in anybody's hands, never appropriated as a commodity or piece of wealth. Power is employed and exercised through a net-like organization. And not only do individuals circulate between its threads; they are always in the position of simultaneously undergoing and exercising this power. In other words, individuals are the vehicles of power, not its points of application." Foucault, *Power/Knowledge: Selected Interviews and Other Writings 1972–1977*, trans. C. Gordon (New York: Pantheon Press, 1980), 98. John Marks summarizes the opinion of many that Foucault takes a "spatial approach to thought" itself, in "A New Image of Thought," *New Formations* 25 (1995), 69, quoted in Andrew Thacker, *Moving through Modernity: Space and Geography in Modernism* (Manchester, UK: Manchester University Press, 2003), 22. Stewart Elden emphasizes that "Foucault's historical studies are spatial through and through," while critics such as Thrift have commented on the "blind spots" in Foucault's thinking about space. See Stewart Elden, *Mapping the Present: Heidegger, Foucault, and the Project of a Spatial History* (London: Continuum, 2001), 152; and Thrift, "Overcome by Space," 53–56.

23. This is a process of "negative definition" in the sense of saying what they are not; it should not be confused with a process involving a "negative" judgment of value or worth.

24. Lewis A. Coser, *The Functions of Social Conflict* (New York: Free Press, 1964), 87, 90; Martin Reisebrodt, "'*Religion': Just Another Modern Western Construction*" (2003), https://divinity.uchicago.edu/sites/default/files/imce/pdfs/webforum/122003/riesebrodtessay.pdf, accessed May 11, 2014.

25. Robert A. Orsi, *The Madonna of 115th Street: Faith and Community in Italian Harlem, 1880–1950*, 3rd ed. (New Haven, CT: Yale University Press, 2010).

26. Herbert Muschamp, "Public Space or Private, a Compulsion to Fill It," *New York Times*, Aug. 27, 2000, www.nytimes.com/2000/08/27/movies/art-architecture-public-space-or-private-a-compulsion-to-fill-it.html accessed July 24, 2014; Walter Benjamin, *The Origin of German Tragic Drama*, trans. John Osborne (London: NLB, 1977), 138–41. "Mourning is the state of mind in which feeling revives the empty world in the form of a mask, and derives an enigmatic satisfaction in contemplating it" (139). Christine Buci-Glucksmann, *Baroque Reason: The Aesthetics of Modernity*, trans. Patrick Camiller (London: Sage, 1994), 71 ("an excavation" and "the world"); Buci-Glucksmann, *The Madness of Vision: On Baroque Aesthetics*, trans Dorothy Z. Baker (Athens: Ohio University Press, 2012), p. 27–28 ("madness"); Carlos Fuentes, "La novela como tragedia: William Faulkner," in *Casa con Dos Puertas* (Mexico City: Joaquín Mortiz, 1970), 67, my translation.

27. Sketches of the New York City churches mentioned here, as well as other New York City churches, civic buildings, and residences incorporating baroque features, are

in the *AIA Guide to New York City*, by Norval White, Eliot Willensky, and Fran Leadon (New York: Oxford University Press, 2010), 233, 202, 826–27, 447, 400, 462–63, and elsewhere. The founding of the shrine to Mary served as a strong statement to Buffalo's Protestants, who in their various denominations accounted for 179 out of 253 churches in the years just after the completion of the shrine. "Buffalo Churches in 1931," Buffalo and Erie County Public Library, www.buffalolib.org/sites/default/files/pdf/genealogy/subject-guides/Buffalo%20Churches%20in%201931.pdf, accessed July 24, 2014; James Napora, "Houses of Worship: A Guide to the Religious Architecture of Buffalo, New York" (master's thesis, 1995), www.buffaloah.com/how/tc.html, accessed July 24, 2014.

The relevant design features of Our Lady of Victory can be seen on the church's website, www.ourladyofvictory.org/virtual-tour/, accessed May 11, 2014.

28. Margaret Marsh, "Suburbanization and the Search for Community: Residential Decentralization in Philadelphia, 1880–1900," *Pennsylvania History* 44 (1977), 102–3.

29. Alexander V. G. Allen, *Phillips Brooks, 1835–1893: Memories of His Life with Extracts of His Letters* (New York: Dutton, 1907), 229; Deborah Mathias Gough, *Christ Church, Philadelphia: The Nation's Church in a Changing City* (Philadelphia: University of Pennsylvania Press, 1995), 282; E. Digby Baltzell, *Philadelphia Gentlemen: The Making of a National Upper Class* (New York: Free Press, 1958), 248, quote on 261; Robert Fishman, *Bourgeois Utopias: The Rise and Fall of Suburbia* (New York: Basic Books, 1987).

30. John R. Stilgoe, *Borderland: Origins of the American Suburb, 1820–1939* (New Haven, CT: Yale University Press, 1988) 156.

31. Martin Reisebrodt, *Pious Passion: The Emergence of Modern Fundamentalism in the United States and Iran*, trans. Don Reneau (Berkeley: University of California Press, 1998), 22, 62; *The Fundamentals: A Testimony to the Truth* (Los Angeles: Bible Institute of Los Angeles, 1917), vol. 4; *Christian Century* 39 (March 16, 1922), 325; Christian Smith, *American Evangelicalism: Embattled and Thriving* (Chicago: University of Chicago Press, 1998).

32. Reisebrodt, *Pious Passion*, 65; Rhys Williams, "American National Identity, The Rise of the Modern City, and the Birth of Protestant Fundamentalism," in *The Fundamentalist City? Religiosity and the Remaking of Urban Space*, ed. Nezar AlSayyad and Mejgan Massoumi (London: Routledge, 2011), 95.

33. In reading liminality this way, I draw upon Victor W. Turner's discussion of the stages of ritual process, extending them to the antistructuring of space. Turner, *The Ritual Process: Structure and Anti-Structure* (Piscataway, NJ: Transaction, 2008), 58.

34. Billy Sunday quoted by Thekla Joiner, *Sin in the City: Chicago and Revivalism, 1880–1920* (Columbia: University of Missouri Press, 2007), 188. The quote of Joiner is also on 188. The fundamentalists' move to the suburbs in the latter part of the twentieth century is described by Darren Dochuk in "'Praying for a Wicked City': Congregation, Community, and the Suburbanization of Fundamentalism," *Religion and American Culture* 13 (2003), 167–203.

35. Charles Hambricke-Stowe, *The Practice of Piety: Puritan Devotional Disciplines in Seventeenth-Century New England* (Chapel Hill: University of North Carolina Press, 1982), 156; Colleen McDannell, *The Christian Home in Victorian America, 1840–1900* (Bloomington: Indiana University Press, 1994); *The Memoirs of Mrs. Elizabeth Bailey* (Boston: Samuel T. Armstrong, 1815), 19, 37; Samuel Merivale, *Daily Devotions for the Closet* (Worcester, MA: Isaiah Thomas/Goulding and Stow, 1808).

36. "The Prayer Closet," *New York Evangelist*, Sept. 20, 1888, 6; "Closet Exercises," *Methodist Magazine and Quarterly Review*, Jan. 1, 1831, 77.

37. McDannell, *Christian Home in Victorian America*, 28; "The Sanctity of the Home," *Gospel Herald*, April 4, 1908, 4; G. K. Newell, "'When Thou Prayest,'" *New York Observer*

and Chronicle, July 26, 1906, 109; "Household Fun," *New York Observer and Chronicle*, June 1, 1876, 172A; "Weekly Sunday School Lesson: Christian Worship," *Indiana Farmer's Guide*, July 26, 1919, 29; Igumen Chariton, *The Art of Prayer: An Orthodox Anthology*, trans. E. Kadloubovsky and E. M. Palmer (1966; New York: Faber and Faber, 1998), 163, and see especially the chapter "The Inner Closet of the Heart," 43–51.

38. "Sentiments to Be Pondered Over by the Christian in the Solitude of the Closet," *Baptist Missionary Magazine*, April 1843, 90; "Closet and Altar," *Congregationalist*, March 24, 1906, 433; "Closet and Altar," *Congregationalist*, March 25, 1897, 417; "Closet and Altar," *Congregationalist*, April 8, 1897, 489; C. H. Spurgeon, *Daily Readings for the Family or the Closet* (New York: Sheldon, 1867), 285; *Gospel Herald* 1, no. 43 (Jan. 16, 1909), 669; "Prayer" *Western Literary Miscellany*, July 1853, 14.

39. Setha M. Low and Denise Lawrence-Zúñiga, *"Locating Culture," in Anthropology of Space and Place: Locating Culture, ed.* Setha M. Low and Denise Lawrence-Zúñiga (Oxford: Blackwell, 2003), 8; Doreen S. Massey, *Space, Place, and Gender* (Minneapolis: University of Minnesota Press, 1994), 10; *Deborah Clarke, Robbing the Mother: Women in Faulkner (Jackson: University Press of Mississippi, 1994), 61; Erica Longfellow, "Public, Private, and the Household in Early Seventeenth-Century England," Journal of British Studies 45 (2006), 315.*

40. *Ruth Madigan and Moira Munro, "The More We Are Together: Domestic Space, Gender, and Privacy," in Ideal Homes? Social Change and Domestic Life, ed. Tony Chapman and Lorna Hockey (London: Routledge, 1999), 61–72; Pierre Bourdieu, "The Kabyle House or the World Reversed," in The Logic of Practice (Stanford, CA: Stanford University Press, 1990), 271–83.*

41. *William Faulkner, Absalom, Absalom! The Corrected Text (New York: Modern Library, 2012), 123; Katrina J. Zeno, Discovering the Feminine Genius (Boston: Pauline Books and Media, 2010), chap. 3, "The Feminine Genius," n.p.; Luce Irigaray, The Sex Which Is Not One (Ithaca, NY: Cornell University Press, 1985), 26; Claire Pajaczkowska and Lola Young,* "Racism, Representation, Psychoanalysis," in *"Race," Culture, and Difference*, ed. James Donald and Ali Rattansi (London: Open University/Sage, 1992), 201; Cynthia A. Freeland, *Feminist Interpretations of Aristotle* (College Park: Pennsylvania State University Press, 1998), 74. Roxanne Mountford, in a study of Protestant women's preaching, asked, "How does a woman earn the respect of an audience conditioned to regard her body as symbolic of a lack (of authority, eloquence, power, substance)?" *The Gendered Pulpit: Preaching in American Protestant Spaces* (Carbondale: Southern Illinois University Press, 2003), 13. In the early twenty-first century, there has been a revival of interest in the prayer closet. See Miriam Pace, "Spiritual Space: People Are Turning Nooks and Crannies into Prayer Closets," *Houston Chronicle*, Aug. 3, 2002, Religion Section, 2.

42. John Corrigan, *Business of the Heart: Religion and Emotion in the Nineteenth Century* (Berkeley: University of California Press, 2002).

Chapter 4

Epigraph: Robert Duncan, "Correspondences," in *The Postmoderns: The New American Poetry*, ed. Donald Merriam Allen and George F. Butterick (New York: Grove Press, 1982), 49.

1. Eva T. Brann, *What, Then, Is Time?* (Oxford: Rowman and Littlefield, 2001), 126.

2. Malcolm L. McPhail, *The Magnetism of the Bible* (Philadelphia: American Sunday School Union, 1909), 178; Alfred Lord Tennyson, "The Mystic," in *Tennyson's Suppressed Poems Now for the First Time Collected*, ed. and annotated by J. C. Thompson (New York: Harper, 1903), 32; Michael Wigglesworth, *The Day of Doom* (Cambridge: Samuel Green, 1666), 2.

3. Charles Beecher, *Spiritual Manifestations* (Boston: Lee and Shepard, 1879), 96–97; Denton J. Snider, *Feeling Psychologically Treated, and Prolomena to Psychology* (St. Louis: Sigma, 1905), 75, 72; "Things Theatrical," *Plaindealer*, March 13, 1936, 3; "Calvin's Digest," *Plaindealer*, June 11, 1943, 7; Thomas Laycock, *Mind and Brain; or, The Correlations of Consciousness and Organization; Systematically Investigated and Applied to Philosophy, Mental Science, and Practice* (New York: Appleton, 1869), 93; John P. Guliver, Egbert C. Smyth, J. Henry Thayer, Charles M. Mead, et al., "A Communication form the Andover Professors," *Independent*, April 13, 1882, 18; Morris Raphael Cohen, *The Meaning of Human History* (LaSalle, IL: Open Court, 1947), 75; "A Chapter on Time," *New Monthly Magazine and Literary Journal*, Jan. 1, 1822, 42, 41; Phillip Fisher, *The Vehement Passions* (Princeton, NJ: Princeton University Press, 2002), 9.

4. "Critique der reinen Vernunft," *Brownson's Quarterly Review*, Oct. 1, 1844, 430; James W. Miles, "Philosophic Theology," *Southern Quarterly Review*, April 1850, 142–43; Laurens P. Hickok, *Rational Psychology; or, The Subjective Idea and the Objective Law of All Intelligence* (Schenectady, NY: G. Y. Van Debogert, 1854), 150; John Bascom, *The Principles of Psychology* (New York: G. P. Putnam, 1869), 132. A useful discussion of Bascom's intuitionism is Robert A. Jones, "John Bascom, 1827–1911: Anti-Positivism and Intuitionism in American Sociology," *American Quarterly* 24 (1972), 501–22.

5. Orestes A. Brownson, "Grounds of Religion," *Boston Quarterly Review* 5 (1842), 398; William James, "The Perception of Time," *Journal of Speculative Philosophy* 20 (1886), 374–407; Rev. Johnston Estep Walter, *Nature and Cognition of Space and Time* (West Newton, PA: Johnston and Penney, 1914), 179; "Ernest Naville: His Works and Opinions," *Methodist Quarterly Review* 23 (1871), 7; "Anthropology," *Journal of Speculative Philosophy* 11 (1877), 314; Frederick William Robertson, *Sermons Preached at Trinity Chapel, Brighton, by the late Rev. Frederick W. Robertson* (New York: Harper, 1871), 334.

6. John Wilkes, ed., *Encyclopaedia Londinensis* (West Smithfield, UK: J. Adland, 1812), 11:608; J. G. Macvicar, *Elements of the Economy of Nature* (Edinburgh: Adam Black, 1830), 569; *Contemporary Review* 25 (Dec. 1874–May 1875), 298.

7. William H. Holcombe, *Our Children in Heaven* (Philadelphia: J. B. Lippincott, 1875), 283–84; E. R. Sproul, *Mystery* (San Francisco: A. L. Bancroft, 1875), 570; S. D. Baldwin, *Armageddon; or, The Overthrow of Romanism and Monarchy* (Cincinnati: Applegate, 1850), 445, 446; Ronald E. Lee, "The Rhetorical Construction of Time in Martin Luther King, Jr.'s 'Letter from Birmingham Jail,'" *Southern Communication Journal* 56 (1991), 283–84; Andrew Jackson Davis, *Arabula; or, The Divine Guest* (Boston: W. White, 1868), 320; R. Huntington Woodman, "Church Music," *New York Evangelist*, Feb. 20, 1896, 22; "Longing," *Continental Monthly* 6 (Oct. 1864), 454.

8. Thoughts on Eternity," *Massachusetts Missionary Magazine*, Feb. 1807, 345; *Our Paper* 10 (Jan. 13, 1894), 21; *Catholic Pulpit* (Baltimore: John Murphy, 1851), 163; Hannah Hobie, "Letter from Hannah Hobie, February 6, 1829," in *Memoir of Hannah Hobbie*, ed. Robert G. Armstrong (New York: American Tract Society, 1837), 133; Susan Allibone, "Diary of Susan Allibone, May, 1834," in *A Life Hid with Christ in God*, ed. Alfred Lee (Philadelphia: J. B. Lippincott, 1856), 95; Elizabeth Lindsay Lomax, "Diary of Elizabeth Lindsay Lomax, May, 1861," in *Leaves from an Old Washington Diary*, ed. Lindsay Lomax Wood (New York: Books, 1943), 155; Handley Dunelm, "The Eternal Prospect," *Living Age*, Nov. 4, 1905, 258; "Wait a Minute!," *Plaindealer*, Jan. 4, 1935, 7; Rev. P. A. Nordell, "Old Testament Word-Studies," *Old Testament Student* 8 (June 1889), 377.

9. "Religion of the Sea," *Lady's Book* 1 (1830), 285; Rev. Frank Crane, "The Ocean," *Independent*, April 11, 1907, 836; "Greatness of Simplicity," *New York Evangelist*, Dec. 18, 1841, 1; "Eternity," *New York Evangelist*, Nov. 26, 1846, 1; Winifred Kirkland, "Some Diffi-

culties in Doing without Eternity," *North American Review* 206 (Oct. 1917), 612; *Methodist Review* 46 (March 1930), 275.

10. An overview of some of the debate about eternity is in W. L. Craig, *God, Time, and Eternity: The Coherence of Theism II: Eternity* (Dordrecht, Netherlands: Kluwer, 2001). "The Metaphysical Idea of Eternity," *New Englander* 34 (April 1875), 222–23; Friedrich Schleiermacher, *The Christian Faith* (English translation of *Der christliche Glaube*, 2nd ed. [Berlin, 1830]), with a foreword by B. A. Gerrish (London: T&T Clark, 1999), 203; Ludwig Wittgenstein, *Tractatus Logico-Philosophicus*, 6.4311 (New York: Harcourt, Brace, 1922), 185; John Ellis McTaggart, "The Relation of Time and Eternity," *Mind* 18 (1909), 343.

11. "Whately's Future State," *Mercersburg Quarterly Review*, July 1856, 23, 31; "The Year 1888—A Retrospect and Prospect," *American Catholic Quarterly Review* 14 (Jan. 1889), 117; Ralph Tyler Flewelling, "The Consciousness of Immortality," *Methodist Review* 39 (March 1923), 232; Dana Luciano, *Arranging Grief: Sacred Time and the Body in Nineteenth-Century America* (New York: New York University Press, 2007), 1. It is important to note that feeling time through intuition and feeling it through the body were not identical ways of knowing, but for many Christians the two greatly overlapped, one informing the other. Sometimes intuition was thought to be a spiritual and abstracted kind of knowing, while at other times it was joined to a recognition of biological states and rhythms. That overlapping was especially of interest to William James, who sought a way to escape some of the philosophical presuppositions of intuitionism through a radical empiricism but at the same time attempted to leave room for it in cognition. Gerald Eugene Myers, *William James: His Life and Thought* (New Haven, CT: Yale University Press, 1986).

12. Walter Benjamin, "Thesis XIII" and "Addendum A," in "On the Concept of History," in *Selected Writings*, vol. 4, *1938–1940*, ed. Howard Eiland and Michael W. Jennings (Cambridge, MA: Harvard University Press, 1993), 394–95, 397; Carlos M. N. Eire, *A Very Brief History of Eternity* (Princeton, NJ: Princeton University Press, 2010), 104–5; Benedict Anderson, *Imagined Communities: Reflections on the Origin and Spread of Nationalism* (London: Verso, 1991). A discussion of Benjamin's theses on history and Jewish and Christian theology is in Stéphane Mosès and Ora Wiskind, "The Theological-Political Model of History in the Thought of Walter Benjamin," *History and Memory* 1 (1989), 5–33. I have benefited from the analyses of historical changes in the keeping and conceptualization of time in Stephen Kern, *The Culture of Time and Space, 1880–1918* (Cambridge, MA: Harvard University Press, 1983); and Stuart Sherman, *Telling Time: Clocks, Diaries, and English Diurnal Form, 1660–1785* (Chicago: University of Chicago Press, 1996). Charles Taylor's remarks in *Philosophical Arguments* (Cambridge, MA: Harvard University Press, 1995) on time and secularity are brief but useful, although he misestimates the history of the spatialization of time (it began much sooner than he admits) in his contention with Heidegger (310n17). Thomas M. Allen, *A Republic in Time: Temporality and Social Imagination in Nineteenth-Century America* (Chapel Hill: University of North Carolina Press, 2008), makes the point that a national community is not as homologous a body as Anderson supposes.

13. Robert Louis Stevenson and Lloyd Osbourne, *The Wrecker* (New York: Scribner's, 1895), 440; Ebenezer Pemberton, "The Life and Character of Mrs. Mary Lloyd," in *Meditations on Divine Subjects: by Mrs. Mary Lloyd. To Which is prefixed, an account of her life and character. By E. Pemberton*, by Mrs. Mary Lloyd (New York: J. Parker, 1750), 25; Benjamin Franklin, *A Collection of the Sayings of Poor Richard* (Boston: Benjamin Mecom, 1758); Winton U. Solberg, *Redeem the Time: The Puritan Sabbath in Early America* (Cambridge, MA: Harvard University Press, 1977); Charles Hambricke-Stowe, *The Practice of Piety: Puritan Devotional Disciplines in Seventeenth-Century New England* (Chapel Hill:

University of North Carolina Press, 1982); Cotton Mather, *A Scriptural Catechism* (Boston: R. Pierce, 1691), 19.

14. Charles Grandison Finney, *Lectures to Professing Christians* (New York: John S. Taylor, 1837), 295.

15. Mark Guy Pearse, *The Gospel for the Day* (London: Charles H. Kelly, 1893), 222; W. Poole Balfern, *Glimpses of Jesus; or, Christ Exalted in the Affections of His People* (New York: Sheldon, Blakeman, 1858), 13.

16. On Kierkegaard's *öjeblikket*, see Victoria S. Harrison, "Kierkegaard's 'Philosophical Fragments': A Clarification," *Religious Studies* 33 (1997), 455–72; John Angell James, *The True Christian* (New York: Robert Carter, 1858), 141. See also Hans Bibfeldt, "On the Paradox of the Unrequited Or/And in Kierkegaard's Diary," in *Visions of Eternity: Before and after Newton*, ed. Martin E. Morton (Toronto: Cercle, 1961), 297–319.

17. Gro Svendsen, "Letter from Gro Svendsen to Nils Knudsen Gudmundsrud, November 27, 1868," in *Frontier Mother: The Letters of Gro Svendsen*, ed. Pauline Farseth and Theodore Blegen (Northfield, MN: Norwegian-American Historical Association, 1950), 88; John Summerfield, "Discourse Seventy-Eighth: The Heavenly Inheritance," in *History and Repository of Pulpit Eloquence*, ed. Henry Clay Fish, 2 vols. (New York: Dodd, Mead, 1850), 1:542.

18. Frank Kermode, *The Sense of an Ending: Studies in the Theory of Fiction with a New Epilogue* (Oxford: Oxford University Press, 2000), 93–126.

19. Eire, *Very Brief History*, 51; Dereck Daschke, "Millennial Destiny: A History of Millennialism in America," in *Introduction to New and Alternative Religions in America*, ed. Eugene V. Gallagher and W. Michael Ashcraft (Westport, CT: Greenwood Press, 2006), 266; Paul S. Boyer, "The Growth of Fundamentalist Apocalyptic in the United States," in *Apocalyptic in the Modern Period and Contemporary Age*, ed. Stephen J. Stein, vol. 3 of *The Encyclopedia of Apocalypticism*, ed. Stephen J. Stein (New York: Continuum, 1999), 160; and Boyer, *When Time Shall Be No More: Prophecy Belief in Modern American Culture* (Cambridge. MA: Harvard University Press, 1992).

20. Bernard McGinn *Visions of the End: Apocalyptic Traditions in the Middle Ages* (New York: Columbia University Press, 1979), 10; Stephen J. Stein, "Apocalypticism outside the Mainstream," in *Apocalyptic in the Modern Period*, 108. The phrase "bewildering diversity" is picked up by Michael Barkun, *A Culture of Conspiracy: Apocalyptic Visions in Contemporary America* (Berkeley: University of California Press, 2003), 15.

21. For parts of this summary and specifically for discussion of the Ita y Parra sermon, I rely on David A. Brading, *Mexican Phoenix: Our Lady of Guadalupe: Image and Tradition across Five Centuries* (Cambridge: Cambridge University Press, 2001), 153.

22. Kristy Nabhan-Warren, *The Virgin of El Barrio: Marian Apparitions, Catholic Evangelizing, and Mexican American Activism* (New York: New York University Press, 2005), 86, 39–40, 87–88. The transmission of Marian traditions to Texas is described in Timothy Matovina, *Guadalupe and Her Faithful: Latino Catholics in San Antonio, from Colonial Origins to the Present* (Baltimore: Johns Hopkins University Press, 2005).

23. Sandra Zimdars-Schwartz, *Encountering Mary: Visions of Mary from La Salette to Medjugorje* (New York: Harper Perennial, 1992), 246–48; William A. Christian Jr., *Apparitions in Late Medieval and Renaissance Spain* (Princeton, NJ: Princeton University Press, 1981); Amy Luebbers stresses the duality of good and evil, conspiracy mentality, and demonization of opponents in a case study of Marian apocalyptic in America in "The Remnant Faithful: A Case Study of Contemporary Apocalyptic Catholicism," *Sociology of Religion* 62 (2001), 221–41; Michael W. Cuneo, "The Vengeful Virgin: Case Studies in Contemporary American Catholic Apocalypticism," in *Millennium, Messiahs, and May-*

hew: Contemporary Apocalyptic Movements, ed. Thomas Robbins and Susan J. Palmer (New York: Routledge, 1997), 175–94.

24. Quoted in Daniel Wojcik, *The End of the World as We Know It: Faith, Fatalism, and the Apocalypse in America* (New York: New York University Press, 1997), 80.

25. Quotes are taken from the collected messages on the Baysiders' Our Lady of the Roses website, www.roses.org/download/msgsall.pdf, accessed May 11, 2014. See entries for Oct. 6, 1976, p. 719; April 10, 1976, p. 635; Sept. 28, 1977, p. 859.

26. Ibid., entries for Dec. 24, 1972, p. 146; Oct. 6, 1970, pp. 21–22; May 30, 1973, p. 204; Sept. 14, 1970, p. 17; Sept. 7, 1971, p. 67. Regarding human conception: "The spirit of life is breathed into the creation of the Eternal Father at the precise moment of infiltration of conception. At the exact moment of infiltration of conception, life begins" (May 10, 1972, p. 102); "In each life there is that moment of recognition of soul" (Nov. 24, 1973, p. 279); April 6, 1974, p. 328; Aug. 13, 1977, p. 839; Douglas Robinson, *American Apocalypses: The Image of the End of the World in American Literature* (Baltimore: Johns Hopkins University Press, 1985), xiii.

27. Walter Elliott, "The Longing for God and Its Fulfillment," *Catholic World* 55 (June 1892), 340.

28. Robert Charles Winthrop and John Winthrop, *Life and Letters of John Winthrop* (Boston: Tichnor and Fields, 1864), 77; Avihu Zakai, *Exile and Kingdom: History and Apocalypse in the Puritan Migration to America* (Cambridge: Cambridge University Press, 1992), 134–35; Theodore Dwight Bozeman, *To Live Ancient Lives: The Primitivist Dimension in Puritanism* (Chapel Hill: University of North Carolina Press, 1988); Baird Tipson, Review of *Avihu Zakai, Exile and Kingdom: History and Apocalypse in the Puritan Migration to America, Church History* 63 (1994), 632; Samuel Danforth, *A Brief Recognition of New England's Errand into the Wilderness* (Cambridge: S.G. and M.J., 1671), 21; Perry Miller, *Errand into the Wilderness* (New York: Harper and Row, 1956); E. Brooks Holifield, *Theology in America: Christian Thought from the Age of the Puritans to the Civil War* (New Haven, CT: Yale University Press, 2003), 77, writes that "no one described the millennial kingdom more expansively than Cotton Mather"; Stephen J. Stein, "A Notebook on the Apocalypse by Jonathan Edwards," *William and Mary Quarterly*, third series, 29 (1972), 623–34; Jonathan Edwards, *Jonathan Edwards: Apocalyptic Writings*, ed. Stephen J. Stein (New Haven, CT: Yale University Press, 1977).

29. W. H. Orr, "What Is Prayer?," *Herald of Gospel Liberty* 79 (April 28, 1887), 264.

30. Jemima Wilkinson, *Some Considerations, Propounded to the Several Sorts and Sects of Professors of This Age* (Providence, RI: Bennett Wheeler, 1779), 88, 75, 81, 92.

31. Stephen J. Stein, *The Shaker Experience in America: A History of the United Society of Believers* (New Haven, CT: Yale University Press, 1992), 118; Frederic McKechnie, "Reform," in *The Manifesto* (East Canterbury, NH: United Societies, 1899), 29:152; Suzanne Youngerman, "'Shaking Is No Foolish Play': An Anthropological Perspective on the American Shakers—Person, Time, Space, and Dance-Ritual" (PhD diss., Columbia University, 1983), 282; Sally Promey, *Spiritual Spectacles: Vision and Image in Mid-nineteenth Century Shakerism* (Bloomington: Indiana University Press, 1993), 135, 96; *Testimonies of the Life, Character, Revelations, and Doctrines of Mother Ann Lee and the Elders with Her* (Albany, NY: Weed, Parsons, 1888), 206, 216, 9, 1, 189, 175, 4, 13, 5.

32. *Testimonies of Mother Ann Lee*, 222.

33. Giacomo Marramao, "Messianism without Delay: On the 'Post-religious' Political Theology of Walter Benjamin," trans. Luca Follis, *Constellations* 15 (2008), 403.

34. Charles Taze Russell, *Studies in the Scriptures* (Brooklyn, NY: Watchtower Bible and Tract Society, 1889), 6:151; Russell quoted in Zoe Knox, "The Watchtower Society and

the End of the Cold War: Interpretations of the End-Times, Superpower Conflict, and the Changing Geo-Political Order," *Journal of the American Academy of Religion* 79 (2011), 1025, which gives this source: "Prospectus," *Zion's Watch Tower and Herald of Christ's Presence* 1/1:1 (CD ROM: *Magazines that Motivate*), 1.

35. Zoe Knox, "Watchtower Society," 1025; David L. Weddle, "A 'New' Generation of Jehovah's Witnesses: Revised Interpretation, Ritual, and Identity," *Nova Religio* 3 (2000), 350–67; "Why Does Life Seem Meaningless?," http://wol.jw.org/en/wol/d/r1/lp-e/2011482; "The Bible Changes Lives," http://wol.jw.org/en/wol/d/r1/lp-e/2012246; "Success—How Do You Measure It?," http://wol.jw.org/en/wol/d/r1/lp-e/2007000; "Jehovah—A God Worth Knowing," http://wol.jw.org/en/wol/d/r1/lp-e/2003121; "Is Death Really the End?," http://wol.jw.org/en/wol/d/r1/lp-e/102007442; "The Good News They Want You to Hear," http://wol.jw.org/en/wol/d/r1/lp-e/1102000103, all documents from the Watchtower Online Library and accessed March 13, 2013.

36. Grant Underwood, *The Millennial World of Early Mormonism* (Urbana: University of Illinois Press, 1993), 26, 24; Richard Bushman, *Joseph Smith and the Beginnings of Mormonism* (Urbana: University of Illinois Press, 1984), 170; Dean C. Jessee, ed., *The Papers of Joseph Smith*, vol. 1, *Autobiographical and Historical Writings* (Salt Lake City: Deseret Book, 1989), 6–7; Rulon T. Burton, ed., *We Believe: Doctrine and Principles of the Church of Latter-day Saints* (Draper, UT: Tabernacle Books, 2004), 176; Orson Pratt, *A Interesting Account of Several Remarkable Visions and of the Late Discovery of Ancient American Records* (Edinburgh: Ballantyne and Hughes, 1840), 30–31; Franklin Dewey Richards, *A Compendium of the Doctrines of the Gospel* (Salt Lake City: Deseret News, 1882), 206; Susan Petersen, "The Great and Dreadful Day: Mormon Folklore of the Apocalypse," *Utah Historical Quarterly* 44 (1976), 368, 377; Massimo Introvigne, "Latter Day Revisited: Contemporary Mormon Millenarianism," in *Millennium, Messiahs, and Mayhew: Contemporary Apocalyptic Movements*, ed. Thomas Robbins and Susan J. Palmer (New York: Routledge, 1997), 235. On the "gathering," see William Mulder, "Mormonism's 'Gathering': An American Doctrine with a Difference," *Church History* 23 (1954), 248–64.

37. Grant Underwood, *The Millenarian World of Early Mormonism* (Urbana: University of Illinois Press, 1999), 12, 45. Underwood nuances this characterization with references to world-building activities that characterized the development of the denomination in the nineteenth century. In his discussion of the Mormon "rhetoric of polarization," Underwood draws on Kennelm Burridge, *New Heaven, New Earth: A Study of Millenarian Activities* (New York: Schocken, 1975), 147.

38. On the development of fundamentalist eschatology in America, see Boyer, *When Time Shall Be No More*; Ernest R. Sandeen, *The Roots of Fundamentalism: British and American Millenarianism, 1800–1930* (Chicago: University of Chicago Press, 1970); Timothy P. Weber, *Living in the Shadow of the Second Coming: American Premillennialism, 1875–1982* (Grand Rapids: Academie Books, 1983); Matthew A. Sutton, "Was FDR the Antichrist? The Birth of Fundamentalist Antiliberalism in a Global Age," *Journal of American History* 98 (2012) 1052–74.

39. Jerry Falwell, *Listen, America!* (New York: Doubleday, 1980), 118, 67, 62; and *Nuclear War and the Second Coming of Jesus Christ* (Lynchburg, VA: Old-Time Gospel Hour, 1983), 15–16; Susan Friend Harding, *The Book of Jerry Falwell: Fundamentalist Language and Politics* (Princeton, NJ: Princeton University Press, 2000), 161–62, Falwell quoted on 159. On American fundamentalist clergy and the jeremiad in the twentieth century, see Andrew Murphy, *Prodigal Nation: Moral Decline and Divine Punishment from New England to 9/11* (New York: Oxford University Press, 2009), 77–124; Mark A Kellner, "Y2K: A Secular Apocalypse," *Christianity Today* 43 (Jan. 11, 1999); *The Collected Works of Pat Robert-*

son: The New Millennium/The New World Order/The Secret Kingdom, 3 books in 1 (New York: Inspirational Press, 1994), 273.

40. Graham ("Communism is a religion") quoted in Darren Dochuk, *From Bible Belt to Sunbelt: Plain-Folk Religion, Grassroots Politics, and the Rise of Evangelical Conservatism* (New York: W. W. Norton, 2011), 139; Billy Graham, *Storm Warning: Whether Global Recession, Terrorists Threats, or Devastating Natural Disasters, These Ominous Shadows Must Bing Us Back to the Gospel* (1992; Nashville, TN: Thomas Nelson, 2010), 163, 109; "The End of the World," *Charlotte Observer*, Oct. 12, 1958, 6-A; "The Flight of Time," *New York Evangelist* 16 (Jan. 2, 1845), 2.

41. James H. Moorhead, "Social Reform and the Divided Conscience of Antebellum Protestantism," *Church History* 48 (1979), 420–21.

42. Mark Hanchard, "Afro-Modernity: Temporality, Politics, and the African Diaspora," *Public Culture* 11 (1999), 254–55.

43. Quoted by Michael J. Mullin, *Africa in America: Slave Acculturation and Resistance in the American South and British Caribbean, 1736–1831* (Urbana: University of Illinois Press, 1992), 119, citing "Management of Slaves," *Southern Cultivator* 4 (March 1846), 44.

44. "Speak Out! Tell It like It Is!," *Afro-American Gazette*, Oct. 18, 1993, 16; Henry Louis Gates Jr., *Figures in Black: Words, Signs, and the "Racial" Self* (New York: Oxford University Press, 1987), 100–101.

45. Lloyd Pressly Pratt, "Progress, Labor, Revolution: The Modern Times of Antebellum African American Life Writing," *Forum on Fiction* 34 (2000), 56–76; Timothy E. Fulop, "'The Future Golden Day of the Race': Millennialism and Black Americans in the Nadir, 1877–1901," *Harvard Theological Review* 84 (1991), 75–99; Maxine Lavon Montgomery, *The Apocalypse in African American Fiction* (Gainesville: University Press of Florida, 1996), 74. Though Dana Luciano does not address specifically the matter of millennial time and race, her discussion of racial time in nineteenth-century literature is useful for its suggestion of how Thomas Jefferson, among other Americans, "understood slavery as an essentially *temporal* inconsistency within the history of the Americas." *Arranging Grief*, 50.

Chapter 5

Epigraph: Elias Canetti, *The Human Province* (New York: Seabury, 1978), 178.

1. Richard Rogers and Samuel Ward, *Two Elizabethan Puritan Diaries*, ed. M. M. Knappen (Chicago: American Society of Church History, 1933), 72; Paula Blank, "Languages of Early Modern Literature in Britain," in *The Cambridge History of Early Modern English Literature*, ed. David Loewenstein and Janel Mueller (Cambridge: Cambridge University Press, 2002), 157.

2. Alexander Campbell and Dolphus Skinner, *A Discussion of the Doctrines of Endless Misery and Universal Salvation* (Utica, NY: C. C. P. Grosh, 1840), 305; Joseph Alleine, *Remaines of that Ecellent Minister of Jesus Christ, Mr. Joseph Alleine* (Boston: John Allen, 1717), 57; Samuel Mather, *A Dead Faith Anatomized* (Boston: Bartholomew Green and John Allen, 1697), 56; Roger Williams, *George Fox Digg'd Out of His Burrowes* (1676; Boston: John Foster, 1696), 92.

3. John Caldwell, *An Impartial Trial of the Spirit Operating in This Part of the World* (Boston: T. Fleet, 1742), 39; J. Williamson Nevin, "Christ the Inspiration of His Own Word," *Reformed Quarterly Review* 29 (Jan. 1882), 21; Edgard Buckingham, "The Truth: What Ought We to Believe?," *Unitarian Review and Religious Magazine* 19 (May 1883), 419; J. B. Ceulemans, "The Cult of Medievalism," *American Catholic Quarterly Review* 40 (Jan.

1915), 61, 72; "Masonic Oration," *American Masonic Register, and Ladies and Gentlemen's Magazine*, April 1, 1821, 288.

4. A. D. Vaud, "The Sunday-School: Lesson for September 7, 1884," *Christian Advocate*, Aug. 28, 1884, 571; "An Argument on Slavery," *Independent*, March 20, 1851, 1; "Prof. Huxley on Evolution," *American Catholic Quarterly Review* 2 (Oct. 1877), 11; Helena Petrovna Blavatsky, *The Secret Doctrine: The Synthesis of Science, Religion, and Philosophy* (Madras, India: Vasanta Press, 1952), 3:488; Lucy Maud Montgomery, "Letter from Lucy Maud Montgomery to Ephraim Weber, September 2, 1909," in *The Green Gables Letters: From L. M. Montgomery to Ephraim Weber, 1905–1909*, ed. Wilfred Eggleston (Toronto: Ryerson Press, 1960), 93; Elmer L. Towns, Ed Stetzer, and Warren Bird, *11 Innovations in the Local Church: How Today's Leaders Can Learn, Discern, and Move into the Future* (Ventura, CA: Regal Books, 2007), 208. The authors of *11 Innovations* cite an interview with an Ohio pastor in 1969 in making this claim.

5. *Lancet* 11 (1827), 526; Dennis Ellard, *A New and Easy Method of the Art of Cutting* (London: T. W. Pocock, 1841), 10; *Bull of His Holiness Leo XII for the Indiction of the Universal Jubilee of 1825* (Baltimore: Lucas, 1826), 14; Adolf van Harnack, *History of Dogman*, trans. Neil Buchanan (Boston: Little, Brown, 1907), 2:91. Harnack nuances his approval of Origen with a historical argument that opens the door for religious innovation or restoration (2:92–93). Charles von Gerock, "Christianity's Most Joyous Fact," *Record of Christian Work* 2 (1884–85), 676.

6. Ralph W. Wyrick, "The Tragedy in Life and Its Break," *Methodist Review* (Sept. 1913), 794; George J. Fritschel, *The Formula of Concord: Its Origin and Contents* (Philadelphia: Lutheran Publication Society, 1916), 51; Charles Pettit M'Ilvaine, *Righteousness by Faith*, 3rd ed. (Philadelphia: Protestant Episcopal Book Society, 1868), 411; *Bull of Leo XII*, 13–14; Adam Clarke, *The New Testament of Our Lord and Saviour Jesus Christ* (Philadelphia: Thomas, Cowperthwait, 1838), 268.

7. Seventh Annual Report of the Pennsylvania Department of Agriculture, part 1 (Pennsylvania: Wm. Stanley Ray, 1901), 102; "Life Line, Radio Transcript, November 4, 1960. Subject: House Committee," *Hearings, Reports and Prints of the Senate Committee on Commerce* (Washington, DC: Government Printing Office, 1960), 1127; "The Story of Buddha," in *The Gospel in All Lands Representing the Missionary Society of the Methodist Episcopal Church*, April 1886, 160; Henry U. Onderdonk, *Sermons and Episcopal Charges* (Philadelphia: C. Sherman, 1851), 263, 264; James E. Talmage, "Knowing and Doing," *The Latter-day Saints Millennial Star* 12 (1850), 374; Joseph Henry Allen, "The Two Worlds One," *Unitarian Review and Religious Magazine* (April 1883), 310; Theodore Parker, *A Discourse of Matters Pertaining to Religion* (London: J. Chapman, 1844), preface.

8. Samuel Greenwood, "Wisdom and Foolishness," *Christian Science Journal* 33 (Oct. 1915–March 1916), 375.

9. "Editorial Notes," *Christian Observer* 96 (March 11, 1908), 1; Elwood C. Hall, "Born of the Spirit, or the First Work of Grace," *Herald of Gospel Liberty* 109 (June 28, 1917), 612; W. O. Holway, "The Sunday School: Second Quarter Lesson XIII," *Zion's Herald* 86 (June 17, 1908), 786; Billy Graham, *How to Be Born Again* (Nashville: Thomas Nelson, 1989), 58; "Religious Communications: On the Love of God," *Christian Observer* 11 (Nov. 1812), 687. This *Christian Observer* (1812) is published in London but also edited and published in Boston.

10. Thomas Gustafson, *Representative Words: Politics, Literature, and the American Language, 1776–1865* (Cambridge, MA: Harvard University Press, 1992), 4, 33, 43.

11. Ibid., 143; E. Brooks Holifield, *Theology in America: Christian Thought from the Age*

of the Puritans to the Civil War (New Haven, CT: Yale University Press, 2003), 174; Amanda Porterfield, *Conceived in Doubt: Religion and Politics in the New American Nation* (Chicago: University of Chicago Press, 2012), 2.

12. Nicholas P. Gilman, "The Scientific Spirit in Theology," *Unitarian Review and Religious Magazine* 12 (Oct. 1879), 7; Ezra S. Gannett, "The Nature and Importance of Our Theology," *Christian Examiner and Religious Miscellany* 47 (July 1849), 107. See "Nominalism," in *The Routledge Companion to Semiotics and Linguistics*, ed. Paul Cobley (London: Routledge, 2010), 276–77. Nominalism in its keenest expression held that ideas themselves do not exist except as names, as empty words. In some historical settings, that extreme form of nominalism held sway. But it was also the case that just as persons blended religious ideas at times, so too did they blend philosophical positions. The Anglo-Irish philosopher George Berkeley (d. 1753) mixed spiritualism and empiricism, nominalism and conceptualism (a more moderate nominalism that allowed for the subjective existence of universals as mental concepts), Christianity and Platonism. American thinkers from Edwards to Emerson sometimes leaned toward Platonism in their philosophical writings but sometimes were less certain about the objective reality of general concepts. Some blamed Darwin for strengthening the nominalist position. The American philosopher Charles S. Peirce urged realism against nominalism, as did the Mercersburg theologian John W. Nevin. Mary Baker Eddy, whose new religion of Christian Science was stridently Platonic, also stressed the emptiness of words to an extent that would have worried even nominalists. *Brownson's Quarterly Review* reproached Unitarians for their nominalism, "which regard[ed] genera and species, the universals of the schoolmen, as empty words or as mere conceptions of mental abstractions with no objective reality." *Brownson's Quarterly Review* 4 (July 1863), 26. As late as the early twenty-first century, however, nominalism remained lively enough as a way of thinking about the world that an editorial in *World* after 9/11 blamed the terrorist attack on "the gods of nominalism, materialism, secularism, and pluralism." Another religious writer affirmed at the same time that "we are all nominalists" in the West. See Robert C. Neville, *Realism in Religion: A Pragmatist's Perspective* (Albany: SUNY Press, 2009), 1; M. Gail Hammer, *American Pragmatism: A Religious Genealogy* (New York: Oxford University Press, 2003), 94–95; William DiPuccio, *The Interior Sense of Scripture: The Sacred Hermeneutics of John W. Nevin* (Macon, GA: Mercer University Press, 1998), 10; Ludwig Wittgenstein, *Critical Assessments*, ed. Stuart Shanker (New York: Routledge, 1986), 1:70; Edwin Herbert Lewis, "Some Definitions of Individualism," *American Journal of Sociology* 17 (1911), 239; "Unitarianism Philosophically and Theologically Examined," *Brownson's Quarterly Review* 4 (July 1863), 282; Richard Cimino, "'No God in Common': American Evangelical Discourse after 9/11," *Review of Religious Research* 47 (2005), 170; Larzer Ziff, *Mark Twain* (New York: Oxford University Press, 2004), 94–95.

13. Horace Bushnell, *God in Christ: Three Discourses* (New York: Charles Scribner's, 1876), 43; Lee J. Makowski, *Horace Bushnell on Christian Character Development* (Lanham, MD: University Press of America, 1999), 34–35; Sidney Ahlstrom, *Theology in America: The Major Protestant Voices from Puritanism to Neo-Orthodoxy* (Indianapolis: Hackett, 2003), 318–19; William Baird, *History of New Testament Research*, vol. 2, *From Jonathan Edwards to Rudolf Bultmann* (Minneapolis: Augsburg Fortress Press, 2003), 38.

14. Grant Wacker, *Heaven Below: Early Pentecostals and American Culture* (Cambridge, MA: Harvard University Press, 2001), 180; and Wacker, "The Foundations of Faith in Primitive Pentecostalism," *Harvard Theological Review* 77 (1984), 354.

15. Malise Ruthven, *Fundamentalism: A Very Short History* (New York: Oxford, 2004),

42; Walter A. Davis, *Death's Dream Kingdom: The American Psyche since 9-11* (Ann Arbor, MI: Pluto, 1996) 123, 127; Peter Harrison, *The Bible, Protestantism, and the Rise of Natural Science* (Cambridge: Cambridge University Press, 1998); Charles Hodge, *Systematic Theology* (London: Thomas Nelson, 1871), 1:164–65; Norman W. Mathers, *Christian Hermeneutics: Dispelling the Myths* (Bloomington, IN: WestBow Press, 2011), 7; Harriet A. Harris, *Fundamentalism and Evangelicals* (Oxford: Clarendon Press of Oxford University Press, 1998); Ernest R. Sandeen, "The Princeton Theology: One Source of Biblical Literalism in American Protestantism," *Church History* 31 (1962), 307–21; Mark A. Noll, "The Bible and Slavery," in *Religion and the American Civil War*, ed. Randall M. Miller, Harry S. Stout, and Charles Reagan Wilson (New York: Oxford University Press, 1998), 47; "How to Interpret Scripture," *Utica Christian Repository* 2 (April 1823), 110; Jeffrey K. Hadden, *Religion in Radical Transition* (New Brunswick, NJ: Transaction, 1970), 62–63. An example of recent research in religious studies that is so inclined is Manuel A. Vasquez, *More Than Belief: A Materialist Theory of Religion* (New York: Oxford University Press, 2011). Thomas Gustafson discusses the ambiguity of legal discourse and how it was present in debate in the early Republic in *Representative Words*. Susan Friend Harding shows how members of Jerry Falwell's church embrace a fundamentalist literalism but at the same time recognize semantic ambiguities in their reading of scripture. *The Book of Jerry Falwell* (Princeton, NJ: Princeton University Press, 2000). A relevant discussion of literalism in religion and law is Peter J. Smith and Robert W. Tuttle, "Biblical Literalism and Constitutional Originalism" (March 1, 2010), GWU Legal Studies Research paper no. 502, available at http://papers.ssrn.com/sol3/papers.cfm?abstract_id=1561933, accessed April 9, 2013; and see also Vincent Crapanzano, *Serving the Word: Literalism in America from Pulpit to Bench* (New York: New Press, 2000), whose analysis overreaches but nevertheless demonstrates collaborations between religious and legal literalism. T. L. Luhrman, in *When God Talks Back: Understanding the American Evangelical Relationship with God* (New York: Knopf, 2013), has made a point of describing how members of the evangelical Vineyard Church in Illinois and California involve themselves in exercises aimed at developing the habit of picturing God to be just as intimately and personally present as a human companion would be. Persons are taught to picture God, to remember experiences of God, to immerse themselves in words about God from the Bible or church doctrines, and to habituate themselves to an everyday life with a God whom you can invite over for a cup of coffee, sit down with, and talk to as a friend. Presented as a species of *kataphatic* prayer—Greek for "to affirm positively"—such exercises are aimed at cultivating "concrete experiences of God's realness." It is an anthropologist's view of a Christian community's effort to accentuate the positive and to behave out of trust that there is, after all, a real core to Christianity that is concrete, meaningful, affirmative, and permanent. At the same time, the author forcefully notes, such persons possess such "an exquisite awareness of doubt" about themselves and others that one must conclude that doubt "is an integral part of what it means to be an evangelical Christian" (xv, 301, 315).

16. Davis, *Death's Dream Kingdom*, 128; Wayne C. Booth, "The Rhetoric of Fundamentalist Conversion Narratives," in *Fundamentalisms Comprehended*, ed. Martin E. Marty and R. Scott Appleby (Chicago: University of Chicago Press, 1995), 376, Kenneth Burke quoted on 76. For example, with regard to Protestants and Catholics, see the interpretations along this line by Jenny Franchot, *Roads to Rome: The Antebellum Protestant Encounter with Catholicism* (Berkeley: University of California Press, 1994); Tracy Fessenden, *Culture and Redemption: Religion, the Secular, and American Literature* (Princeton,

NJ: Princeton University Press, 2006); and Elizabeth Fenton, *Religious Liberties: Anti-Catholicism and Liberal Democracy in Nineteenth-Century U.S. Literature and Culture* (New York: Oxford University Press, 2011). John Henry Clippinger recently has argued, in *A Crowd of One: The Future of Individual Identity* (New York: Perseus, Public Affairs, 2007), 155:

> The notion that the most evolved and efficient mechanism for protecting identity should have a "negative definition" of identity runs counter to common-sense notions of personal identity. Yet much of the information about who you are comes from your reaction to those around you. . . . This could not happen if your identity were fixed and defined in the positive. Since neither physical nor social identity can be defined that way, there is no bounded definition as to who you are—both individuals and societies have the potential to be highly adaptive, and that is a great survival advantage.

17. Philip Hamburger, *Separation of Church and State* (Cambridge, MA: Harvard University Press, 2002); David Sehat, *The Myth of American Religious Freedom* (New York: Oxford University Press, 2011); Winnifred Fallers Sullivan, *The Impossibility of Religious Freedom* (Princeton, NJ: Princeton University Press, 2007).

18. Candy Gunther Brown, *The Word in the World: Evangelical Writing, Publishing, and Reading in America, 1789–1880* (Chapel Hill: University of North Carolina Press, 2004); David Paul Nord, *Faith in Reading: Religious Publishing and the Birth of Mass Media in America* (New York: Oxford University Press, 2004); Barton Price, "Evangelical Periodicals and the Making of America's Heartland, 1789–1900" (PhD diss., Florida State University, 2011).

19. Henry Sloane Coffin, "Why I Am a Presbyterian," *Forum* 75 (March 1926), 374; Walter M. Langtry, "Has the Supernatural Ceased? Revelation and Miracle," *Christian Observer* 97 (Oct. 20, 1909), 4; E. D. Howe, *Mormonism Unvailed; or, A Faithful Account of That Singular Imposition and Delusion* (Painesville, OH: By the author, 1834), https://archive.org/details/mormonismunvaile00howe, accessed May 14, 2014; Robert Abanes, *One Nation under Gods: A History of the Mormon Church* (New York: Four Walls Eight Windows, 2005), 390.

20. "A Picture of an Apostate Christian," *Lutheran Church Review* 21 (1902), 454–55; see also 634, 158; John Schroeder, *Heresies of Catholicism: The Apostate Church* (Lincoln, NE: iUniverse, 2003), 241; *Month and Catholic Review* 24 (1881), 574; "The Test of Religion," *Christian Telescope and Universalist Miscellany* 3 (Dec. 16, 1826), 124; "Is Spiritism a Development of Christianity," *American Catholic Quarterly Review* 8 (Jan. 1883), 160, 168, 170; "Recent Attacks on the Bible," *Church Weekly* 5 (Nov. 1863), 641; "Various Objections and Criticism," *Brownson's Quarterly Review* 2 (Oct. 1, 1861), 429; "The Times—Theologically Considered," *Charleston Gospel Messenger and Protestant Episcopal Register* 27 (Aug. 1850), 129; Hosea Ballou, "Criteria of False and True Preaching," *Universalist Expositor*, July 1830, 33.

21. Hiram Mattison, *A Scriptural Defense of the Doctrine of the Trinity; or, A Check to Modern Arianism* (New York: Lewis Colby, 1846), iv–v; *Popular Amusements: An Appeal to Methodists* (New York: Carlton and Porter, 1868); "Dr. Mattison's Theological Works," in *The Resurrection of the Dead*, by Hiram Mattison (Philadelphia: Perkinpine and Higgins, 1866), back matter; Edward Thompson, *Work Here, Rest Hereafter; The Life and Character of Rev. Hiram Mattison, D.D.* (New York: N. Tibbals, 1870), 25–27; A. Gregory Schneider,

"A Conflict of Associations: The National Camp-Meeting Association for the Promotion of Holiness versus the Methodist Episcopal Church," *Church History* 66 (1997), 269.

22. Hiram Mattison, *The Immortality of the Soul* (Philadelphia: Perkinpine and Higgins, 1864); Mattison, *Resurrection of the Dead.*

23. Alister McGrath, *Heresy: A History of Defending the Truth* (New York: HarperOne, 2009), 82; "On the Attempt to Deprive Unitarians of the Name Christians," *Christian Disciple and Theological Review* 4 (Sept. 1, 1822), 314.

24. Henri Tajfel, *Differentiation between Social Groups: Studies in the Social Psychology of Intergroup Relations* (New York: Academic Press, 1978); Bruce Fireman and William A. Gamson, "Utilitarian Logic in the Resource Mobilization Perspective," in *The Dynamics of Social Movements: Resource Mobilization, Social Control, and Tactics*, ed. Mayer N. Zald and John D. McCarthy (Cambridge, MA: Winthrop, 1979), 8–44; Susan Haber, *"They Shall Purify Themselves": Essays on Purity in Early Judaism* (Atlanta: Society of Biblical Literature, 2008), 157; John G. Gager, *Origins of Anti-Semitism: Attitudes towards Judaism in Pagan and Christian Antiquity* (New York: Oxford University Press, 1983); Evert-Jan Vledder, *Conflict in the Miracle Stories: A Socio-Exegetical Study of Matthew 8 and 9* (Sheffield, England: Sheffield Academic Press, 1997), 103; Mikael Telbe, *Christ-Believers in Ephesus: A Textual Analysis of Early Christian Identity* (Tübingen: Mohr Siebeck, 2009), 140; Christian Smith, *American Evangelicalism: Embattled and Thriving* (Chicago: University of Chicago Press, 1998); Kai Erikson, *Wayward Puritans: A Study in the Sociology of Deviance* (New York: Wiley, 1966), 64; Jolle Demmers, *Theories of Violent Conflict: An Introduction* (New York: Routledge, 2012), 21; D. H. Lawrence, *Studies in Classic American Literature* (New York: Viking, 1923), 3.

25. John Corrigan and Lynn S. Neal, *Religious Intolerance in America: A Documentary History* (Chapel Hill: University of North Carolina Press, 2010).

26. Alan Wolfe, *The Transformation of American Religion: How We Actually Live Our Faith* (Chicago: University of Chicago Press, 2003), 45; "U. S. Religious Knowledge Survey," Pew Forum on Religion and Public Life, www.pewforum.org/U-S-Religious-Knowledge-Survey-Who-Knows-What-About-Religion.aspx, accessed April 10, 2013.

27. Bill J. Leonard, *Baptists in America* (New York: Columbia University Press, 2005), 64, 65, 66; David A. Harvey, "TV Preacher Jimmy Swaggart: Why Does He Say Those Awful Things About Catholics?," in *The God Pumpers: Religion in the Electronic Age*, ed. Marshall W. Fishwick and Ray B. Browne (Bowling Green, OH: Bowling Green State University Popular Press, 1987), 97, 94.

28. John R. Rice, *False Doctrines* (1970; Murfreesboro, TN: Sword of the Lord, 1990), 7, 8, 410, 400, 412; Rice, *The Power of Pentecost* (Wheaton, IL: Sword of the Lord, 1949), 350. Rice was strongly opposed to the Federal Council of Churches. *False Doctrines*, 62.

29. Richard Hofstadter, *The Paranoid Style in American Politics and Other Essays* (New York: Vintage, 1967), 16; Robert Alan Goldberg, *Enemies Within: The Culture of Conspiracy in Modern America* (New Haven, CT: Yale University Press, 2001), x; David H. Bennett, *The Party of Fear: From Nativist Movements to the New Right in American History* (Chapel Hill: University of North Carolina Press, 1988), 20; Robert S. Levine, *Conspiracy and Romance: Studies in Brockden Brown, Cooper, Hawthorne, and Melville* (New York: Cambridge University Press, 1989); John Corrigan, "New Israel, New Amalek: Biblical Exhortations to Religious Violence," in *Jeremiah to Jihad: Religion, Violence, and America*, ed. Jonathan Ebel and John Carlson (Berkeley: University of California Press, 2012), 111–27.

30. Eli Sagan, *The Honey and the Hemlock: Democracy and Paranoia in Ancient Athens and Modern America* (New York: Basic Books, 1991); Timothy Tackett, "Conspiracy Obses-

sion in a Time of Revolution: French Elites and the Origins of the Terror, 1789–1792," *American Historical Review* 105 (2000), 712; James H. Moorhead, "Apocalypticism in Mainstream Protestantism, 1800 to the Present," in *The Encyclopedia of Apocalypticism*, ed. Stephen J. Stein (New York: Continuum, 1999), 103.

31. Mary Douglas, *Natural Symbols: Explorations in Cosmology* (New York: Pantheon, 1970); "False Teaching within the Church," *Christian Observer* 90 (March 5, 1902), 3; Albert Barnes, *Notes, Explanatory and Practical, on the Gospels: Designed for Sunday School Teachers and Bible Classes* (New York: Harper, 1869), 60.

Index